John R. W. Stott and others
Urbana 70

InterVarsity Press
Downers Grove, Illinois 60515

Unless otherwise noted, the
Scripture quotations in this
publication are from the Revised
Standard Version of the Bible,
copyrighted 1946 and 1952 by
the Division of Christian Education
of the National Council of the
Churches of Christ in the U.S.A.
and used by permission.

ISBN 0-87784-757-6
Library of Congress Catalog
Card Number: 70-157168

Printed in the United States of
America

CONTENTS

PREFACE

Proclaim liberation to the captives, preach sight to the blind, set at liberty them that are bruised, go into all the world and tell men that are bound mentally, spiritually and physically, "The liberator has come!"

With these words Tom Skinner ended his address to 12,300 Urbana 70 conventioneers. With these words he epitomized the spirit that prevailed throughout the four-day conference that ended the year of 1970 for students from 48 states and 72 countries.

An exciting sense of urgency and concern permeated the conference. John Stott's daily exposition of John 13–17 set each day into the context of Jesus' mission to the world. The talks by Samuel Escobar, Tom Skinner, George Taylor, Myron Augsburger, all concentrated on the necessity for the church to face social issues–race, poverty, political revolution. Those by Leighton Ford, C. Peter Wagner, Warren Webster, Ted Ward, Byang Kato, Dennis Clark and C. Stacey Woods concentrated on the spiritual needs of the global village. And the talks by David Howard, Paul Little, John W. Alexander and Samuel Kamaleson directed the conventioneers' attention to themselves—their needs, their training, their potential in God's plan for all men to hear the good news of Christ the Liberator.

This collection is more than a record of what was said during one short week. These addresses represent a new dimension in mission thinking. They will reverberate in the minds of thousands of delegates for years to come. They will be the beginning of a new era in many students' lives. And they will—we trust by the mercy and power of God—become for readers of this book not only food for thought but encouragement to action.

On the last night of the convention John W. Alexander closed his message, "Where Do We Go from Here?" by reading Revelation 7:9-12. Here is the great vision of multitudes of men and angels falling on their faces and singing glory to God. As Dr. Alexander says,

If the Lord Jesus Christ is residing within us, you and I are going to be there. People will be there from other nations, other tribes, other races, other languages, other classes. There will be no middle class, no upper class, no lower class. And together we will hear them sing, "Blessing and glory and wisdom and thanksgiving and honor and power and might be to our God for ever and ever! Amen."

CONVENTION SPEAKERS

John W. Alexander is President of Inter-Varsity Christian Fellowship—USA, Madison, Wisconsin. Previously he served as Chairman of the Department of Geography at the University of Wisconsin. His publications include *Fire in My Bones,* a Scripture memory system for university students.

Myron S. Augsburger is President of Eastern Mennonite College and Seminary, Harrisburg, Virginia. As Chairman of the Board of Inter-Church, Inc., he has been cited by *TIME* magazine as one of the ten most influential "preachers of the active gospel" in America. He has written a number of books, including, most recently, *Faith for a Secular World.*

Dennis Clark is Bible Minister and Evangelist for the Bible and Medical Missionary Fellowship and consultant in communications for David C. Cook Foundation. He is the author of the recently-published book *The Third World and Mission.*

Samuel Escobar is Editor of *Certeza* and all Spanish publishing for the International Fellowship of Evangelical Students, Cordoba,

Argentina. He has served on the IFES staff in Argentina, Brazil and Spain.

Leighton Ford is Associate Evangelist with the Billy Graham Evangelistic Association. He has frequently spoken to university students and has preached to large audiences on every continent. He is also the author of a number of books including *The Christian Persuader, One Way to Change the World* and *Letters to a New Christian.*

David M. Howard is Missionary Director of Inter-Varsity Christian Fellowship and Director of the Student Foreign Missions Fellowship. He served for 15 years with the Latin America Mission and is the author of *Hammered as Gold* and *Student Power in World Evangelism.*

Samuel Kamaleson is pastor of the Emmanuel Methodist Church, Madras, India. As a candidate for a Ph.D. at Emory University, he is currently on a one-year assignment at Walnut Hill Methodist Church, Dallas, Texas.

Byang H. Kato is now working with the Sudan Interior Mission, Kagoro, Nigeria. He was formerly the General Secretary of the Evangelical Churches of West Africa, representing churches which have grown out of the SIM ministry in Nigeria.

Paul E. Little is the Director of Urbana 70, Assistant to the President of Inter-Varsity Christian Fellowship, and Associate Professor of Evangelism, Trinity Evangelical Divinity School, Deerfield, Ill. He is the author of *How to Give Away Your Faith, Know Why You Believe,* and *Know What You Believe.*

Tom Skinner is an evangelist with Tom Skinner Associates, Brooklyn, New York. In his autobiography, *Black and Free,* he tells the story of his life in Harlem and his radical transformation from a gang leader to a Christian evangelist. He has also written *Words of Revolution* and *How Black Is the Gospel?*

John R. W. Stott is Rector of All Souls Church, London, and honorary chaplain to Her Majesty, the Queen of England. As a minister, he is best known for his exposition of Scripture. He has written many books, including *Basic Christianity* and, more recently, *Christ the Controversialist* and *One People.*

George J. Taylor is Professor of Practical Theology and Pastoral Psychology at Seminario Biblico Latinoamericano (Latin America Mission), San José, Costa Rica. He has also served as a professor at the University of Costa Rica.

C. Peter Wagner is Associate General Director, Andes Evangelical Mission. He has served as a visiting lecturer at Fuller Theological Seminary and is the author of a number of books, the most recent of which is *Latin American Theology.*

Ted Ward is Director, Learning Systems Institute, and Professor of Education at Michigan State University, East Lansing, Michigan. His experience includes research, training and field work in England, France, Germany, Switzerland, Brazil, Bolivia, Colombia, Israel and the Philippines.

Warren W. Webster works with the Conservative Baptist Foreign Missions Society, West Pakistan. He has been a visiting instructor at Fuller Theological Seminary and has contributed to Urbana missionary conferences in 1964 and 1967.

C. Stacey Woods is General Secretary of the International Fellowship of Evangelical Students, Lausanne, Switzerland. He was the first staff member for Inter-Varsity Christian Fellowship in the United States and has worked with this movement from its inception. He is also the author of many articles in *HIS* magazine and other Christian publications.

THE UPPER ROOM DISCOURSE (JOHN 13—17)

John R. W. Stott

THE FOOT-WASHING LORD AND SAVIOR (JOHN 13)

The gospel of John is divided into two approximately equal halves. The first half (chaps. 1–12), after the prologue, tells the story of Christ's three years of public ministry from his recognition by John the Baptist to his triumphal entry into Jerusalem. The second half (chaps. 13–21) describes the events of a single weekend from the Thursday night when he entered the Upper Room to the Sunday morning when he rose again from the dead.

We are to study the Upper Room discourse, with which the second half of the gospel of John begins. John 13–17 are perhaps the most sacred chapters in the whole Bible. If Scripture may be likened to the temple, these chapters are the inner sanctuary of the temple. As we read them, we seem to step into the Holy of Holies in which the very presence of God is made manifest. We are permitted to enter the mind of the Master, as he revealed to the apostles his innermost thoughts about his imminent departure through death and the coming of the Holy Spirit to replace him, about his own return at the end to take his people to himself, and about the responsibilities of the Christian and the church during the interim period between his departure and his return.

So these chapters contain Jesus Christ's last words of instruction to his apostles. Before the sun sets again his limbs will have been stretched out on the cross. Within less than twenty-four hours he will be dead. Although a few sentences from the lips of the risen Christ have been preserved, it is these chapters which contain the final message of his earthly career.

John's description of what happened in the Upper Room begins not with a word but with a deed—the astonishing deed of the foot washing.

Before we consider it, let me say something about the relation between the words and the deeds of Jesus. The gospels are a record of his words and works, or, as the evangelists call them, of his "mighty works" and "gracious words." The two belong essentially together, for his deeds dramatized his words, while his words interpreted his deeds.

In a sense, the whole career of Jesus was one mighty deed of salvation, interpreted by all his recorded words. In another sense, this one deed was broken up into many deeds, each an acted parable containing some hidden truth.

Some were miraculous deeds, as when he healed the sick, raised the dead, multiplied the loaves and fishes and withered the fig tree by a curse.

Others were nonmiraculous, as when he cleansed the temple, rode into Jerusalem on a donkey and took the bread and the cup into his hands.

But each deed was a sign whose significance is explained either by Jesus himself or by the evangelist who records the incident.

The washing of the apostles' feet belongs to the second category. It was a nonmiraculous deed, but it was still a sign. It possessed much more significance than appears on the surface, for it was not an ordinary act of footwashing. After all, their feet had been washed many times before and would be washed many more times in the future. But there was something special about this occasion. It was a deliberate parable by which Jesus was teaching at least three truths.

I. A parable of the mission Jesus undertook for us

Before describing the incident, John introduces it carefully. His preface is more elaborate than for any other event (vv. 1-3).

To begin with, he emphasizes the time context, when it took place. It was "before the feast of the Passover, when Jesus knew that his hour had come to depart out of this world to the Father . . ." (v. 1).

It is impossible here to go into the problem of the Passion chronology and the apparent discrepancy between the synoptic evangelists (who say that the Last Supper was a Passover meal) and John (who says that it took place "before the feast of the Passover"), except to say that there is evidence in the Dead Sea Scrolls that some Jews ate the Passover meal a day earlier than the official date.[1] For our purpose it is sufficient to see that the context was the Passover, the feast which commemorated that first redemption by sacrifice from the judgment of God, an event which was a shadow of the final sacrifice and redemption of Christ, the "hour" for which he had come into the world. Jesus "knew that his hour had come."

In addition to his description of the occasion (the Passover and the "hour"), John introduces the *dramatis personae,* the chief actors in the drama, both seen and unseen. On the other hand, he tells us (v. 2) that "the devil had already put it into the heart of Judas Iscariot, Simon's son, to betray him," and still further (v. 3) that "the Father had given all things into his [Jesus'] hands" and that Jesus "had come from God and was going to God." Thus behind the coming confrontation between Jesus and Judas there stood the Father and the devil. The devil had made Judas his tool; but the Father had made Jesus his heir.

Moreover, John emphasizes that Jesus *knew* this. He knew his origin and his destiny (v. 3), and that his hour had come (v. 1). So, knowing these things, he dramatized his whole career in microcosm before its final denouement took place.

He "rose from supper" (v. 4), just as he had risen from his eternal throne. He "laid aside his garments"—his girdle and outer garment—just as he had laid aside his glory. He then took the form of a servant, for he "girded himself with a towel" (a badge of servitude), just as he had taken the form of a servant when girding himself with our humanity. Next he humbled himself to such an extent that (v. 5) "he poured water into a basin, and began to wash the disciples' feet, and to wipe them with the towel with which he was girded," just as he humbled himself and became obedient unto death, even death on a cross, in order to cleanse us from our sins. Finally (v. 12), "When he had washed their feet, and taken his garments," he sat down again, just as (to quote Hebrews 1:3) "When he had made purification for sins, he sat down at the right hand of the Majesty on high."

Indeed, this incident described by John in such detail seems to be a divinely provided visual aid to illustrate the theological statement of Philippians 2:6-9, where the apostle Paul writes that Christ "emptied himself" (of his glory), took "the form of a servant," was "born in the likeness of men" and then "humbled himself and became obedient unto death. . . . Therefore God has highly exalted him. . . ."

As we contemplate the majestic sweep of this perspective, we should be filled with wonder and praise. For Paul writes that, although Christ was eternally "in the form of God," he humbled himself to death before being exalted to heaven. John tells us that he knew he had come from God and was going to God. And Christ himself exhibited this by symbolic actions.

For me there is no clearer or more compelling evidence for the deity of Jesus than the extraordinary paradox between his lofty claims and his lowly conduct. Christ claimed to have come from God and (as we shall see in verse 13) to be the Lord and teacher of men. Yet here he is on his hands and knees washing their feet. Their Lord became their servant.

II. A parable of the salvation Jesus offers to us

The washing of the apostles' feet was a picture (and was intended to be a picture) of another kind of washing, what the Episcopal Prayer Book calls a "heavenly washing." It symbolized the washing away of sin through the death Christ was about to die. To give it its proper theological name, it was a symbol of *salvation.*

It is not fanciful to see in the footwashing a parable of salvation.

Jesus indicated as much when he said to Peter (v. 7), "What I am doing you do not know now, but afterward you will understand."

At least two aspects of salvation are vividly illustrated here; namely, its necessity and its nature.

A. The necessity of salvation

Simon Peter in his protest is typical of every sinner whom Christ would save. First came the incredulous question (v. 6): "Lord, do you wash my feet?" Then followed the indignant expostulation (v. 8): "You shall never wash my feet"—never, not even when I have understood what you are doing, as you say I shall.

It is not difficult to appreciate Peter's acute embarrassment. Was it really necessary for him to admit that his feet were dirty and needed to be washed? Then to humble himself to let Jesus perform a slave's duty in washing them? And moreover to let Jesus do it in public while everyone was watching? Was it necessary for Peter to suffer these public indignities? The pride of Peter rebelled against the humility of Christ. Professor Tasker comments in his note on verse 37, where Peter boasts that he is ready to die for Christ, "Peter would much rather wash Jesus' feet than that Jesus should wash his feet; he would prefer to lay down his life for Jesus than that Jesus should lay down His life for him."[2]

There is in each of us the same sinful pride, a fundamental unwillingness to admit that we are unclean and need to be washed, to acknowledge that our need of cleansing took Christ to his cross, and then to allow Jesus Christ to wash us.

We find it humiliating to confess that we are guilty sinners and that only Jesus Christ can save us. We cry out with Peter in vehement protest, "Lord, never!" We prefer to remain in our dirt rather than humble ourselves to let Jesus Christ make us clean.

So Christ says to us, as he did to Peter (v. 8), "If I do not wash you, you have no part in me." Or, as the New English Bible puts it: "If I do not wash you, you are not in fellowship with me."

We cannot escape these basic truths. They are in fact the *prolegomena* to the gospel. We are defiled by sin and guilt. Being unclean, we are unfit for the company of Christ. Until and unless Christ washes us and makes us clean, we can enjoy no fellowship with him.

B. **The nature of salvation**

We have seen that salvation is a washing. Now we must see that it is a washing of two kinds or in two stages.

"Simon Peter said to him, 'Lord, not my feet only but also my hands and my head!' Jesus said to him, 'He who has bathed does not need to wash, except for his feet, but he is clean all over; and you are clean, but not all of you.' For he knew who was to betray him; that was why he said, 'You are not all clean' " (vv. 9-11).

Notice that once Peter had humbled himself to let Jesus wash his feet, he demanded that his hands and his head should be washed as well. In other words, he went from one extreme to the other. Most of us manifest a tendency to religious extremism. It is not easy to be a balanced Christian.

But Jesus replied that a *bath* is one thing; a washing of the *feet* is another. They had already taken a bath, as a result of which (v. 10) they were clean (cf. 15:3). Not all of them were clean, it is true. Judas was not clean, for Judas had refused a bath. But the rest had bathed. So all *they* needed now was a washing of their feet.

The social customs to which Jesus was alluding were commonly practiced in his day. Before going out to a meal or a party, the guest would take a bath. Walking in sandals through the dusty streets of the town, however, his feet would get dirty again. So, on arrival at his friend's house, a servant would wash his feet. But he would not need another bath.

The spiritual truth thus illustrated should be plain. When we first come to Christ we get a bath. It is the complete cleansing called "justification," the complete change called "regeneration." It is publicly set forth in baptism and is called, in Titus 3:5-6, "the washing [*loutron,* literally a "bath"] of regeneration and renewal in the Holy Spirit, which he poured out upon us richly through Jesus Christ our Savior." Moreover, it is unique and unrepeatable. Because we fall into sin, however, and get spattered with mud in the dirty streets of the world, we need to keep coming to Christ for forgiveness, so that his blood may keep cleansing us from all sin. But we do not need another justification, another new birth. That is why we come to the Lord's Supper repeatedly, whereas we are baptized only once. Baptism is the bath, the sign (some people call it the "sacrament") of justification, while the Lord's Supper is the footwashing (indeed, in the synoptic gospels the institution of the Lord's Supper replaces the footwashing), the sign or sacrament of that continuous forgiveness which is available to us through the bloodshedding of Christ.

Looking back, we can now see that Peter made two mistakes. First, he protested against being washed by Jesus at all. Then, he asked for a bath when he needed only a footwashing.

The same two mistakes are commonly made today. Some people are too proud to come to Christ for cleansing of any kind. They do not even relent later, as Peter did. No. Like Judas, they persist in their sin, and perish.

Others come to Christ and are cleansed but then become overscrupulous in their conscience. They imagine that every time they sin, they lose their salvation and need another bath, another justification. They have an inadequate view of the greatness of Christ's salvation.

We can avoid these two mistakes if we distinguish clearly between justification (which is unique) and forgiveness (which is a continuous necessity). Then we shall come humbly to Jesus Christ for both—only once in penitence and faith for the bath of acceptance with God, then every day, every moment of the day, in the same penitence and faith, for our feet to be kept clean.

III. A parable of the mutual love Jesus expects from us

John clearly saw in the action of Jesus a picture or parable of love. For he writes in verse 1 that what Jesus did, he did to illustrate that, "having loved his own who were in the world, he loved them to the end [or "to the uttermost"]." But John also saw that this love of Christ, displayed in the washing of the apostles' feet, was to be a pattern of our love for each other.

We need to look carefully at verses 13-17: "You call me Teacher and Lord; and you are right, for so I am. If I then, your Lord and Teacher, have washed your feet, you also ought to wash one another's feet. For I have given you an example, that you also should do as I have done to you. Truly, truly, I say to you, a servant is not greater than his master; nor is he who is sent greater than he who sent him. If you know these things, blessed are you if you do them."

Here Jesus designates himself as our "Teacher and Lord." These were "the ordinary titles of respect paid to a Rabbi."[3] But in adopting them himself, Jesus insisted that they were no mere courtesy titles. You are right to call me this, he said. I am in *fact* what you call me in *title.* "If I then, your Lord and Teacher, have washed your feet, you also ought to wash one another's feet." I have set an example for you to follow. I have given an instruction for you to accept. I have issued a command for you to obey. "If you know these things, blessed are you if you do them" (v. 17)–an additional beatitude to those in the Sermon on the Mount.

I wonder if there is any more urgent need in the contemporary church than that professed disciples of Jesus should take their profession seriously. It is no use *calling* Jesus Christ our Teacher and Lord if we do not *treat* him as such. He is not only our Savior, who washes us from our sins. He is also our Teacher to instruct us and our Lord to command us. If we are Christians, we should gladly accept toward Jesus Christ a position of voluntary subordination. As his pupils we are under his instruction; as his slaves, we are under his authority. And true freedom is found in assuming Christ's yoke, not in discarding it.

This means that we shall derive our views both of Christian doctrine and of Christian behavior from Jesus Christ. We shall not presume either to disagree with what he taught or to disobey what he commanded. In particular, since "a servant is not greater than his master" (v. 16), we must follow his example.

It is interesting (and rather sad) that the church, in its endeavor to obey Christ's command, has tended to do so with an excessive and unimaginative literalism. He said that we should wash one another's feet. So the church has done so, even in the western world, without making any allowance for the fact that ours is not a Palestinian culture, that we wear shoes not sandals, that the streets are cleaner nowadays, that in any case we drive rather than walk to parties, and that if we did walk, a servant would not meet us on arrival and proceed to wash our feet!

This is an instructive example of the need for us to get at the principle behind each command of Scripture and obey it, without being bound to the precise cultural form which it took in first-century Palestine.

It was natural that one of the qualifications of Asian Christian widows before they were officially enrolled for church service was this: "She must be well attested for her good deeds, as one who has brought up children, shown hospitality, *washed the feet of the saints,* relieved the afflicted, and devoted herself to doing good in every way" (1 Tim. 5:9-10).

But footwashing later became an occasional and ceremonial act. According to Canon 3 of the 17th Synod of Toledo (A.D. 694) footwashing was made obligatory on Maundy Thursday "throughout the churches of Spain and Gaul." It is still practiced in some Protestant groups, I believe by Mennonites and United Brethren, while Seventh Day Adventists do it regularly on the twelfth sabbath of each quarter and call it "the ordinance of humility."

It has tended to be a performance by leaders of Church and State, however, as a symbol of their humility. Thus in 1530 Cardinal Wolsey "washed, wiped and kissed the feet of 59 poor men at Peterborough."[4] Still today, in the Church of the Holy Sepulchre in Jerusalem, the Patriarch of the Greek Orthodox Church washes the right foot of 12 senior clergy representing the apostles, while in Rome the Pope does likewise, a custom restored by John XXIII after a lapse of about ninety years.

One of the most interesting examples is to be found among English kings and queens. The first record is of King John who at Rochester in 1213 washed the feet of the poor. He also gave thirteen pence to each of thirteen men, which came to be known as the Royal Maundy.

Similarly, there is an entry in the Chapels Royal Register that "on Maundy Thursday, April 16th 1685, our gracious King James ye 2nd, was'd, wip'd and kiss'd the feet of 52 poor men with wonderful humility."

The last sovereign who is known to have continued this practice was William III on Maundy Thursday, 1698, but 234 years later (in 1932) King George V revived it, although without the footwashing.

The distribution of the Royal Maundy still continues today. The recipients are elderly people who have given a lifetime of voluntary service and are in financial need, and their number is the same as the years of the Queen's age. Green, white and red purses are distributed to them, containing specially minted silver coins in lieu of food and clothing. Although there is no footwashing, the officials still wear white linen towels as aprons, and all the principal participants including the Sovereign still carry nosegays of fragrant herbs and flowers—as they did in the days of the Plague against the risk of infection.[5]

We need now to ask what fundamental principle lay behind the action of Jesus in washing the apostles' feet and in commanding us to do likewise. Surely the footwashing teaches that true love, Christian love, contains at least two essential elements.

A. **Love involves service**

Love is not merely sentiment or emotion. It takes more than sentiment to wash the dirty feet of men, ignoring the smell and the indignity of it. Love is service rather than sentiment. Luke tells us that in the Upper Room there had been a dispute about precedence, which of them was the greatest. In his reply Jesus said, "Let the leader become as one who serves." He went on: "For which is the greater, one who sits at table, or one who serves? Is it not the one who sits at table? But I am among you as one who serves" (Lk. 22:24-27).

Perhaps before supper Jesus had waited to see if one of them would volunteer to be the servant of the others and wash their feet. If so, he waited in vain. Instead of serving one another, they argued with one another and maybe even competed with one another for the best places at table.

Of course, if one of them had volunteered to do the servant's dirty work, the others would no doubt have been delighted. They would have revelled in being waited on hand and foot. Marcus Dods recalls in his commentary the description Suetonius gives of the Emperor Caligula who "was fond of making some of the senators wait at his table *succinctos linteo,* that is, in the guise of waiters."[6] It was great fun to turn senators into waiters. It gave a tremendous fillip to his pride. He would never have dreamed of waiting on them. So too these disciples of Jesus. They thought of themselves as apostles not waiters, as masters not servants. It was for someone else to do the dirty work, not for them.

As a result, supper began with everybody's feet unwashed. So "during supper" (v. 2) Jesus himself did what none of them had been willing to do before supper. He became their servant. *He* washed their feet. He exhibited the truth that genuine love issues in service.

Some years later, Paul wrote "through love be servants of one another" (Gal. 5:13). It is no good claiming to love people if we are not prepared to serve them. Sometimes when we say we love somebody, what we really mean is that we want to possess him and use him and manipulate him. We want him to serve us, rather than being willing ourselves to serve him.

B. **Love involves sacrifice**

True love always gives in order to serve, sacrifices itself in order to serve others. Before he could wash and wipe their feet, Jesus rose from supper, laid aside his garment and girded himself with a slave's apron. He humbled himself to do it, just as he emptied himself and humbled himself when he came into the world to die for our sins.

It will be the same for us. If the love in our hearts is Christ's love, we shall not shrink from sacrificial service, from a service which is costly in energy, dignity, money or time. Sacrifice and service always belong together where true love exists and operates. For love always serves, and the service of others is impossible without self-sacrifice.

This principle of sacrificial service is not only illustrated in what Jesus did in washing the apostles' feet but is also deliberately contrasted with the action of Judas in betraying him. The announcement of the betrayal (vv. 18-30) immediately follows the footwashing (vv. 1-17). Already in verses 18-20 Jesus quotes the Scripture which Judas will fulfil (Ps. 41:9): "He who ate my bread has lifted his heel against me." Then in the following verses Jesus gives the "sop" (the morsel which symbolizes special honor) to Judas. As Professor Tasker writes, "in accepting *the sop* Judas shows himself completely impervious to the appeal of love; and from that moment he is wholly the tool of Satan."[7]

The love of Jesus Christ shines all the more brightly when it is seen against the dark background of Judas' treachery. The whole Upper Room seems to blaze with the light of love as Christ washes their feet. Outside is the dominion of darkness (cf. Luke 22:53). We are not surprised therefore, when Judas leaves and goes out, that John adds, "and it was night" (v. 30). In Archbishop William Temple's opinion, "There are no more pregnant words in the whole of literature than these–*and it was night*."[8] In his first letter John elaborates the truth that light belongs with love, and darkness with hate.

The contrast between Jesus and Judas is painted in stark tones. Judas "betrayed" Jesus, that is, gave him up, or gave him away. It is hardly accidental that the very same verb is used in the New Testament of Christ giving himself for us (e.g., in Gal. 2:20). Indeed, John uses this verb for Christ's last act, when he "gave up his spirit" (19:30).

We may say, therefore, that Judas sacrificed Christ in order to serve himself, whereas Christ sacrificed himself in order to serve others.

Every man to some degree is and behaves either like Judas or like Jesus. As Calvin writes, "The love of ourselves and of our neighbour no more agree than do fire and water."[9] So we have to choose. Satan puts it into men's hearts, as he did into the heart of Judas (v. 2, cf. v. 27), to serve themselves and sacrifice others. But Christ leads his people to serve others and sacrifice themselves to do so, to wash people's feet in humility, and to wipe them also, for love never leaves a job half done but, like Christ, completes it.

This love (or sacrificial service), which Christ has illustrated by his own action and by predicting the contrasting action of Judas, he goes on to state in the form of "a new commandment": "A new commandment I give to you, that you love one another; even as I have loved you, that you also love one another" (v. 34).

It is now not enough to love our neighbor *as* we love ourselves (although, to be sure, this is already a very high standard). We are now to love our neighbor *more* than we love ourselves, and so to give ourselves up for him as Christ loved us and gave himself for us.

It is by such love, the love which sacrifices and serves, that all men will learn that we are Christ's disciples (v. 35), because it is only by such love that we shall bear Christ's likeness.

Tertullian in his *Apology* (written about the end of the second century A.D.) describes how the money voluntarily contributed by Christians to church funds was used to relieve the poor, orphans, the elderly, the shipwrecked, prisoners and other needy people. "It is the exercise of this sort of love," he added, which was the chief "brand" of Christians–though some pagans regarded it as a brand of evil. " 'See,' say they, 'how they love each other'; for they themselves hate each other: and 'see how ready they are to die for each other'; for they themselves are more ready to slay each other."[10] It is a tragedy that these words of pagan astonishment about Christian love have seemed more often a parody than a reality.

We have now seen the principle which Jesus has taught by example (in the footwashing) and by contrast (with the treachery of Judas) and by statement (in the words of the new commandment).

We have also considered the dead and unimaginative literalism of those who have sought to obey the commandment by an actual, though ceremonial, washing of some people's feet sometimes.

Are there not better ways of obeying this command to love? Are there not many lowly, menial, foot-washing jobs waiting to be done which we commonly shirk? It was not beneath the dignity of Jesus to put on a slave's apron, get down on his knees and dirty his hands in the service of others. Is it beneath ours? His ministry was not only spiritual; it was social and practical as well. He did not only preach; he served. Think of some of the needy people we tend to neglect.

In 1878 when William Booth's Salvation Army had just been so named, men from all over the world began to enlist. One man, who had once dreamed of himself as a bishop, crossed the Atlantic from America to England to enlist. He was a Methodist minister, Samuel Logan Brengle. And he now turned from a fine pastorate to join Booth's Salvation Army. Brengle later became the Army's first American-born commissioner. But at first Booth accepted his services reluctantly and grudgingly. Booth said to Brengle, "You've been your own boss too long." And in order to instill humility into Brengle, he set him to work cleaning the boots of the other trainees. And Brengle said to himself, "Have I followed my own fancy across the Atlantic in order to black boots?" And then as in a vision he saw Jesus bending over the feet of rough, unlettered fishermen. "Lord," he whispered, "you washed their feet; I will black their boots."[11]

Is Christ calling us to some hidden backroom job "serving tables," when we would rather be in the limelight of publicity? Is he calling us to spend time with somebody who is lonely or emotionally unstable or mentally sick, when we would rather relax with our friends? Or to give ourselves in genuine friendship–not superficial but sacrificial–to someone hooked on drugs, and stand by him faithfully during the painful period of withdrawal? Is he calling us to work with penitence and without paternalism in a rundown inner city area or ghetto? Or are we meant to offer our lives in Christ's service in a developing country abroad–as a doctor, nurse, teacher, agriculturalist or social worker–when it would be more lucrative and more respectable to pursue our profession at home? Or should we stay at home and get involved with people in the secular community –perhaps with hippies, whom Ted Schroder (one of my colleagues in London) has described as "the largest unreached tribe in the world today." He has added, "We don't learn their language, we don't study their culture, we don't live among them."

It is in such ways as these that we are to follow the example of Jesus our Teacher and Lord today, washing people's feet, sacrificing ourselves to serve them. As he girded himself with a towel, we are (in Peter's expressive phrase) to clothe ourselves with humility (1 Pet. 5:5). I do not think it would be an exaggeration to say that if there is no humble service in our lives, nothing comparable to Christ's washing of the apostles' feet, we can hardly qualify as the disciples of Jesus. For a disciple is not above his teacher, nor a servant above his lord.

Let Richard Baxter sum up this challenge for us:

> O then, let us hear these arguments of Christ, whenever we feel ourselves grow dull and careless: "Did I die for them, and wilt not thou look after them? Were they worth my blood, and are they not worth thy labour? Did I come down from heaven to earth, to seek and to save that which was lost; and wilt thou not go to the next door or street or village to seek them? How small is thy labour and condescension as to mine! I debased myself to this, but it is thy honour to be so employed."[12]

As we look back over the chapter we have been studying, we can perhaps grasp what Jesus meant when he said (v. 7): "What I am doing you do not know now, but afterward you will understand." There is much more in this drama than meets the eye. It sets forth the glory of Jesus Christ himself, and especially the glory of his cross.

As we watch and listen, it seems that Jesus deliberately portrays himself in a threefold role.

First, as the *Son of God made flesh.*

His series of actions, from his rising from supper to his resuming his place after he has washed their feet, sets forth the whole sweep of his mission, from glory to glory.

Second, as the *Savior of sinners.*

The main object of the servant role he assumed, according to Isaiah 53, was to bear sin and to die for sin. He did it to wash us clean from our sins.

Third, as our *Teacher and Lord.*

He set us an example, showing us the way of sacrificial service, and commanding us to follow.

Moreover, in each of the three parables told by the footwashing, there is some allusion to the cross.

For the cross is the center of Christ's mission; it is to *this* he humbled himself.

The cross is the means of the sinner's salvation; it is by *this* that he makes us clean.

And the cross is the pattern of the believer's love; it is to *this* that he calls us today.

In these ways the footwashing foreshadows the yet greater work of the cross.

Notes

[1] See, for example, E. Earle Ellis, *The World of St. John* (Nashville: Abingdon Press, 1965), p. 48.

[2] R. V. G. Tasker, *The Gospel according to St. John* (Grand Rapids: Eerdmans, 1960), p. 155.

[3] Alfred Plummer, *The Gospel according to St. John* (New York: Cambridge University Press, 1881), p. 266.

[4] B. F. Westcott, *St. John's Gospel* (Grand Rapids: Eerdmans, 1950 [First published in *The Speaker's Bible,* 1880]), p. 192.

[5] Peter A. Wright, *The Pictorial History of the Royal Maundy* (1968).

[6] Marcus Dods, *The Gospel of St. John* (London: Hodder and Stoughton, 1897), p. 815.

[7] Tasker, p. 159.

[8] Archbishop William Temple, *Readings in St. John's Gospel* (New York: St. Martin's Press, 1945 [First published in 1939/40 by Macmillan, London]), p. 218.

[9] John Calvin, *The Gospel according to St. John* (London: Oliver and Boyd, 1962 [First published in 1553]), II, 71.

[10] Tertullian, *Apology,* chap. xxxix.

[11] Richard Collier, *The General Next to God* (Glasgow: Collins, 1965), p. 72.

[12] Richard Baxter, *The Reformed Pastor* (London: Epworth, 1939 [First published in 1656]), pp. 121-22.

THE TWO COMINGS OF CHRIST (JOHN 14)

At the beginning of this chapter (v. 1) and again near its end (v. 27) Jesus issues the same command, namely, "Let not your hearts be troubled." He is alluding to a form of heart trouble from which the whole world suffers. Yet no cardiologist on earth can cure it. Nor can transplant surgery take it away.

Mind you, there is much in human experience to cause spiritual heart trouble; and to suffer from it is by no means always sinful. Even Jesus himself was not immune. The very same verb is used by John three times to describe Jesus' distress. At the sight of people weeping over Lazarus' death, at the prospect of his own death and at the thought of his betrayal by Judas, we read, Jesus "was troubled in spirit" (11:33; 12:27; 13:21).

What John records for us in this chapter is the Great Physician's diagnosis of the condition, and the remedy which he goes on to propose.

The chief cause of the apostles' heart trouble was the imminent departure of their Master. He had just told them in clear and unmistakable terms that he was going to leave them. "Little children," he had said, "yet a little while I am with you. You will seek me; and as I said to the Jews so now I say to you, 'Where I am going you cannot come.' " Peter expostulated: "Lord, where are you going?" And again, "Lord, why cannot I follow you now? I will lay down my life for you." To this Jesus replied: "Will you lay down your life for me? Truly, truly, I say to you, the cock will not crow, till you have denied me three times" (Jn. 13:33, 36-38).

It was this prospect of being left, of being abandoned by Jesus, which gave them heart trouble—especially when they grasped that it would involve his death, and that betrayal by Judas and denial by Peter would somehow contribute to it. Their hearts trembled with anxious foreboding. As Jesus was to say a little later (16:5-6), "now I am going to him who sent me" and "because I have said these things to you, sorrow has filled your hearts."

Perhaps they remembered a previous occasion on which Jesus had left them only temporarily. They were in a boat, crossing the lake. But he was still on the land. He had gone up into the hills by himself to pray. After they had lost his presence, the night came on and a storm broke out. The wind rose and was against them. The waves threatened to engulf them. And they were in the dark. Their hearts failed them for fear. Then suddenly about the fourth watch of the night Jesus came to them, walking on the water. And when they had taken him into the boat, the wind ceased and there was a great calm (Mk. 6:45-52).

In fact, this is precisely what Christ promises to them now. He is going away, it is true. But there is no need for them to be troubled or afraid, however hard the times may be. For he is going to come back to them and all will be well.

So the cure for spiritual heart trouble is faith. As Bishop J. C. Ryle puts it in his commentary, "We have . . . in this passage a precious remedy against an old disease. That disease is trouble of heart. That remedy is faith."[1]

What Jesus said to them is this: "Let not your hearts be troubled; believe in God, believe also in me" (v. 1). Both verbs are the same and in the same present tense (*pisteuete*). They may be either indicative and therefore statements ("you believe") or imperative and therefore commands ("believe!"). It seems probable that both are commands, as in the Revised Standard Version, and could be translated: "Keep believing in God, keep believing also in me."

Moreover, the faith in Christ which cures heart trouble is specific rather than general. It is faith in Christ's promised coming and so in his promised presence. These are the promises of Christ to which faith clings: "I go . . . I will come again" (v. 3) and "I will not leave you desolate; I will come to you" (v. 18).

Although both promises contain the same verb, meaning "I am coming" or "I will come," yet a careful look at the context makes it plain that each promise refers to a different occasion. The first (v. 1) is to Christ's final coming in glory on the last day, while the second (v. 18) is to his intermediate coming through the Spirit on the day of Pentecost.

This differentiation between the two comings of Christ is made clear in another way. At each coming there will be a reception, Christ says. But who receives whom will be different. According to verse 3, when Christ comes, he will receive them into heaven to dwell with him. According to verses 17 and 18, when Christ comes, they will do what the world cannot do, namely, receive him into their hearts so that he may dwell with them.

Further, the Greek word for "mansions" or "resting places" is used of both, and occurs nowhere else in the New Testament. When we go to dwell with Christ *we* find a resting place (v. 3), and when he comes to dwell with us *he* finds a resting place (v. 23).

It is only when we truly believe these promises of Jesus Christ—that he has not left us for ever, but that he has come back in the Spirit and that he will come back in power and great glory—that we shall be cured of spiritual heart trouble and enjoy peace.

I. Christ's ultimate coming (vv. 1-14)

We have already seen that Christ's first prohibition of fear was spoken at the prospect of his death. It is almost equally appropriate in prospect of ours. Indeed, this passage is often (and rightly) read at funerals and memorial services. Neither death nor the prospect of death should trouble the Christian's heart.

Yet many are troubled. When Jesus told the apostles that he was going and that they could not immediately follow him, their questions came thick and fast.

Peter asked, "Lord, where are you going? . . . Lord, why cannot I follow you now?" (13:36-37).

Thomas asked, "Lord, we do not know where you are going; how can we know the way?" (14:5).

Philip asked, "Lord, show us the Father, and we shall be satisfied" (14:8).

And what Peter, Thomas and Philip asked in their bewilderment, we too ask in our different ways today. "Lord, where? Lord, why? Lord, how?" we inquire, especially in the face of death.

Men have always been afraid of death. "No rational man can die without uneasy apprehension," said Dr. Johnson. And according to Rousseau, "He who pretends to face death without fear is a liar." Still today death is the great unmentionable. A leading doctor said to me in London a few years ago, "I have seen death often; but I have never faced death myself."

In a sense, the sufficient Christian answer to all our questions is this: "Trust God; trust me." The whole New Testament tells us that Jesus Christ has "abolished" or defeated death. He is the resurrection and the life. He holds in his hand the keys of death and of Hades. Quietly and confidently we can therefore trust him.

Nevertheless, in his grace he goes further than a general command to trust him. He spells out in some detail why we may trust him and so not be afraid of death (or for that matter of life either). He makes four affirmations about himself as the basis of our trust: "I go to prepare a place for you" (v. 2), "I will come again" (v. 3a), "I will take you to myself" (v. 3b) and "I am the way" (v. 6).

A. **I go to prepare a place for you (v. 2)**

These words imply not only that the separation will be temporary ("I go . . . I come"), but that it will be a separation with a view to a reunion ("I go in order to prepare a place for you").

So Jesus bids us think of death not as a leap into the dark unknown, but as a journey to a prepared place. It will not be like arriving in a strange town in a foreign land, where you know nobody, nobody is expecting you and you haven't even made a hotel reservation. No. Just as Jesus had sent two of his disciples ahead into the city to prepare for him to eat the passover (Mk. 14:12-16), so now he would go ahead to prepare for them. In the familiar and true expression death is "going home" to a place prepared in our Father's house.

Shortly before the final surrender of what was Biafra in 1969, one hospital was crowded with 800 wounded soldiers, many of whom were described as "alive, yet half-rotten." One morning a night nurse reported: "A patient died the death of a Christian last night." His name was Okon Bassey, a paraplegic. He had clasped his hands together, prayed aloud for forgiveness, praised the Lord and asked that God's will be done. Finally he said, "Lord, take me home," and he died.[2]

In the Father's house, Jesus added, there are "many mansions" (AV). This word is very misleading, for you can hardly have many mansions in one house! It comes from the Latin word *mansiones* (*mansio* meaning a dwelling or habitation) which the early English translators in the Vulgate had simply transliterated into English. The Scottish word *manse* and the French *maison* are derived from the same root.

The Greek word is *monai* and means "dwelling places." It can refer to temporary resting places, like the coaching stages of a journey in olden days. Thus, William Temple writes "the *resting-places (monai)* are wayside caravanserais–shelters at stages along the road where travellers may rest on their journey."[3] He goes on to apply the image to "the stages of our spiritual growth" in *this* life.[4] Other commentators follow Origen in applying the metaphor to the next life, like Westcott who claims that "the contrasted notions of repose and progress are combined in this vision of the future."[5] Indeed, some writers have based upon this word entirely unwarranted speculations about the nature of heaven, universalistic dreams that everybody who has died is in heaven, the only difference between them being that they are at various stages of development.

However, the emphasis Jesus is making seems to be not on the temporary nature of the resting places (we know from verse 24 that a "resting place" may be permanent), but on the refreshment and security to be found there, and also the ample spaciousness, for there are "many" of them. As Calvin comments, Christ says "that the mansions are many, not that they are different or unlike, but that there are sufficient for a great number."[6]

B. **I will come again (v. 3a)**

Here is a second promise of Christ calculated to reassure us. Having gone ahead to prepare a place for us, he does not expect us to travel there on our own. Instead, he promises to come back in person to fetch us.

The primary reference is to his personal return in power and glory, which will herald the general resurrection and our final state. But it seems legitimate to find a secondary reference to death, at which it may be said that Christ comes to take us to himself. Is it fanciful to suppose that when the dying martyr Stephen said he saw Jesus *standing* at God's right hand, Jesus had in fact risen from his throne in order to fetch or welcome him?

C. **I will take you to myself (v. 3b)**

Christ is to be our destination as well as our escort. *He* comes to take us, and he takes us to *himself.*

This is the essential New Testament revelation about the next life for believers, whether the reference is to the final state after the resurrection or to the intermediate state between death and resurrection. Of the intermediate state Paul said he had a "desire to depart and be *with Christ,* for that is far better" (Phil. 1:23, cf. 2 Cor. 5:8). Of the final state he wrote "so we shall always be *with the Lord*" (1 Thess. 4:17).

There is no need for us to speculate about the precise nature of heaven. We are assured on the authority of Jesus Christ that it is the house and home of his Father and ours (there are twenty-two references to the Father in this chapter), that this home is a prepared place containing many rooms or resting places, and that he himself will be there. What more do we need to know? To be certain that where he is, there we shall be also should be enough to satisfy our curiosity and allay our fears.

D. **I am the way (v. 6)**

It is a beautiful truth that the Lord Jesus Christ, who is himself our heavenly destination, is in addition our forerunner (who has gone ahead to prepare the way), our personal escort (who comes to fetch us) and the way by which we travel there.

The sense in which Jesus Christ is "the way" to the Father is suggested by the other two expressions; namely, that he is also "the truth and the life," that is, the truth about God and the very life of God.

These are the two great offices of Jesus Christ. First, he reveals the Father to us, for he is the Truth and shows truth to us. Second, he reconciles us to the Father, for he is the Life and gives life to us. Moreover, in both directions (revealing God to man and reconciling man to God) he is the only mediator. So he says here, "No one comes to the Father, but by me," as he says elsewhere, "No one knows the Father, except the Son and anyone to whom the Son chooses to reveal him" (Mt. 11:27).

The emphasis in this passage, however, is on the Son's work of revelation. "If you had known me, you would have known my Father also," he says (v. 7), and again, "He who has seen me has seen the Father" (v. 9). What Jesus is asserting here is not the personal identity of the Father and the Son, but a mutual indwelling (v. 10): "Do you not believe that I am in the Father and the Father in me?" It is as a result of this indwelling that the words which the Son speaks are the Father's words, and the works which the Son performs are the Father's works (vv. 10b-11).

Next comes a short parenthesis in which (vv. 12-14), having spoken of his own works, Christ goes on to speak of ours which will continue his: "Truly, truly, I say to you, he who believes in me will also do the works that I do; and greater works than these will he do, because I go to the Father" (v. 12).

It is not uncommon to meet devout Christians (whose zeal is greater than their wisdom) who believe that these words should be interpreted literally and materially, and that we are to perform more spectacular miracles even than Christ. I submit to you that it cannot possibly mean this. If it did, we would presumably be able to feed fifty thousand people with a few loaves and fishes instead of five thousand, still storms in the ocean instead of in a lake and resuscitate a man who has been dead fourteen days instead of only four.

There are two better interpretations, either alone or in combination.

The first is that our works are to be greater *in extent rather than in character,* or, as William Temple puts it, "in scale, if not in quality." He continues: "It is a greater thing to have founded hospitals all over Europe and in many parts of Asia and Africa, than to have healed some scores or some hundreds of sick folk in Palestine. . . . His works are no longer limited to Palestine but are diffused over the world."[7]

The second and more likely interpretation is that our works are to be greater *spiritually rather than materially.* At least since Augustine's exposition of this verse, it has been recognized that the conversion of the Gentiles by the preaching of the disciples of Christ is a greater work than Christ ever did himself. Thus Calvin refers to "the wonderful conversion of the world in which his divinity was displayed more powerfully than when he lived among men."[8] Bishop Ryle enlarges on this: "In short, 'greater works' mean more conversions. There is no greater work possible than the conversion of a soul."[9] A little later he continues:

> The meaning of these words must be sought in the *moral* and *spiritual* miracles which followed the preaching of the Apostles after the day of Pentecost. It could not be truly said that the *physical* miracles worked by the Apostles in the Acts were greater than those worked by Christ. But it is equally certain that after the day of Pentecost they did far more wonderful works by God's blessing in converting souls than our Lord did. On no occasion did Jesus convert 3,000 at one time, and a "great company of priests."[10]

I myself believe that we have liberty to combine both explanations. The works of the Christian can be greater than the works of Christ both extensively and spiritually. As Alfred Plummer puts it, "Christ's work was confined to Palestine and had but small success; the Apostles went everywhere, and converted thousands."[11]

Such "greater works" would be possible, Jesus said, because he was going to the Father (v. 12). From there he would send the Holy Spirit. There also he would intercede for his people. And these "greater works" would be granted not just to those who labor, but especially to those who pray in the name of Christ, that is, through Christ as mediator. For, "if you ask anything in my name," Jesus added, assuming always that it is in accordance with the Father's will, "I will do it" (vv. 13-14).

These, then, are the four positive assertions about the second coming of Christ which he gave to the apostles in order to cure their spiritual heart trouble. And the same promises (if we believe them) will calm our fears in the face of death. Already he is preparing a place for us. Already he is the way along which we are traveling. One day (at his appearing or in a secondary sense at our death) he will come himself to fetch us and he will take us to himself.

It is those believers who thus keep their eyes on Christ as the Forerunner, the Way, the Escort and the Destination, whose hearts are set free from the fear of death.

Rather they will be like Augustus Toplady. A friend visited him just before his death, felt his pulse and told him that his heart was evidently beating weaker and weaker every day. Toplady replied immediately with the sweetest smile: "Why, that is a good sign that my death is fast approaching and, blessed be God, I can add that my heart beats every day stronger and stronger for glory."[12]

Another example is Henry Venn, who retired from being Vicar of Huddersfield and came to live in Clapham next to his son John's rectory in 1796. When told that he was dying, "the prospect made him so jubilant and high-spirited that his doctor said that his joy at dying kept him alive a further fortnight!"[13]

II. Christ's intermediate coming (John 14:15-26 and parts of John 16)

The glorious prospect of our Lord's final coming and presence does not mean that he is altogether absent now.

In verse 18 he says, "I will not leave you desolate." The word means literally "orphans" or "alone in the world" (J. B. Phillips). He has just called them his "little children" (13:33) because he loves them with a father's love. So when he goes, they will be like orphans, although Westcott is right to add that "the very word which describes their sorrow confirms their sonship."[14]

Jesus knows that they will feel bereaved, that already sorrow has filled their hearts (16:6) and that later they will "weep and lament" (16:20). But he will not leave them bereft. "I will not leave you desolate," he says, "I will come to you."

What is this coming of Christ? As a result of it, although the world will not see him again, he is able to say to them, "you will see me" and, moreover, "you will live" (v. 19) and "you will know" (v. 20). That is, when he comes to them, their sight will be restored, their life intensified and their knowledge increased. What is this coming, as a result of which they will see and live and know?

Jesus elaborates his promise in John 16:16 and the following verses in the repeated phrase, "A little while, and you will see me no more; again a little while, and you will see me." The apostles themselves were puzzled by these words, and commentators have been puzzled ever since. Some think that the reference is to the resurrection, and that the second "little while" after which they would see Christ was the short period elapsing between his death and his resurrection. But it must mean more than that. The blessings which this renewed sight of Christ would bring would be permanent. They would not be available only for forty days before he disappeared again. Further, this "sight" of Christ seems to refer to spiritual vision, so that the promise "you shall see me" is the consequence of his other promise "I will manifest myself to him" (v. 21).

Verses 21-23 are "exceeding great and precious promises." If I am not greatly mistaken they are some of the most precious promises Christ ever uttered, for they relate to the deepest longing of every Christian believer, which is to know Christ better. As Bishop Ryle has written, "There is more of heaven on earth to be obtained than most Christians are aware of."[15]

Two great lessons are taught in these verses.

The first is that Christ reveals himself to his lovers. The Jews were expecting Christ to manifest himself to the world, for "the nations" had been promised him as his inheritance (Ps. 2:8). It is to this expectation that the other Judas alluded when he asked (v. 22), "Lord, how is it that you will manifest yourself to us, and not to the world?" But, just as the risen Christ manifested himself only to certain chosen witnesses, so he manifests himself today to the few, not the many. And the few are not just those who believe in him (v. 12), but those who love him (v. 15). He keeps his secrets for his friends, to those of whose devotion he is sure: "He who loves me will be loved by my Father, and I will love him and manifest myself to him" (v. 21).

The second lesson is that Christ's lovers prove their love by their obedience. "If you love me, you will keep my commandments," he has said (v. 15). And again, "He who has my commandments and keeps them, he it is who loves me" (v. 21). Just as in the Old Testament (especially in Deuteronomy) Israel was to love God and obey his commandments, so in the New Testament Christ expects his people to love and obey him.

If we want to convince Jesus Christ that we love him, there is only one way to do so. It is neither to make protestations of our devotion, nor to work up feelings of affection toward him, nor to sing hymns of personal piety, nor even to give ourselves to the service of humanity. It is to obey his commandments. Jesus demonstrated his love for the Father by his obedience ("I do as the Father has commanded me," v. 31); we must demonstrate our love for Christ by our obedience.

Thus the test of love is obedience, and the reward of love is a self-manifestation of Christ.

Having seen this, we must again press our question: How does Christ come to us and manifest himself to us? And how will his other promise be fulfilled that both he and his Father will come to us and make their home with us (v. 23)?

The answer is that Christ comes to us through the Holy Spirit, and this takes us back to verses 15-17: "If you love me, you will keep my commandments. And I will pray the Father, and he will give you another Counselor, to be with you for ever, even the Spirit of truth, whom the world cannot receive, because it neither sees him nor knows him; you know him, for he dwells with you, and will be in you."

Notice that Christ now says of the Holy Spirit what he has previously said (v. 7) of the Father, namely, "you know him." Just as the apostles knew the Father because they knew the Son, so they also knew the Spirit because they knew the Son. Although each Person of the Trinity is eternally distinct from the others (so that the Son can speak of the Father and of the Spirit as being each a separate *he*), yet the three Persons are so completely one in their essential being that to know one is to know the others. In particular, Jesus said, it is impossible to know the Son without thereby knowing the Father and the Spirit as well. Do you know Christ? Then you also know the Father. Do you know Christ? Then you also know the Spirit. We must not separate the three Persons of the Trinity.

Notice also how Christ refers to the Spirit in the Upper Room discourse. He is "the Holy Spirit" (v. 26), holy himself and the promoter of holiness. He is "the Spirit of truth" (14:17; 15:26; 16:13), true himself and the teacher of truth. He is also the Comforter, the Paraclete, a word meaning both specifically "advocate" and more generally one called in to help, whether to comfort or to counsel. As such he is not only "the helper" but "another helper" (v. 16)–"other" not in the sense of "different" (*heteros*) but in the sense of "second" (*allos*). Jesus was their first helper or comforter. When he had gone, he would send another, he said. And this second comforter would in a real sense be Jesus himself, returned to them in the person of the Holy Spirit, so that he could say: "I will not leave you desolate; I will come to you" (v. 18).

Moreover, after Pentecost Christ's presence with his people would be even better than it had been before. He says so plainly in 16:7: "Nevertheless I tell you the truth: it is to your advantage that I go away, for if I do not go away, the Counselor will not come to you; but if I go, I will send him to you."

This saying must have astonished the apostles. Could they believe their ears? Had Jesus really said that it would be to their advantage that he should go? Had he actually stated that they would be better off without him than with him? How could that be possible?

Christ's answer to their unspoken questions was that the Holy Spirit would replace him, and that his own presence through the Spirit after Pentecost would bring greater benefits than his presence on earth in the flesh. Indeed, Jesus insisted on this by his formula "I tell you the truth."

We may summarize these increased benefits under the two headings of the greater availability and the wider ministry of the Holy Spirit.

A. The greater availability of the Holy Spirit

I guess that we have all sometimes looked on the apostles with envy. We have probably all said to ourselves: "If only I had been with

Jesus, and glimpsed the glory of his face and heard the music of his voice! If only I had watched him make the lame walk, the deaf hear, the blind see and the dumb speak!" This kind of aspiration is natural enough, but it is mistaken. For if we have Christ through the Spirit now, we have the advantage over those who knew him only in the flesh. This is because the Spirit makes Christ available to us continuously and universally.

Jesus emphasized this to the apostles by saying that through the Spirit he would be with them "forever" (14:16). They would enjoy his presence no longer spasmodically or temporarily, but without interruption or end. Further, this constant presence of Jesus through the Spirit would be possible because he would no longer be merely "with" them but actually "in" them (v. 17) and so could never be separated from them.

The great benefit of this presence of Christ with his people through the Spirit, an eternal presence because an internal presence, is well illustrated by Henry Drummond.

> Suppose He had not gone away; suppose He were here now. Suppose He were still in the Holy Land, at Jerusalem. Every ship that started for the East would be crowded with Christian pilgrims. Every train flying through Europe would be thronged with people going to see Jesus. Every mail-bag would be full of letters from those in difficulty and trial. Suppose you are in one of those ships. The port, when you arrive after the long voyage, is blocked with vessels of every flag. With much difficulty you land, and join one of the long trains starting for Jerusalem. Far as the eye can reach, the caravans move over the desert in an endless stream. As you approach the Holy City you see a dark, seething mass stretching for leagues and leagues between you and its glittering spires. You have come to see Jesus; but you will never see Him.

B. **The wider ministry of the Holy Spirit**

In general, we may say that the function of the Holy Spirit in these days of the New Covenant is to make Christ known, to apply to believers all the benefits of Christ's words and work. For neither the revelation nor the redemption of God in and through Jesus Christ can benefit us until the Holy Spirit makes them ours in personal enjoyment.

There are four paragraphs in John 14–16, about the ministry of the Holy Spirit, which it may be helpful to bring together here. The references are 14:25-26; 15:26-27; 16:8-11; and 16:12-15.

Each of these paragraphs has a main verb which summarizes the particular work of the Spirit which is in mind. Christ promised his apostles that the Spirit would bring his teaching to their remembrance (14:26), bear witness to him before the world (15:26), convince the world of sin, righteousness and judgment (16:8) and guide them into all the truth (16:13).

According to the first promise the Spirit's ministry is a *reminding* ministry, according to the second a *witnessing* ministry, according to the third a *convincing* (or convicting) ministry and according to the fourth a *teaching* ministry. The first and fourth refer to his ministry to the church, and the second and third refer to his ministry to the world. I propose, therefore, to take them in that order.

1. The Spirit will recall Christ's teaching (14:25-26)

He will "bring to your remembrance all that I have said to you." This promise was addressed first and foremost to the apostles. I do not doubt that it has a secondary reference to us, in that the Holy Spirit is able to stimulate our mind in the task of Scripture memorization. But the primary reference is without doubt to the apostles who were gathered round the Lord in the Upper Room. This is evident from the context, especially from a study of the pronoun "you." Thus Jesus said, "These things I have spoken to *you,* while I am still with *you.* But the Counselor . . . will teach *you* all things, and bring to *your* remembrance all that I have said to *you.*" The word comes five times and on each occasion must refer to the same group. The "you" whom the Spirit will remind of Christ's teaching are the "you" to whom Christ had spoken while he was still with them.

The fulfillment of this great promise is to be seen in the writing of the New Testament, and in particular of the gospels. Whatever may be said about the custom of Jewish rabbis to get their disciples to learn their instruction by heart, about the tenacious Oriental memory, about the many collections of Christ's sayings, about the period of oral transmission and about the use of Christ's teaching in worship, evangelism and the instruction of converts, we owe the gospels ultimately to the work of the Holy Spirit in recalling Christ's teaching to the mind and memory of the original hearers, and indeed in interpreting it to them. So Jesus says (v. 26) that the Father will send the Spirit *in his name,* as his representative, to take his place, to continue and complete his teaching work.

"Under the inspiration and in the illumination of the other Advocate," writes Professor Tasker in his commentary, "the words spoken to them by Jesus on earth will not only be recalled, but become radiant with hitherto unsuspected meaning."[16] Archbishop Temple adds, "Especially will He make those days in Galilee and Jerusalem live again and yield up their secret."[17]

2. **The Spirit will bear witness to Christ (15:26-27)**

"But when the Counselor comes, whom I shall send to you from the Father, even the Spirit of truth, who proceeds from the Father, he will bear witness to me; and you also are witnesses, because you have been with me from the beginning."

The context, as we shall see when we study John 15, is that of a hostile and persecuting world (vv. 18-25). It is before this world that the Spirit and the apostles are to bear witness.

Again, it is not *our* witness in the first place to which Jesus is alluding, but theirs, the witness of those he could describe as having been with him "from the beginning" (v. 27).

In other words, the Holy Spirit's purpose in recalling Christ's teaching to them was not that they should guard it like some priceless treasure for themselves, but that they should share it with the world. The gospels are not biography; they are testimony.

3. **The Spirit will convict of sin, righteousness and judgment (16:8-11)**

"And when he comes, he will convince the world of sin and of righteousness and of judgment."

This is another aspect of the Spirit's ministry—to the world rather than the church, that is, to unbelievers, not believers.

It is also portrayed in legal terms, although now the Spirit is not giving evidence so much as securing a conviction. He convinces or convicts the world of three things—sin, righteousness and judgment.

That is to say, he makes these three moral categories (which men otherwise despise and dismiss) a solemn reality.

We might perhaps sum up this ministry of the Holy Spirit by saying that he convinces the world of the gravity of sin, the possibility of righteousness and the certainty of judgment. In each case he brings forth evidence by which to secure the conviction.

The Spirit convinces the world of sin, Jesus said, "because they do not believe in me" (v. 9). Jesus Christ is the light come into the world, but men love darkness rather than light. As Professor Tasker comments, "The root of sin lies in the desire of men to live their lives in self-centered independence, disowning any allegiance to Jesus."[18]

The Spirit convinces the world of righteousness, Jesus said, "because I go to the Father, and you will see me no more" (v. 10). The departure of Jesus to the Father would be by his resurrection and ascension. These would vindicate his sin-bearing death as a finished and satisfactory work, and so convince men that righteousness can be theirs through Christ.

The Spirit convinces the world of judgment, Jesus said, "because the ruler of this world is judged" (v. 11). Again Jesus is looking forward to his death, resurrection and ascension by which he would win a decisive victory over the devil. In these events the judgment had already begun. If therefore the ruler of the world had been judged, the world he rules will one day be judged also.

So it is, Jesus taught, that the Holy Spirit uses men's unbelief to prove the gravity of their sin, Christ's triumph to prove the possibility of their righteousness, and the devil's overthrow to prove the certainty of their judgment. The fact of sin and the solemn alternatives of righteousness or judgment become vital realities only when the Holy Spirit is doing his convicting work.

4. **The Spirit will lead into all the truth (16:12-15)**

Already in 14:26 Jesus has said that the Holy Spirit "will teach you all things." He now elaborates this promise: "I have yet many things to say to you, but you cannot bear them now. When the Spirit of truth comes, he will guide you into all the truth; for he will not speak on his own authority, but whatever he hears he will speak, and he will declare to you the things that are to come. He will glorify me, for he will take what is mine and declare it to you. All that the Father has is mine; therefore I said that he will take what is mine and declare it to you."

As in the Holy Spirit's reminding ministry (14:25-26), so in his teaching ministry here, it is essential to see that the primary reference is to the apostles. For this promise has been misapplied both by Catholics and by liberal Protestants.

The Catholic applies it to the *church* and claims that, as the Spirit teaches the church, the church's teaching has supreme authority. The liberal Protestant applies it to the *individual,* and claims that as the Spirit teaches the individual, his own reason has supreme authority. But the evangelical applies it to the *apostles* and claims that, as the Spirit inspired the apostles, it is their teaching (in the New Testament) which has supreme authority.

Again this is clear from the identity of the "you." The "you" whom the Holy Spirit will "guide into all the truth" (v. 13) is the very same "you" to whom Jesus had "many things to say" but who could not "bear them now" (v. 12).

We are now in a position to put together Christ's promises regarding the Holy Spirit's ministry to the apostles. According to 14:25-26 Christ had spoken certain things to the apostles, and the Spirit would bring these to their remembrance. According to 16:12-13 Christ had many more things to speak to the apostles which they could not then bear, and the Spirit would lead them into all the truth.

In other words, the Spirit's ministry to the apostles would be both a reminding and a supplementing ministry. He would remind them of what Christ had said to them and supplement it with what Christ had not been able to say.

Both promises were fulfilled in the writing of the New Testament, the gospels being the product of the Spirit's reminding ministry and the epistles the product of the Spirit's supplementing ministry.

This is not to say that the Holy Spirit has been idle in the subsequent, post-apostolic history of the church, but rather that his ministry has changed. He was leading the apostles into all the truth; he has been leading the church into an understanding of the truth into which he led the apostles. His work through the apostles was one of revelation; his work in the church is one of illumination, enlightening our minds to grasp what he has revealed.

And what is this truth into which the Spirit led the apostles? In two words, it is "Jesus Christ." The Spirit of truth led the apostles into all the truth, because Jesus Christ is the truth, as he said (14:6). Hence, the other phrases in 16:13-15.

"He will declare to you the things that are to come." It may be that this should be translated "the coming things" and that it refers to Christ's coming death, resurrection, ascension and gift of the Spirit as well as to his return at the end of time.

"He will glorify me," that is to say, he will manifest me or make me known.

"He will take what is mine and declare it to you," and in so doing he will glorify or reveal the Father also.

Here then is the wider ministry of the Holy Spirit, continuing, extending and applying the ministry of Christ. It is a fourfold work, and the Lord Jesus Christ himself is central to each aspect of it. Whether the Spirit is working with Christians or non-Christians, with the church or the world, his is a Christ-centered ministry.

First, he reminded the apostles of all Christ's earthly teaching. Then he supplemented and completed it, leading them into all the truth, revealing Christ to them in all his fullness. Thirdly, through the resulting teaching of the apostles (now preserved in the New Testament) the Spirit has ever since been convicting the world of sin, righteousness and judgment in relation to Christ. Fourthly, through the same unique apostolic testimony, faithfully expounded and personally attested by subsequent generations, the Spirit has been bearing witness to Christ.

It is Christ whose teaching the Spirit recalled to the apostles' minds. It is Christ whom the Spirit revealed to them as he led them into all the truth. It is Christ concerning whom the Spirit convicts the world of sin, righteousness and judgment. And it is Christ to whom the Spirit bears witness before the world.

The work of the Spirit can never be considered apart from Jesus Christ. He is the Spirit of Christ. His paramount concern is to reveal Christ to us and to form Christ in us.

We come now to the last five verses of Chapter 14 (vv. 27-31), in which Jesus returns to the theme of his imminent departure. Again he tells them not to let their hearts be troubled (v. 27). Instead, he says to them, "Shalom [Peace]." Yet his is no casual greeting. The peace he promises to give them is not the world's peace (shallow and transitory) but his own peace (deep and lasting): "Peace I leave with you; my peace I give to you; not as the world gives do I give to you."

Matthew Henry puts it like this, with quaintness and charm:

> When Christ was about to leave the world, He made His will; His soul He committed to His Father; His body He bequeathed to Joseph. . . . His clothes fell to the soldiers; His mother He left to the care of John. But what should He leave to His poor disciples, that had left all for Him? Silver and gold He had none; but He left them that which was infinitely better, His peace.[19]

But how is it possible to enjoy peace? How can we be delivered from the fear of death? How can we endure the trials of life and the persecutions of the world?

There are details in the concluding verses of John 14 which we have no time to elucidate. Yet the essence of the message is in verse 28: "You heard me say to you, 'I go away, and *I will come to you.*' " That is the answer. The ruler of this world (the devil) was also coming (v. 30), but (literally) he had "nothing" in Christ—no foothold in his life, no power or authority over him. For Christ always did his Father's will (v. 31).

C. H. Dodd suggests that the last words of the chapter, "Rise, let us go hence," may be a moral, not a physical, exhortation. He argues that the usual reference of the Greek verb is to an advancing enemy, that the enemy here may be the devil, and that Christ's words may mean, "Up, let us march to meet him."[20]

So then, after the devil has done his worst, when the world imagines that Jesus Christ is finished, he will return—first in the Spirit to continue his work, then in glory to consummate it.

It is in these sure comings of Christ that we can find rest and peace. He promises to come to us now, to manifest himself to us now, today, through the Spirit who glorifies him, if we love him and prove our love by our obedience.

And he promises to come again on the last day, to manifest himself in power and great glory, and to take us to himself.

These promises are sufficient to cure the most acute spiritual heart attack. As he said at the beginning of the chapter, "Let not your hearts be troubled; believe in God, believe also in me."

Notes

[1]Bishop J. C. Ryle, *Expository Thoughts on the Gospels* (Grand Rapids: Zondervan, n.d. [First published in 1856]), V, 277.
[2]Bill Roberts, *Life and Death among the Ibos* (London: Scripture Union, 1970), pp. 85-86.
[3]Temple, p. 226.
[4]*Ibid.*, p. 228.
[5]Westcott, p. 200.
[6]Calvin, p. 74.
[7]Temple, p. 235.
[8]Calvin, p. 80.
[9]Ryle, p. 297.
[10]*Ibid.*, p. 301.
[11]Plummer, p. 277.
[12]Bishop J. C. Ryle, *Christian Leaders*, p. 370.
[13]Michael Hennell, *John Venn and the Clapham Sect* (London: Lutterworth, 1958), p. 151.
[14]Westcott, p. 206.
[15]Ryle, *Expository Thoughts*, p. 313.
[16]Tasker, p. 168.
[17]Temple, p. 247.
[18]Tasker, pp. 179-80.
[19]Matthew Henry, *An Exposition of the Old and New Testament* (1706), p. 470.
[20]C. H. Dodd, *The Fourth Gospel*, pp. 406-09 as quoted by Tasker, pp. 169-70.

THE THREEFOLD DUTY OF THE CHRISTIAN (JOHN 15)

In John 14 Christ has described the cure for spiritual heart trouble, namely, faith in himself and in his two comings. In John 15 he indicates our duty between these two comings; that is, after he has come back through the Spirit but before he has come back in glory.

Our Christian duty is threefold–first, to ourselves; next, to each other in the Christian fellowship; and third, to society as a whole. And this threefold duty is elaborated in the three paragraphs which constitute this chapter. We are to abide in Christ (vv. 1-11), to love one another (vv. 12-17) and to witness to Christ before the world (vv. 18-27).

This is Jesus Christ's own portrait of a balanced Christian disciple. It concerns his three major relationships–to the Lord, to the church and to the world.

I. **The Christian and the Lord (vv. 1-11)**

"Abide in me, and I in you. As the branch cannot bear fruit by itself, unless it abides in the vine, neither can you, unless you abide in me. I am the vine, you are the branches. He who abides in me, and I in him, he it is that bears much fruit, for apart from me you can do nothing" (vv. 4-5).

We are all familiar with this allegory of the vine and the branches, although we do not know what suggested it to Jesus. It may have been "the fruit of the vine" to which he has referred, the emblem of his blood (Mk. 14:23-25) or the gigantic golden vine which decorated the Temple gates and had grape clusters over six feet long. Or possibly there was a vine growing outside the house, whose tendrils were climbing over the wall and even into the Upper Room itself. More probably, Jesus was thinking of Israel, the choice vine which God had planted in Canaan.

Whatever suggested the allegory to his mind, it is a forceful one. "I am the true vine," he said. "My Father is the vinedresser [or *gardener,* NEB]," and "you are the branches" (vv. 1-5).

The essential message of the allegory is plain: It is just as much God's will for his people to be fruitful as it is the function of a vine to bear fruit. Two questions then immediately arise about Christian fruitfulness. The first concerns its nature (what it is), the second its secret (how it can be secured).

A. **The nature of Christian fruitfulness**

It is surprising how many imagine that "fruitfulness" means success in winning people for Christ and that the fruitful Christian is the Christian effective in soul-winning.

I remember receiving a letter from a girl student some time ago who was in spiritual distress because she said she had never won anybody to Christ, although (she said) Christ had promised that she could be fruitful. In my reply I said that she could indeed be fruitful, but that this did not necessarily mean that she would be successful. What God required of her in witness was that she should be faithful, not successful; she must be content to leave the results of her witness to God.

However, there are many modern scholars who take the same view. For example, Principal John Marsh writes in his commentary,

"The true vine would bear fruit; that is to say, the Church would and could and must evangelize."[1]

Nevertheless, with great respect, this interpretation has very doubtful biblical warrant. The ingathering of souls is indeed likened to the reaping of the grain harvest (e.g., Mt. 9:37-38 and Jn. 4:35-38), but hardly if at all to the fruit bearing of a vine or vineyard.

What then is the fruitfulness of which Jesus spoke? If we compare Scripture with Scripture, we do not have far to seek for an answer. We have already seen that in the Old Testament Israel was likened to a vine, indeed a "luxuriant vine" (Hos. 10:1) planted by God. Listen to Psalm 80: 8-9: "Thou didst bring a vine out of Egypt; thou didst drive out the nations and plant it. Thou didst clear the ground for it; it took deep root and filled the land." And now Jesus says: "I am the real vine." The adjective is *alethinos,* not *alethes,* not meaning true as opposed to false, but genuine as opposed to spurious and the reality as opposed to the shadow. He seems to have meant that he and his people in the Christian community would embody the ideal of the vine, of which disobedient Israel was only a rather pathetic apology.

We still have to ask what the "fruit" of the vine is. The prophet Isaiah tells us. He sang a song of the vineyard: "My beloved had a vineyard on a very fertile hill. He digged it and cleared it of stones, and planted it with choice vines; he built a watchtower in the midst of it, and hewed out a wine vat in it; and he looked for it to yield grapes, but it yielded wild grapes" (Is. 5:1-2). A similar lamentation occurs in Jeremiah: "I planted you a choice vine, wholly of pure seed. How then have you turned degenerate and become a wild vine?" (2:21).

Isaiah concludes his song with an explanation of the grapes and the wild grapes: "The vineyard of the Lord of hosts is the house of Israel, and the men of Judah are his pleasant planting; and he looked for justice, but behold, bloodshed; for righteousness, but behold, a cry" (5:7). The prophet then continues with a series of woes against greedy landowners and drunkards, against the nation's irresponsible leaders who were neglecting the ignorant and hungry, destroying moral values (calling evil good and good evil) and perverting justice in the law courts (vv. 8-23). In other words, the fruitfulness which God looked for in his people, and could not find, was righteous conduct, the moral qualities of justice, self-control, fair dealing and compassion toward the needy.

This coincides with the New Testament in which "the fruit of the Spirit" (the fruitfulness which the Holy Spirit produces in the lives of God's people) is "love, joy, peace, patience, kindness, goodness, faithfulness, meekness and self-control," nine graces which make the Christian believer Christlike. In fact, I do not hesitate to say that fruitfulness means Christlikeness.

God's purpose for his people is not only that we should be "clean" through Christ's teaching (v. 3), but that we should be "fruitful," "bearing fruit in every good work" (Col. 1:10); not only that we should be justified, but also that we should be sanctified. This is the fruit he looks for and expects. He could not find it in Israel; may he find it in us!

B. The secret of Christian fruitfulness

Perhaps I should rather say the "secrets" in the plural, because there are two. The first is the pruning of the branches by the vinedresser, and the second the abiding of the branches in the vine.

1. The pruning

God the Father is pictured as an indefatigable gardener. A branch that is already bearing fruit he prunes, in order to make it bear more fruit (v. 2b). He is not content to leave well enough alone; he wants what is well to be better. He is anxious that the fruitful branch will become more fruitful. So he prunes it for its own sake.

Jesus does not explain specifically what this pruning is. But we need not doubt that pain, sorrow, sickness and suffering, loss, bereavement, disappointment and frustrated ambition are all part of the pruning activity of God the gardener. Not that this is a complete explanation of the meaning of suffering. But it is a partial explanation. Much suffering is the pruning of the heavenly husbandman, or (changing the metaphor) the chastening of the Heavenly Father: "He disciplines us for our good, that we may share his holiness" (Heb. 12:10).

Now pruning is a drastic process. The amateur gardener knows this, as well as the professional horticulturist. The bush or shrub is cut right back, usually in the autumn, without any reserve or pity.

To the uninitiated it looks very cruel. Sometimes only a stump is left—naked, jagged, scarred, mutilated—to face the storms and the cold of the winter. But when the spring and the summer return, there is much fruit. The sharp pruning knife has after all brought a blessing.

So when a time of pruning comes in our Christian lives, we need to remember this teaching of Jesus. The painful pruning knife is in safe hands. It is the wise and loving vinedresser who wields the knife, as it is the wise and loving Father who wields the rod. His purpose is never wanton, never destructive, but always wholly beneficent. It is not to wound but to bless, not to deny us any good but to bring us a greater good, namely, to make us more fruitful still.

God's people of every age have been able to testify that suffering of some sort has proved a great means to holiness. Thus we read in Psalm 119: "Before I was afflicted I went astray; but now I keep thy word" (v. 67). Again, "It is good for me that I was afflicted, that I might learn thy statutes" (v. 71).

Malcolm Muggeridge has put it like this:

> Supposing you eliminated suffering, what a dreadful place the world would be! I would almost rather eliminate happiness. The world would be the most ghastly place because everything that corrects the tendency of this unspeakable little creature, man, to feel over-important and over-pleased with himself would disappear. He's bad enough now but he would be absolutely intolerable if he never suffered.[2]

Indeed, I would go further and suggest that some form of suffering is virtually indispensable to holiness. As Peter puts it, "Whoever has suffered in the flesh has ceased from sin" (1 Pet. 4:1). I sometimes wonder if the real test of our moral appetite, of whether we truly know what it means to "hunger and thirst after righteousness," is that we come to God and say, "Father, I am willing for *anything,* for any suffering however painful, if only you will use it as a means to make me like Christ."

Before we leave this first condition of fruitfulness, notice that pruning is not the only work which the heavenly vinedresser does. If he cuts back the fruitful branch, in order that it may bear more fruit, the fruitless branch (which bears no fruit at all) he cuts right out: "Every branch of mine that bears no fruit, he takes away" (v.

2a). That is, the branch that does not produce is removed altogether.

The historical reference is surely to Judas who, although one of the apostles, has already been described as "not clean" (13:10-11). His attachment to Christ was purely external; he was not a true branch in the vine. "Fruitless" branches appear in the allegory to represent church members, nominally but not vitally united to Christ. The fate of such branches is to be cast forth, to wither, to be gathered, thrown into the fire and burnt (v. 6). Marcus Dods draws attention to this succession of verbs, as emphasizing "the inevitableness and the completeness of the destruction."[3] As Jesus said elsewhere, "Every plant which my heavenly Father has not planted will be rooted up" (Mt. 15:13).

2. **The abiding**

If the first secret of fruitfulness is the pruning of the branch by the vinedresser, the second is the abiding of the branch in the vine. It is on this that the emphasis is laid. In Calvin's words, "This is the conclusion and application of the whole parable."[4]

What does it mean to "abide in Christ"? Perhaps we should start by recalling that every Christian is "in Christ." In essence, to be a Christian is neither to believe certain doctrines of the Christian creed, nor to attend certain services of the Christian church, nor to follow certain precepts of the Christian ethic (important as all these are in their place), but rather to be personally, vitally, organically related to Jesus Christ himself. The New Testament description of a Christian is that he is "in Christ," and to be "in Christ" means not to be inside him but to be united to him. The Christian is in Christ in the sense that a branch is "in" the vine, or a limb is "in" the body.

Now to "abide" in Christ is to develop this already existing relationship. More exactly, we are to abide in Christ and to allow Christ to abide in us. We must not miss that our duty is double, reciprocal: "Abide in me, and I in you" (v. 4). "He who abides in me, and I in him, he it is that bears much fruit" (v. 5). And these things are not the same, nor do they depend on the same conditions.

If Christ is to abide in us, we must let him do so. We must allow him, almost passively, to be what he is, our Lord and Lifegiver. We must yield to his control, look for his enabling and humbly rely on him to supply our need.

But if we are to abide in Christ, there are active steps which we must take. Let me quote Bishop Ryle's paraphrase of our Lord's command: "Abide in me. Cling to me. Stick fast to me. Live the life of close and intimate communion with me. Get nearer and nearer to me. Roll every burden on me. Cast your whole weight on me. Never let go your hold on me for a moment. . . ."[5] In particular, we must be diligent in our use of the so-called "means of grace." That is, we must spend time each day seeking Christ's face in Scripture and in prayer. We must be disciplined in our attendance at public worship and at the Lord's Supper. It is in these and other ways that we must actively pursue Christ and learn to abide in him. As William Temple put it, "All forms of Christian worship, all forms of Christian discipline, have this as their object. Whatever leads to this is good; whatever hinders this is bad; whatever does not bear on this is futile."[6]

The more disciplined we are in our set times of devotion, the more easy it will become to live the rest of our time in the presence of God. Brother Lawrence is the classic example of this. His real name was Herman of Loraine. After working as a soldier and a footman he was admitted to a Carmelite community in Paris in 1666 as a lay brother and became the society's cook. He was "a great awkward fellow who broke everying," and he was lame. But "in his business in the kitchen (to which he had naturally a great aversion)" he learned to practice the presence of God. "When the appointed times of prayer were passed," we are told, "he found no difference, because he still continued with God." Finally he could say, "I am come to a state wherein it would be as difficult for me not to think of God as it was at first to accustom myself to it. . . . In short, I am assured beyond all doubt that my soul has been with God above these thirty years."

Such abiding in Christ, and Christ in us, is absolutely indispensable to holiness: "He who abides in me, and I in him, he it is that bears much fruit." Thus the Christian is likened to a fruit tree, not a Christmas tree. For the fruit *grows* on a fruit tree, whereas the decorations are only *tied* on to a Christmas tree. The holiness of some professing Christians is Christmas-tree holiness. It is a purely artificial decoration, an external conformity to Christian standards. Authentic Christian holiness is a visible manifestation of the invisible

Christ-life within. As the fruit ripens naturally when the branch is abiding in the vine, so Christian character develops naturally when the Christian is abiding in Christ.

The opposite is also true. "As the branch *cannot* bear fruit by itself, unless it abides in the vine, neither *can* you, unless you abide in me. . . . For apart from me you *can* do nothing" (vv. 4-5). We must weigh carefully what Christ says we "can" and "cannot" do. We are probably familiar with the biblical doctrine of human inability (that no man can come to Christ unless the Father draws him); here is the biblical doctrine of Christian inability (that no believer can bear fruit without Christ).

It clearly does not mean that we can do absolutely nothing apart from Christ. We can. We frequently do. We can do our academic work and get a good degree without Christ; many do. It is possible to be a good parent or husband or wife without Christ. We can live our life, manage our home, do our job without any special grace of Jesus Christ. But we cannot be "fruitful," that is to say, we cannot be Christlike Christians without abiding in Christ. We cannot "lead a life worthy of the Lord, fully pleasing to him, bearing fruit in every good work" (Col. 1:10).

Once again we need to humble ourselves. As we have to allow Christ to wash us and make us clean, so we must also allow him to abide in us, and we in him, if he is to make us fruitful.

Am I speaking to a Christian who is conscious of bearing very little fruit? Then is it that we are bearing little fruit because we are not abiding in Christ? And is it that we are not abiding in Christ because this would be to adopt an attitude of dependence on him, and to be dependent on others is thought to be weak and spineless? Well, we should certainly want to be rid of drug dependence, but we can never be rid of Christ dependence. We are as dependent on Christ for fruitfulness as we are for cleansing. And we shall never learn to abide in Christ until we have despaired of ever becoming fruitful by ourselves.

But when we despair of ourselves, we shall humble ourselves. When we humble ourselves, we shall abide in Christ and let him abide in us. When we abide in Christ, we shall bear fruit. And then further good consequences will follow, which are listed in verses 7-11.

First, our prayers will be answered: "Ask whatever you will, and it shall be done for you" (v. 7). Calvin wisely comments, "When He promises to grant whatever we wish, He does not permit an undisciplined asking."[7] It is only when Christ's words abide in us that our prayers will be answered. Then we can ask what we will and it shall be done, because we shall will only what he wills.

Second, our Father will be glorified (v. 8) because his purpose in putting us in Christ and pruning us when we are in Christ is that we shall be fruitful.

Third, our Christian discipleship will be demonstrated (v. 8) because we shall be keeping Christ's commandments and abiding in his love, as he keeps his Father's commandments and abides in his love (vv. 9-10).

Fourth, our joy will be full through experiencing Christ's own joy within us (v. 11).

Looking back over this first paragraph, we can see that we have no excuse for fruitlessness. With such a vinedresser to prune us and with such a vine to abide in, God says to us as he did to Israel, "What more was there to do for my vineyard that I have not done in it?" He has made every possible provision for our fruitfulness. So he looks for grapes–good, ripe, luscious grapes–in his vineyard. He expects us, and has a right to expect us, to become increasingly fruitful, increasingly like Christ.

II. The Christian and the church (vv. 12-17)

Christ turns now from our duty in relation to himself (to abide in him) to our duty in relation to each other (to love one another). This second paragraph of the chapter begins and ends with the same command (vv. 12, 17).

So we learn that the Christian life is not just a personal and private relationship to Jesus Christ. It also involves mutual love, which in its turn implies membership in the Christian church. For we cannot belong to Christ without thereby belonging to his people as well. It was John Wesley who said that to turn Christianity into a solitary religion is to destroy it. To be sure, it has its solitary aspect (the individual Christian abiding in Christ, as each branch abides in the vine); but it has its corporate aspect also (for all the branches are members of the same vine). I understand that California now has its drive-in church, advertized by the inviting sign, "Worship in the privacy of your own automobile." But that is not New Testament Christianity.

Let me ask you: Are you a conscientious member of a local Christian church? Every Christian should be a church member. Lone-wolf Christianity is not biblical Christianity. If God is our Father, we are brothers and sisters and must express our family life in corporate activities.

True, no part of the visible church is perfect. Billy Graham gives sound advice when he urges us to look for the perfect church, and, when we find it, to join it. But we must remember, he adds, that when we join it, it ceases to be perfect.

It is unfortunately true that some churches are so compromised in their loyalty to Jesus Christ that what they appear to offer the newcomer is rejection rather than acceptance. If that is your experience, all I can say to you is, "Persevere!" Do not accept this non-acceptance as an acceptable alternative. Claim the membership which is yours by right, if you are Christ's.

C. S. Lewis gives a humorous description of his first attempts to join the church and of the discomfort he felt:

> The idea of churchmanship was to me wholly unattractive. . . . But though I liked clergymen as I liked bears, I had as little wish to be in the Church as in the zoo. It was, to begin with, a kind of collective; a wearisome "get-together" affair. . . . To me, religion ought to have been a matter of good men praying alone and meeting by twos and threes to talk of spiritual matters. And then the fussy, time-wasting botheration of it all! The bells, the crowds, the umbrellas, the notices, the bustle, the perpetual arranging and organising. Hymns were (and are) extremely disagreeable to me. Of all musical instruments I liked (and like) the organ least. . . .[8]

Now the chief characteristic of church members should be mutual love: "This is my commandment, that you love one another as I have loved you" (v. 12) and "This I command you, to love one another" (v. 17). At least two parts of this mutual love are noteworthy.

A. **Love is obligatory**

Jesus has already issued his "new commandment" to love each other as he has loved us (13:34). Here, too, in both verses 12 and 17, to love one another is a "command."

"But," someone will no doubt protest, "this is quite intolerable. Love is not a fit subject for commandments. Love is an emotion—strong, uninvited, uncontrollable—and you cannot command me to love or not to love. You must not tell me to stop loving someone I do love or to start loving someone I don't. I cannot help it. I cannot help myself. I am at love's command; love is not at mine."

This kind of talk betrays much misunderstanding about the true nature of love. We may be sure that Jesus did not issue commands which cannot be obeyed. Since he commanded us to love each other (even elsewhere, our enemies), we must conclude that the loving he meant is not the victim of our emotions, but the servant of our will. We may not feel like loving somebody, but we are commanded to do so. We have to learn deliberately to set our love on people whom we do not naturally like.

This is the love of God. Moses expressed it long ago to the children of Israel: "It was not because you were more in number than any other people that the Lord set his love upon you and chose you, for you were the fewest of all peoples; but it is because the Lord loves you" (Deut. 7:7-8). This is the logic of divine love. He loves you because he loves you. There is no explanation of the love of God except the love of God. His love is not aroused by its object, but only by itself.

And we are to love others with God's love. Paul could write to the Philippians how greatly he loved them and yearned for them all "with the affection [or better, *compassion*] of Christ Jesus" (1:8). We must not therefore restrict our love to those we are fond of or with whom we have some natural affinity. Others may belong to a different race and rank. We may appear to have nothing in common with each other. Yet we are to love all men because God made them and Christ died for them, and especially to love each other because we are brethren in the same family. We must set our love upon one another in prayer and in practical service, seeking each other's good actively, for this is the meaning of love. How one longs to see such love displayed in the contemporary church!

B. **Love is sacrificial**

Christ's command to love is not vague and undefined, but precise. We are to love each other *as he has loved us* (v. 12). This seems to be the "newness" of the "new commandment." No longer are we to love others as we love ourselves. Now we are to love others as Christ loved us.

Verse 13 indicates the greatness of Christ's love: "Greater love has no man than this, that a man lay down his life for his friends." This statement is not contradicted by Romans 5:10 in which we are told that Christ died for his enemies. The context here is one of mutual friendship, and Christ is saying that no man can love his friends more than by laying down his life (the emphatic word) for them. Not that we are to wait for the opportunity to perform heroic deeds of self-sacrifice, for life is full of opportunities for lesser sacrifices. As John put it, "If anyone has the world's goods and sees his brother in need, yet closes his heart against him, how does God's love abide in him?" (1 Jn. 3:17). God's love, if it is in us, will lead us to share what we have with others–our money, possessions, time, friendship, home and knowledge of Christ.

There follows in verses 14-16 something of a digression on the implications of friendship. Having said that the greatest proof of friendship is self-sacrifice, Jesus immediately adds, "You are my friends" (v. 14), implying that he is going to prove his friendship for them by dying for them.

Why did Christ call his apostles his friends, as God called Abraham his friend (Is. 41:8; Jas. 2:23)? The essential difference between being a servant (in modern terms, an employee) and a friend is that the boss does not tell his staff either his plans or his secrets. He reserves his confidences for his friends. So Jesus calls the apostles "friends" because he has made known to them what the Father had made known to him. They had been the recipients of this special privileged revelation.

Indeed, Christ had chosen them for this very purpose (v. 16; cf. 6:70; 13:18; and Lk. 6:13); they had not chosen him. They were to "go," their mission being to share his special revelation with others. They were also to "bear fruit," representing Christ by their life as well as by their teaching, by a ripe Christian character which would "abide" (cf. 1 Cor. 13:13), and as a result of which their prayers would be answered.

Although these verses (like others which we have considered before) refer in the first instance to the apostles whom Christ had chosen and to whom he had made known the Father's words, nevertheless they have a secondary application to us and to all Christ's followers. It is to us also that he says, "No longer do I call you servants . . . I have called you friends" (v. 15).

We must be careful how we interpret this statement, however. We cannot legitimately press it into meaning that the Christian life is nothing but friendship with Jesus and that we are no longer required either to serve or to obey him, because the concepts of submission and obedience have been abolished for the Christian. This would be a very superficial interpretation, as the context makes plain. Did Jesus not say earlier (13:13), "You call me Teacher and Lord; and you are right, for so I am"? Did he not add (v. 16), "A servant is not greater than his master"–an epigram he is about to repeat in verse 20? Does he not also say here (15:14), "You are my friends if you do what I command you"? It would be unthinkable that we should say such a thing to our friends and make their obedience a condition of our friendship!

All this shows that friendship with Jesus Christ is not like ordinary friendship. The fact that he calls us "friends" gives us no liberty to assume that everything in human friendship has its equivalent in our friendship with Christ. It is always dangerous to argue from an analogy.

No. Jesus tells us the precise point at which the friendship analogy is made, namely that he tells us his secrets, which he would not tell us if we were only his servants. It is the same truth as he has expressed in 14:21, where he promised to manifest himself to us. Just as he manifests himself to his lovers, so he makes himself known to his friends.

Let us take the fullest possible advantage of this privilege of friendship with Christ. Let us press on to know him. Let us share the ambition of a sixteen-year-old Ugandan boy who once said to me with great earnestness, "Sir, I want to be intimate with Jesus."

But let us not presume on this friendship with Christ. It does not make us his equals. In other ways, we are still his servants, his subordinates, and are glad and proud to be such. The apostles, whom Jesus here called "friends," continued to call themselves his "slaves." He expects us to keep his commandments (v. 10), to do what he commands us (v. 14).

This brings us back to the chief commandment with which this paragraph begins and ends, namely, that we love one another. For all of us within the Christian community, sacrificial love is obligatory.

So far, Christ has spoken of our duties in relation to himself and to each other. Is that all? Is the Christian life to be understood in terms merely of fellowship with Christ and with each other? Are Christians in the end only a self-absorbed, self-regarding coterie whose interests are limited to themselves and their Lord? No, no. We are called also to be involved in the world.

III. **The Christian and the world (vv. 18-27)**

By the "world" Jesus meant the godless world of unbelievers, which in John's own words lies "in the power of the evil one" (1 Jn. 5:19). It is what we call "secular society," a community which rejects or ignores Christ, and of which Satan is both prince and god.

Jesus tells us here both what the world's attitude to the church will be, and what the church's attitude to the world should be.

A. **The world's attitude to the church (vv. 18-25)**

This is an attitude of hostility, of antagonism. "If the world hates you, know that it has hated me before it hated you" (v. 18). It is remarkable that Christ passes from the *love* which we ought to have for one another to the *hate* which the world will have for us.

The world hates the church because it hates Christ, the Lord of the church (v. 18), although it hates him without a cause (v. 25), and because Christ has chosen the church out of the world (v. 19b). Of course, when the church is worldly, the world loves the church: "If you were of the world, the world would love its own" (v. 19a). But when the church remembers its calling to be different from the world, the world hates the church. As William Temple puts it, the world "would not hate angels for being angelic; but it does hate men for being Christians. It grudges them their new character; it is tormented by their peace; it is infuriated by their joy."[9]

None of this is surprising (v. 20) because "a servant is not greater than his master." When Jesus used this epigram previously, it was to show that a servant must love as his master has loved (13:16); now he uses it to show that a servant will be hated as his master has been hated.

The world does not stop at hatred; its hatred of the church issues in persecution: "If they persecuted me, they will persecute you" (v. 20b).

Jesus then immediately goes on to say that the cause of the world's hostility is their ignorance of God (v. 21). Nevertheless, they are without excuse. If he had not come and *spoken* to them, and if he had not *done* among them the works which no one else had done, they would not have been as guilty as they were. As it is, his words and works made their opposition to him inexcusable (vv. 22-24).

This, then, is the world's attitude to the church. The world hates the church as it hated Christ, and it persecutes the church as it persecuted Christ.

Historically, this has proved to be true. Dietrich Bonhoeffer, who was himself executed in the Flossenburg concentration camp by direct order of Himmler on April 9, 1945, wrote this about persecution in his book, *The Cost of Discipleship* (1937):

> Suffering . . . is the badge of the true Christian. The disciple is not above his master. . . . Luther reckoned suffering among the marks of the true church, and one of the memoranda drawn up in preparation for the Augsburg Confession similarly defines the church as the community of those "who are persecuted and martyred for the gospel's sake." . . . Discipleship means allegiance to the suffering Christ, and it is therefore not at all surprising that Christians should be called upon to suffer. . . .[10]

A personal friend of mine, who is a medical missionary in a Muslim country, wrote recently of bitter attacks on Christian missionaries in a national newspaper—attacks which were answered by silence. My friend went on:

> It seems to be our lot as Christians to be misunderstood, criticized, and opposed by the world; and while the poor, the diseased, the blind, and the spiritually hungry come to us in their need, and in their hundreds, some of the wise, the rich,

and the self-sufficient spend their time slandering and opposing us, as they did when the Lord Jesus lived among them in the flesh. . . . It is the greatest privilege in the world to be spat upon for his sake. Oh that we were more worthy of it!

The individual Christian shares the church's lot. The more wholehearted each of us is in allegiance to Jesus Christ, the less popular we are likely to become in secular society. As Jesus said in the eighth and last beatitude (thus demonstrating that persecution is to characterize every Christian): "Blessed are those who are persecuted for righteousness' sake, for theirs is the kingdom of heaven" (Mt. 5:10).

B. **The church's attitude to the world (vv. 26-27)**

Here then is this hostile, hating, persecuting world. How are we to react to it?

Certainly not in resentment, retaliation or revenge; we are forbidden to return evil for evil. Nor are we to withdraw from contact with the world in order to escape its opposition or lick our wounds in self-pity. What then? We are to stay in the world in order to witness. We are to go out into the world, as Jesus will say later (17:18; 20:21), into this hating, persecuting world, as his ambassadors. In the name of Christ we are to love those who hate us and to commend Christ to them as their Savior. Let the world persecute the church, the church must evangelize the world.

From the last two verses of the chapter (26-27) we can learn four important truths about Christian witness.

First, it is witness before the world. We must read verses 26-27 against the background of verses 18-25. Persecution, far from being an excuse for silence, is actually a challenge to witness.

Second, it is witness to Christ. "He will bear witness to me," literally, "concerning me." This shows that *testimony* is not a synonym for *autobiography*! When we are truly witnessing, we are not talking about ourselves, but about Christ, although we may indeed illustrate what we say about Christ from our own experience of him.

Third, it is witness by the Holy Spirit. What Jesus said is this: "But when the Counselor comes, whom I shall send to you from the Father, even the Spirit of truth, who proceeds from the Father,

He will bear witness to me" (v. 26). The Holy Spirit is the chief witness to Christ before the hostile world. It is not that we shall bear witness and that the Spirit will confirm our witness (although this is what Peter said in Acts 5:32), but that the Spirit will bear witness and that we will ourselves confirm it. The Holy Spirit is "the Spirit of Truth." One of his chief functions is to bear witness to Christ, to open the eyes of the blind to see the truth as it is in Jesus. For "no one can say 'Jesus is Lord' except by the Holy Spirit" (1 Cor. 12:3). And the whole of Scripture—Old and New Testaments together—is his written testimony to Christ. He is also the Paraclete, the divine advocate, pleading Christ's cause before an unbelieving world.

Fourth, it is witness through the church. Jesus adds (v. 27): "And you also are witnesses, because you have been with me from the beginning." So there are two witnesses, the Spirit and the church, the Spirit through the church, so that in the mouth of two witnesses the testimony may be established.

Once again, the immediate reference is to the apostles. It is they who have been with Christ "from the beginning" (cf. Mk. 3:14; Lk. 1:2; Jn. 16:4; Acts 1:21-22) and whose eye-witness experience was one of their indispensable qualifications as apostles. And the apostolic witness to Jesus (preserved forever in the New Testament) will always remain the primary witness. Ours is a secondary witness, for the Christ to whom we bear testimony is the apostles' Christ; there is no other.

Thus the Christian witness is witness borne to Christ before the world by the Spirit through the church. And *every* Christian is called to participate in this testimony, to let his light (which is Christ's light) shine before men.

Let me quote Malcolm Muggeridge again:

> Sometimes on foolish television and radio panels, or being interviewed, someone asks me what I most want, what I should most like to do in the little that remains of my life, and I always nowadays truthfully answer, and it *is* truthful, "I should like my light to shine, even if only very fitfully, like a match struck in a dark cavernous night and then flickering out."

John 15 contains our Lord's account of the Christian's duty during the period which elapses between his two comings. It is a threefold duty, in widening circles. At the center of the inner circle is Christ himself, our Lord and Savior. Next comes our duty to each other in the fellowship of his church, and thirdly our duty to the outside rebellious world.

It is very easy to become an unbalanced Christian. Some concentrate on their fellowship with Christ in the church and woefully neglect their Christian duty of service and witness in the secular world. Others are so determined to serve man in the secular city that they neglect their fellowship with Christ and with Christ's people. Let us not neglect any duty in favor of the others. Let us seek rather to fulfil them all.

Let us also remember, that in each duty it is Jesus Christ himself who is central. First, we are to abide in *Christ.* Second, we are to love one another as *Christ* loved us. Third, we are to witness to *Christ* before the world.

This is the balanced, integrated, satisfying, Christ-centered life of a Christian. May God enable each of us to live it today!

Notes

[1] John Marsh, *The Gospel of St. John* (Baltimore: Penguin, 1968), p. 520.
[2] Malcolm Muggeridge, *Jesus Rediscovered* (Glasgow: Collins-Fontana, 1969), pp. 158-59.
[3] Dods, p. 829.
[4] Calvin, p. 95.
[5] Ryle, *Expository Thoughts,* p. 335.
[6] Temple, p. 258.
[7] Calvin, p. 96.
[8] C. S. Lewis, *Surprised by Joy* (London: Geoffrey Bles, 1955), p. 220-21.
[9] Temple, p. 272.
[10] Dietrich Bonhoeffer, *The Cost of Discipleship* (1937), p. 74.
[11] Muggeridge, p. 91.

THE MASTER'S FINAL PRAYER (JOHN 17)

John 17 is without doubt one of the most profound chapters of the Bible. A single hour is a hopelessly inadequate time in which to attempt to fathom it. Whole books have been written to expound it. In fact, Thomas Manton, a seventeenth-century Puritan minister who at one time was Oliver Cromwell's chaplain, preached a series of forty-five sermons on it.

Another commentator was Marcus Rainsford, the Irish clergyman who exercised an influential ministry of biblical preaching in St. John's Church, Belgrave Square, London, from 1866 to his death in 1897, and was a friend of D. L. Moody. His exposition of John 17 is now published under the title *Our Lord Prays for His Own.*

Both these expositions run to about 450 pages. What can we hope to accomplish in one study? If we were to meditate on this chapter all our lives, we would not be able to fathom its depths. In one brief hour we can only paddle in its shallows.

"When Jesus had spoken these words, he lifted up his eyes to heaven and said, 'Father. . .' " (v. 1). Having spoken to the apostles, Jesus now speaks to his Father, and thus waters with prayer the seeds of instruction which he has been sowing. Those of us who are preachers and teachers can learn a valuable lesson here. As Calvin puts it, "Doctrine is cold unless it is given divine efficacy. He therefore shows teachers an example, that they should not only occupy themselves in sowing the Word, but by mixing their prayers with it should implore God's help, that His blessing should make their work fruitful."[1]

Next, we must notice how Jesus approaches God before he utters any petition. He says, "Father, the hour has come" (v. 1). This address ("Father") and this assertion ("the hour has come") together form an essential introduction and background to the prayer which follows. The whole prayer is colored by this double awareness.

First, it is a prayer of the Son of God. Indeed, although we know that on occasions Jesus continued all night in prayer to God (e.g., Lk. 6:12), yet this is the only prayer of any length which has been recorded. Jesus evidently prayed it aloud. As a result, we are given the great privilege of overhearing the Son communing with the Father. Five times he repeats this address–the "Abba" which Professor Joachim Jeremias, after scouring all Jewish literature, has declared to be unique: "Father" (v. 1), "Father" (v. 5), "holy Father" (v. 11), "Father" (v. 24) and "righteous Father" (v. 25).

Second, it is a prayer prayed on the eve of his passion. "The hour has come," he says. Twice already he has referred to the arrival of his "hour," the hour of his death, the hour for which he had entered the world (12:23; 13:1). Previously he kept saying "my hour has not yet come." Now at last "the hour has come." He knows that he is about to die for the sins of the world, then to rise from death, to return to the Father and to send the Holy Spirit.

It is a marvellous providence of God that there has been preserved for posterity such a prayer by such a person at such an hour.

The prayer of Jesus is composed of a threefold petition–first for himself (vv. 1-5) as he faces the climax of his earthly career; second for his apostles (vv. 6-19), to whom he has manifested the Father's name (v. 6); and third for those who would later believe in him through the apostles' testimony (vv. 20-26).

His petitions are that he may be glorified, that the apostles may be sanctified and that the church may be unified.

I. The glorification of the Son (vv. 1-5)

Jesus prays twice for his glorification. At the end of verse 1, "Father, . . . glorify thy Son." And at the beginning of verse 5, "Father, glorify thou me." What did he mean?

We have already noted that the glory of God is the revelation or manifestation of God. God himself in his essential being is invisible and even incomprehensible. No one has ever seen God (1:18); all that men have ever seen or known of him is his "glory." This glory has been defined as "the outward shining of the inward being of God." "Glory is the display of the fulness of God . . . as the light of the sun is the glory of the sun."[2] God's glory is seen partly in nature ("The heavens are telling the glory of God," Ps. 19:1), but especially in Christ, who is described as the reflection or effulgence of his glory (Heb. 1:3), so that "the light of the knowledge of the glory of God" shines "in the face of Christ" (2 Cor. 4:6).

So then the verb "to glorify" means to reveal or manifest God. Jesus has already said in 16:14 that the Holy Spirit will glorify him, that is, make him known. Now he prays that the Father will glorify him or make him known.

If this is the meaning of the prayer, to what event or experience is Jesus alluding? How did he expect his prayer to be answered? By what means would the Father glorify the Son?

These verses mention three means.

A. The Son would be glorified in the cross (vv. 1-4)

There can be no doubt of the close connection in the mind of Christ between his death on the cross and his glorification. When certain Greeks asked to see him, he spoke immediately of his death, which he described as the hour when he would be glorified: "The hour has come for the Son of man to be glorified. . . . Unless a grain of wheat falls into the earth and dies, it remains alone; but if it dies, it bears much fruit" (12:23-24). Again in the Upper Room, as soon as Judas had left, Jesus said to the eleven: "*Now* is the Son of man glorified" and "God will . . . glorify him *at once*" (13:31-32).

The same link is plain here too: "the hour has come; glorify thy Son." The hour of his death would be the hour of his glorification.

But how could this be? We tend to think of the cross in terms of shame, not of glory. Certainly, a crucified criminal was regarded by the Romans as unspeakably degraded, and by the Jews as being under the curse of God. How then could Christ refer to himself as glorified in such a death, when others would consider him as rejected by men and accursed by God?

The answer is that on the cross he was glorified in the sense of being revealed or manifested. He had already manifested his glory in his miracles. They were "signs" displaying his claims and character (e.g., 2:11). But the greatest sign of all was his death. If we want to see Jesus Christ as he is, we must look at the cross. The cross is the clearest and brightest revelation of his nature and purpose.

Nevertheless, a question may enter our minds at this point. How is it that Christ could pray for his own glorification? Even when we grasp the meaning of the word, is not the prayer somewhat self-centered? No. Rather, the reverse. For the ultimate ends of his own glorification (for which he prayed) were first the glory of God and second the salvation of men.

First, the glory of God: "Father, . . . glorify thy Son that [thereby] the Son may glorify thee." The glory of the Father and of the Son are indissolubly connected. Since the Son is the glory of the Father, and since the glory of the Son is the glory of the only begotten of the Father (1:14), whenever the Son is glorified the Father is glorified also (cf. 14:13).

Now the cross is a marvelous display of the holiness, justice and love of God in Christ. We see his holiness in his hatred of sin and refusal to compromise with it, his justice in his condemning it, even in the person of his Son, and his love in his securing the salvation of sinners at such enormous cost. As Calvin expressed it while expounding John 13:31, "For in the cross of Christ, as in a splendid theatre, the incomparable goodness of God is set before the whole world. The glory of God shines, indeed, in all creatures on high and below, but never more brightly than in the cross. . . ."[3]

Second, if the glorification of Christ on the cross brought glory to God, it also brought salvation to man.

"Since thou hast given him power [literally "authority"] over all flesh, to give eternal life. . ." (v. 2): This seems to express another ground or reason for Christ's desire for his own glorification. It contains a whole complex of profound truths. It tells us that the Father has given the Son authority over all flesh; and that the purpose of this gift of authority is that the Son should not only execute judgment (5:27), but also give eternal life to all whom the Father has given him.

Notice this series of divine gifts. The Father "gives" the elect to the Son and "gives" authority to the Son to "give" them eternal life. Further, this eternal life (which the Son gives them) consists of the knowledge of God, who is the only true (literally "real") God, as opposed to images which are fantasy. It is the intimate, personal, dynamic, increasing knowledge both of the Father and of his Son Jesus Christ, whom the Father sent.

But such knowledge of God is impossible without the cross. For the cross is the revelation of God, without which we cannot "know" him truly. And the cross is the means of our reconciliation to God, without which we cannot "know" him personally.

So then Christ prays for his own glorification on the cross, both in order that by it the Father may be made known as the Savior he is, and in order that by it sinners may come to know him, and so receive eternal life. The ultimate end of Christ's prayer being God's glory and man's salvation, it cannot be said to be selfish.

This brings us to the second stage in the process of the Son's glorification.

B. The Son would be glorified in heaven

"I glorified thee on earth, having accomplished the work which thou gavest me to do; and now, Father, glorify thou me in thy own presence with the glory which I had with thee before the world was made" (v. 4-5).

These verses obviously refer to heaven and prepare the way for the petition of verse 24 that Christ's people may behold his glory.

Christ's glory is conceived now not as actually set forth in and by his sufferings, but as the consequence of them. Jesus certainly spoke like this after the resurrection when he said it was necessary for the Christ to "suffer these things and enter into his glory" (Lk. 24:26). And the apostles Paul and Peter wrote in these terms also.

So here Jesus prays that he may resume the position he had before the world was made and that his glory (which had been veiled on earth) may again be fully displayed in heaven.

In this second prayer the reciprocal glorification of the Father and the Son is once more expressed: "I glorified you on earth," he says (having accomplished the work you gave me to do); "now, Father, will you glorify me in heaven. . . ."

Putting the two prayers together, one sees a remarkable progression. It is as if he prays, "Father, please glorify me on the cross, that I may thereby glorify you. I have already glorified you on earth, so now please glorify me in heaven."

We cannot leave this first petition of Christ's for his own glorification without considering the third means by which it would be effected, although it is not mentioned until the second paragraph. It is this:

C. **The Son would be glorified in the church**
"I am glorified in them" (v. 10).

If the glorification (revelation) of Christ were restricted to the cross and to heaven, we would be in grave difficulties. For neither of these revelations is immediately accessible to us. Time in the one case and space in the other have to some extent removed them from us. True, the witness of the biblical writers makes the cross contemporary in the sense that it placards it before our eyes (see Gal. 3:1). Yet Christ's glorification on the cross did happen nearly two thousand years ago, and his glorification in heaven is to us invisible and virtually incomprehensible.

Is there no means, we may legitimately ask, by which Jesus Christ is glorified in the here and now, accessibly, visibly, conprehensibly? Yes, there is! He is glorified in his people, just as (incidentally) according to 15:8 the Father is glorified in the fruitful Christian.

The followers of Jesus Christ, redeemed by his blood and renewed by his Spirit, are intended to exhibit his glory on earth. True, not till Christ returns will he be fully glorified in his people (2 Thess. 1:10). But already his people can make him known if they are being transformed by his Spirit into his image from one degree of glory to another (2 Cor. 3:18).

It is a solemn and splendid truth that between the glorification of

Christ in history and in heaven there is another glorification in the present and on earth, namely, in his church. The same Lord Jesus, whose glory was once seen on the cross and will finally be seen in heaven, is now to be seen, or is meant to be seen, in his people. "I am glorified in them," he says. "Mortified Christians are the glory of Christ."[4]

A Sudanese national once said of the Anglican bishop in the Sudan: "When I see Bishop Gelsthorpe, I think I see the Lord Jesus."

Once Sadu Sundar Singh came to an Indian home, knocked at the door and a little girl went to open it. She took one look at him and ran back into the kitchen. Her mother said, "Who is it?" The girl replied, "I don't know, but he has such a lovely face, I think it must be Jesus."

Not merely in the words you say,
Not only in your deeds confessed,
But in the most unconscious way
Is Christ expressed.

Is it a beatific smile?
A holy light upon your brow?
Oh no! I felt His presence
When you laughed just now.

To me, 'twas not the truth you taught,
To you so clear, to me still dim,
But when you came you brought
A sense of Him.

And from your eyes He beckons me,
And from your heart His love is shed,
Till I lose sight of you and see
The Christ instead.

In the second paragraph of Christ's prayer the subject changes. He has been praying for himself; he prays now for others, for certain men whom the Father has given him. These are the apostles, and he prays for their sanctification.

II. The sanctification of the apostles (vv. 6-19)

There are clear indications in the text (as throughout Jn. 13–17) that the primary reference of these verses is to the apostles whom Christ had chosen and who were gathered round him in the Upper Room. Thus, he has in a special way manifested God's name to them (v. 6) and given them God's words (v. 8). And none of them is lost, he says (v. 12), but only "the son of perdition." Since many of Christ's contemporaries had rejected him and were lost, this must refer to the apostles among whom only Judas had proved reprobate. He then prays (v. 20) for subsequent believers, who would come to faith "through their word," that is, through the apostles' testimony either heard while they were alive or later read in the New Testament.

Nevertheless, although the immediate reference is to the apostles, the way Christ describes them and the prayers he prays for them are also applicable to us.

Underlying this second paragraph is the basic biblical truth that there are two distinct human communities. The larger community Jesus calls "the world" or (as we might say) secular society; the other and smaller community he calls those whom the Father has given him out of the world. That they are the Father's gift to the Son is repeated several times (vv. 2, 6a and b, 9, possibly 11-12, 24), and as Marcus Rainsford says, we do not know which to admire more–"the grace which gave us to Christ or gave Christ to us."[5] Listen to verse 9 (and cf. 15:19): "I am praying for them; I am not praying for the world but for those whom thou hast given me, for they are thine." Here the two communities are clearly set over against one another.

At least from the call of Abraham onward God's purpose has been to call out from the world a people for himself. Sometimes the two communities are depicted as two kingdoms: the kingdom of light and the kingdom of darkness, the kingdom of God (the sphere of his rule) and the kingdom of Satan; and sometimes as two cities: the holy city Jerusalem and the great city Babylon, so that the story of the Bible is a tale of two cities. To blur the distinction between them is fatal to a true understanding of Scripture.

How then does Jesus refer to his people? He actually gives an elaborate description of them and their situation (from v. 6 to the beginning of v. 11); he does not begin to pray for them until the end of verse 11. He emphasizes two facts about them.

First, *they do not belong to the world.*

On the contrary, as we have seen, they have been given to Christ out of the world. And Christ, to whom they have been given, has revealed to them the nature of God and given them the Word of God, so that they have been brought to Christian knowledge and to Christian faith. "I have manifested thy name to the men whom thou gavest me out of the world" and "they have kept thy word" (v. 6). As a result "they know . . ." (v. 7). Similarly, "I have given them the words which thou gavest me" and "they have received them" (v. 8). As a result, "they know in truth . . . and they have believed" the divine origin of the revelation.

This is the first fact about the apostles and indeed about the whole Christian community. The Father has given us to Christ out of the world, and Christ has given us that true knowledge of God which is eternal life. So we no longer belong to the world. We belong to God. We know God. We belong to Christ, and Christ is glorified in us (v. 10).

That brings us to the second fact about the Christian community, namely that *they continue to live in the world.*

"I am no more in the world," Jesus says (v. 11), for he is about to leave the world and go to the Father. "But," he immediately adds, "they are in the world."

Although we have been given to Christ out of the world and have thus been transferred from one community to the other, we still live in the world out of which we have been taken. For although the two communities are spiritually distinct, they are not socially segregated. On the contrary, we have a solemn responsibility, now that Christ himself has left the world, to remain in it as his representatives and to make known to others the revelation which he has made known to us.

Let us keep clearly in our minds these two characteristics of the Christian community; namely, first that we do not belong to the world (because we have been given to Christ out of it) and secondly that we do continue to live in the world. It is only against the background of this description of us that we can appreciate Christ's prayer for us.

For what does Christ pray? In two words, the burden of his prayer is *keep them.* He prays that the holy Father will keep them holy or distinct, keep them in the unique position which they occupy, keep them true to what they are, as being in the world though not of the world.

More particularly, his petitions are as follows: "Keep them in thy name" (v. 11) and "keep them from the evil one" (v. 15). He makes it clear that he does not pray that they should be taken out of the world (v. 15), but that while remaining in the world they should be "kept," kept by the power of God, kept a distinct people, kept in the truth and in righteousness of life. We must look at these two petitions more closely.

First, *he prays that they may be kept in the Father's name* (vv. 11-13).

I will not weary you with the various possible translations of the petition of verse 11, according to whether the preposition means "*in* thy name" or "*through* thy name," and whether the relative pronoun should be "whom" (referring to the apostles) or "which" (referring to the name). It is sufficient to say that for myself I believe the context supports the RSV rendering: "Keep them *in* thy name *which* thou hast given me."

That is to say, the Father had given his name to Christ (the revelation of his nature), and Christ had given it to the apostles (v. 6, "I have manifested thy name . . ."). During his earthly ministry, while he was still with them, Christ kept them in the Father's name (v. 12). But now that he was leaving them, he prayed that the Father himself would keep them in it, that is, faithful to it.

And the object of Christ's prayer for their loyalty was "that they may be one," referring here first and foremost to the unity of the apostolic band. Christ's prayer was answered. Although there is in the New Testament a rich variety of apostolic instruction, the apostles speak with a single voice because they were kept true to the revelation which Christ had given them.

Still today loyalty to revealed truth is the major means to Christian unity. Unity which is not according to God's truth is not according to God's will either.

This, then, was the first necessity for the apostles. If they were to fulfil their calling to live as Christ's ambassadors in the world, they must be loyal to the revelation which he had given them. Then they would present a powerful, united testimony to the world. Otherwise, they would be useless. It is the first necessity for us also.

Next, *he prays that they may be kept from the evil one.*

His prayer in verse 15 is not that the Father should take them out of the world, but that he should keep them from evil in the world or from the evil one who is the world's ruler and god.

That is, he prays that they should remain in the world without becoming contaminated by it; that they should be what he was—at one and the same time "a friend of sinners" and "separated from sinners" (Mt. 11:19; Heb. 7:26); that they should be both "worldly" (involved in the life of the world) and "holy" (distinct from the standards of the world) simultaneously; that they should maintain what has been called a "holy worldliness," being in it while not of it, like a rose blooming in midwinter or a lily growing on a dung heap.

So important and controversial is this issue today, that I feel I must enlarge on it. What is to be the Christian's attitude to "the world," which is mentioned nineteen times in this chapter?

First, *the Christian attitude to the world should not be one of withdrawal.*

Withdrawal was the attitude of the Pharisees (whose very name means "separatists"), but Jesus did not want his followers to be Christian Pharisees. Yet Christian pharisaism is common. It is also understandable, being due sometimes to the fear of persecution (Jesus mentions the world's hatred in verse 14) and sometimes to the fear of contamination. It is this that made the hermits flee into the desert in the fourth century A. D. and led to the development of monasticism in the Middle Ages.

And the spirit of monasticism still lingers. Some of our evangelical Christian fellowships are in reality monasteries, although without the stone walls and without the name. For they are enclosed communities. Indeed, so-called "secular Christianity" is partly a reaction against this very thing, against the exaggerated pietism of much evangelical Christianity, against a religion which is divorced from life in the world, against religious people whose preoccupation with another world is so unbalanced that it leads them to contract out of all responsibility for this world.

Every Christian should consider Christ's prayer and say to

himself, "Jesus did not pray that God would take me out of the world; have I effectively taken myself out of it? Or am I deeply concerned with this world and involved in its life and its pain?"

Second, *the Christian attitude to the world should not be one of conformity.*

If we are not to withdraw from the world, we are not to conform to the world either. If Christ did not pray that we should be taken out of it, he did pray that we should be kept from the evil in it, in fact that we should remain what we are, namely "not of the world" (v. 16).

Yet this second option (conformity) is understandably attractive, and high motives have often animated those who have embraced it.

They are anxious not to be cut off from their contemporaries, but rather to identify with them; anxious to break down barriers, not to erect them.

But this right and proper anxiety has led some to become assimilated to the world (its outlook and its standards) and to erase the distinction between the church and the world.

Others, the advocates of a secular Christianity, say that they have given up religion (worship and prayer) in favor of social action. Their sphere of concern is no longer the church, but the secular city. They have abandoned all other-worldliness for a thorough-going worldliness and replaced metaphysics with politics.

One sympathizes with their protest against a false and separatist religion, which has no concern for the world. But these two contradict the prayer of Jesus. His prayer was indeed "do not remove them from the world," but it was also "keep them in your name, your revelation, your truth; keep them from evil; keep them from adopting either the world's philosophy or the world's ethical standards; keep them in the world, but keep them distinct from the world, in the truth and the righteousness which they maintain."

So then, in view of Christ's prayer for us, we have no liberty either to withdraw from the world (the characteristic fault of the evangelical) or to conform to the world (the characteristic fault of the ecumenical). We cannot escape the church-world tension either by opting out of the world or by giving in to it. What then is Christ's way?

Third, *the Christian attitude to the world should be one of mission* (vv. 17-19).

And the mission Christ intended involved witness as well as service, a mission undertaken by those to whom he had entrusted his word (v. 14). So he says in verse 18, "As thou didst send me into the world, so I have sent them into the world."

It is remarkable that Christians who live *in* the world, and are not removed *from* the world, should nevertheless need to be sent *into* the world! It is evidently possible to be "in" it without actually going "into" it, possible to be a resident without being a witness.

It now becomes clear why Christ prayed that his apostles might be "kept" in the Father's name and from the evil one. He was not concerned merely that what had been achieved in his earthly ministry should be consolidated and that those he had won should be preserved. His purpose was that his apostles, remaining in the world after he had left it and remaining with the revelation which he had given them, should share it, spread it and make it known.

It seems that the petition of verse 17, "Sanctify them in the truth" (better "by the truth"), implies this. The sanctification he desired for them was that they should be set apart not just from evil but for mission. Certainly verse 19 has this meaning of "sanctify" and the RSV translates the same verb, "For their sake I *consecrate* myself. . . ." Further, the means of their consecration to Christ's mission was the truth, the word which he had given them. God's revelation does "sanctify" in the sense of making us holy; it also "consecrates" in the sense of commissioning us. It places upon us an obligation to pass it on.

How we are to do this emerges from verse 18. Here Christ says that he has sent his apostles into the world as the Father had sent him, a truth which is repeated in 20:21 after the resurrection in the form of a commission: "As the Father has sent me, even so I send you." Thus Jesus makes his mission the pattern of the church's mission. We are sent into the world in the same way as he was, which was the way of identification.

Jesus did not attempt to perform his mission from a distance, any more than the Apollo mission could have been fulfilled without an actual landing on the moon. And Jesus did more than "land" on earth. The Apollo astronauts took with them to the moon all the accoutrements of the earth–earth's oxygen, earth's food and clothing and instruments (they could not have survived otherwise). But when Jesus "landed" on the earth, he did not bring heaven's accoutrements with him. On the contrary, he brought nothing except himself. He laid aside heaven's splendor. He entered earth's conditions. He assumed human nature, human flesh, human life. He identified himself with us in our lowliness and our limitations. On the cross he even took upon himself our sin and guilt.

It is to a costly identification like this that we are called today—not to stand aloof from the world, but to enter it, to penetrate it, for Christ.

Our Christian calling is not to shout the gospel at people from a distance, but to enter their thought-world, in order to be able to interpret the gospel to them. This is our mission, and it makes us missionaries.

A missionary is not just someone who crosses a physical barrier (an ocean, a swamp or a mountain), to share the gospel with the people on the other side, but someone who crosses a cultural barrier in order to do so, someone who takes pains to learn another language and understand another culture in order to communicate the gospel.

In this sense every true Christian witness is a missionary, even though he stays at home. For Western secularism is to the Christian just as much a foreign culture as Islam or Hinduism.

The principle of the incarnation challenges us not to cut ourselves off from the foreign, secular culture around us, nor to become assimilated to it, but to accept the pain and the peril of entering it, of understanding its thought forms and learning its language, while remaining ourselves distinct from it. In the words of the present Archbishop of Canterbury, "We state and commend the faith only in so far as we go out and put ourselves with loving sympathy inside the doubts of the doubting, the questions of the questioners, and the loneliness of those who have lost their way."[6]

So the true Christian attitude to the world is one of mission. It is the only way to avoid the pitfalls to which the church-world tension exposes us. If we are sent into the world, we cannot withdraw from it. If we are sent into the world, we cannot conform to it either, or we shall lose both our message and our power. It is involvement in mission, witness and service which will keep the church both in the world and not of the world, both worldly and holy.

So the Christian calling is at one and the same time to worldliness (in the sense of living in the world), to holiness (in the sense of being kept from the world's evil) and to mission (in the sense of going into the world in the name of Christ as servants and witnesses).

All this is the "sanctification" for which Christ prayed. It is summed up in the three prepositions, that the Christian is "in" the world, not "of" the world, but sent "into" the world.

And Jesus Christ himself is our perfect example. He tells us in verse 19 that he "consecrated himself." He lived in the world; he did not withdraw. He remained pure, holy and distinct; he did not conform. He came not to be served but to serve—to live, to suffer and to die for others.

So he prays, "As thou didst send me into the world, so I have sent them into the world."

We come now to the third section of Christ's prayer.

III. **The unification of the church (vv. 20-26)**

Indeed, as Thomas Manton expressed it, "This prayer is a standing monument of Christ's affection to the Church."[7] "I do not pray for these only, but also for those who believe in me through their word." Here Christ distinguishes between the apostles for whom he has just been praying and those who would later believe in him through their teaching.

His chief prayer for this church of the future is its unity. There can be no doubt about this because it is repeated at least three times for emphasis: "that they may all be one" (v. 21), "that they may be one even as we are one" (v. 22) and "that they may become perfectly one" (v. 23).

These are well known prayers. They are probably quoted more frequently than any other petitions of John 17. They have come to be the proof texts of the ecumenical movement. But there are many who are familiar with these phrases who are ignorant of their context and are therefore unbalanced and even mistaken in their interpretation. It is important that we subject them to a careful and critical scrutiny.

Let us consider four aspects of the church's unity for which Christ prayed: its nature (what it is), its means (how it may be secured), its purpose (why it should be desired) and its goal (when it will be consummated).

A. The nature of the church's unity (what it is)

Let's look again at verses 20-21 and try to grasp the two kinds of church unity Christ prays for: "I do not pray for these only, but also for those who believe in me through their word, that they may all be one; even as thou, Father, art in me, and I in thee, that they also may be in us. . . ."

First, there is *unity with the apostles.*

We have already seen that in verse 20 Jesus alludes to two groups, conveniently designated in the RSV "these" (i.e., the apostles) and "those" (i.e., subsequent believers). It seems beyond question that the "all" of verse 21, whose unity Christ desires, are a combination of "these" and "those."

Let me elaborate on this. The Lord Jesus peers with prophetic eyes into the future. He sees generation after generation of his followers. He calls them "believers," for they will believe in him, and they will believe in him through the apostles' words.

This is a description of every single Christian believer from the Day of Pentecost onward, including ourselves. We have put our trust in Christ, and we have done it through the apostles' teaching. If the apostles had not borne their unique testimony to Jesus Christ and if their unique firsthand testimony had not been recorded and preserved in the New Testament, we could never have believed in Jesus. True, we probably came to believe in him through the witness of some contemporary Christian—a preacher or relative or friend—but theirs was a secondary testimony, an endorsement from personal experience of the apostles' testimony. The Christ they were witnessing to was the apostles' Christ, the Christ of the New Testament witness. There is no other.

Here then are the two groups—the little band of chosen apostles ("these") and the huge company who will believe in Jesus through their word ("those"). And Christ's prayer is that "all" (both "these" and "those") may be one.

It is first and foremost a prayer that there may be a historical continuity between the church of the first century and the church of subsequent centuries; that the church's faith may not change but remain recognizably the same; that the church of every age may merit the title "apostolic" because it is loyal to the teaching of the apostles.

This kind of church unity was clearly understood in the earliest days. We are distinctly told that the very first converts (the 3,000 who were converted on the Day of Pentecost) "devoted themselves to the apostles' teaching and fellowship" (Acts 2:42). It is not surprising that two verses later we read that "all who believed were together." Similarly, the apostle John who here records this prayer of Jesus is clear about its implications, for in his first letter he writes, "that which we [the apostles] have seen and heard we proclaim also to you, so that you may have fellowship with us; and our fellowship is with the Father and with his Son Jesus Christ" (1:3). And the apostle Paul asserts that the church is one, a single building, God's temple, because it is constructed "upon the foundation of the apostles and prophets, Christ Jesus himself being the cornerstone" (Eph. 2:20).

So the first aspect of the church's unity is unity with the apostles.

Secondly, there is *unity with the Father and the Son.*

The latter part of verse 21 seems to be a separate sentence: "even as thou, Father, art in me, and I in thee, that they also may be in us."

This is a staggering petition, namely, that as there is a mutual indwelling between the Father and the Son within the Godhead, so there should be a mutual indwelling between the church and the Godhead. The prayer "that they also may be in us" is a prayer that the church may be organically united to the Father and the Son, sharing the divine life.

And now let us put these two unities together. The unity of the church for which Christ prayed was not primarily that we may be one with each other, but first that we may be one with the apostles and second that we may be one with the Father and the Son. The first speaks of a common truth, the second of a common life. And both are needed to unite the church.

For the two greatest potential enemies of Christian unity are time and space. It is these which separate believers from each other. But the same apostolic truth spans the successive generations of the church, and the same divine life animates all believers of the same generation. So when we share in these, the disruptive powers of time and space are conquered, and we enjoy the unity for which Christ prayed.

Mind you, to define thus the unity Christ desired does not exempt us from the quest for the church's visible unity, namely, the mutual recognition between churches in which there is a free interchange of members and ministers. However, such a union and intercommunion, although very desirable in themselves, are certainly not pleasing to Christ or a fulfilment of his prayer unless they are the visible expression of a shared apostolic truth on the one hand and a shared divine life on the other.

B. **The means to the church's unity (how it may be secured)**

It is only logical that the *means* employed to secure the church's unity will be consistent with the *nature* of the unity being sought. So if the church's unity is a unity with the apostles in their teaching, the unity will be fostered as the teaching is fostered. And if the church's unity is a unity with the Father and the Son in their life, the unity will be fostered as the life is fostered. This is exactly what we find in Christ's prayer.

First, *common truth is a means to unity.*

"The glory which thou hast given me I have given to them, that they may be one even as we are one" (v. 22).

We have already seen that the word *glory* means "revelation." The glory which the Father gave the Son and the Son gave the apostles is the revelation of himself. It is by this revelation, and by loyalty to it, that unity will be secured.

This is a recurrent theme of John 17, which is too often ignored. The repeated prayer "that they may be one" is through the Name in verse 11, through the Word in verse 20 and through the Glory in verse 22. And these three are the same, for the Name, the Word and the Glory are all expressions for the same revelation of God in Christ, of his nature, being, mind and will.

It is sometimes said that "doctrine divides," but Jesus Christ evidently believed the opposite. Unity amongst the apostles themselves would be secured by their loyalty to the divine Name, he said (v. 11), and unity in the later church would be secured in the same way, by our receiving the glory or revelation of God (v. 22). It is not by neglecting Christ or the apostolic witness to Christ that the church's unity will be secured. Rather the reverse. The unity of the church is unity in the truth. Every quest for the reunion of the church should be a quest for the reformation of the church according to God's Word.

As Hugh Latimer said in one of his sermons, "Unity must be according to God's holy word, or else it were better war than peace. We ought never to regard unity so much that we forsake God's word for her sake."

Second, *common life is a means to unity.*

"I in them and thou in me, that they may become perfectly one . . ." (v. 23).

Here the "perfect oneness" for which Christ prayed is made to depend on a mutual indwelling, the Son indwelling the church as the Father indwells the Son. Thus the horizontal (oneness with each other) is made to depend on the vertical (oneness with Christ).

William Temple expresses this admirably: "The way to the union of Christendom does not lie through committee-rooms, though there is a task of formulation to be done there. It lies through personal union with the Lord so deep and real as to be comparable with His union with the Father."[8]

C. **The purpose of the church's unity (why it should be desired)**

This has already been stated in the verses we have been studying.

"So that the world may believe that thou hast sent me" (v. 21).

"So that the world may know that thou hast sent me and hast loved them even as thou hast loved me" (v. 23).

In both cases the conjunction (*hina*) expresses not just the consequence of the church's unity, but the very object and purpose of it. Christ prays that those who believe in him (v. 20) may so live in unity that others will come to believe in him too (vv. 21, 23). Thus faith begets faith, and believers multiply, through the unity which they enjoy–unity with the apostles, unity with the Father and the Son, and so unity with each other. Since this unity transcends the barriers of race and rank, Alfred Plummer is right to call it "a moral miracle"[9]; it is a sign to elicit faith.

Bishop Stephen Neill gives an eloquent description of it:

Within the fellowship of those who are bound together by

> personal loyalty to Jesus Christ, the relationship of love reaches an intimacy and intensity unknown elsewhere. Friendship between the friends of Jesus of Nazareth is unlike any other friendship. This ought to be normal experience within the Christian community. . . . Where it is experienced, especially across the barriers of race, nationality, and language, it is one of the most convincing evidences of the continuing activity of Jesus among men.[10]

But where it is not apparent, unbelievers remain in their unbelief. As Manton puts it, "Divisions in the church breed atheism in the world."[11]

D. The goal of the church's unity (when it will be consummated)

It is significant that in the final verses of Christ's prayer (vv. 24-26) Jesus looks beyond history to eternity. For it is only then–in heaven–that the church's unity will be consummated.

Notice that Jesus begins verse 24 with the words "Father, I will" (AV). This is the most remarkable prayer ever prayed. It is quite unlike any prayer that we have the liberty to pray. For all our prayers are variations on the theme, "Not my will but yours be done." Yet here Jesus says, "Father, I will. . . ." He seems to pass beyond the realm of prayer to the expression of his will, because it is identical with the Father's will.

What does Jesus will? He desires that his people (who have been given to him by the Father) will be with him where he is and will then behold his glory which had been given to him before the foundation of the world. Already the apostles have received his glory (v. 22), displayed especially in his words and signs. But one day they would behold it unclouded and unveiled, in the full revelation of his person in heaven. In Manton's words, "When Christ made his will, heaven is one of the legacies which he bequeathed to us. This was his last will and testament, 'Father, I will.' . . . Heaven is ours, a legacy left us by Christ."[12]

This is all we need to know about the life of heaven. In heaven we shall both be with Christ and see him as he is. Again and again the apostles repeat these promises, that in heaven we shall enjoy the company of Christ and be granted the vision of Christ.

And this vision of Christ will be the vision of God. It will complete the process of revelation begun by Christ on earth. The great difference between the church and the world (v. 25) is that the world does not know God. But Christ knows him. Further, Christ has made him known to his people (vv. 6, 26). And what he has done he will continue to do ("I made known to them thy name, and I will make it known") both through the Holy Spirit on earth and in the beatific vision in heaven.

This knowledge of God, however, will not be one of intellectual apprehension alone, but of personal relationship, of love. For the end result of the Son's revelation of the Father will be that we may enjoy the very same love with which the Father has loved the Son (v. 26).

This final unity, comprehending the Father, the Son and the church in love, is not only beyond our experience, but beyond our imagination, even our comprehension as well. At least we should not miss the fact that it is a unity of love based on a unity of knowledge, the knowledge of the divine name. And this brings us back to where we started in verse 3, for such knowledge of God is eternal life.

In conclusion, let us look back over the prayer we have tried to analyze. In particular, what does Christ pray for his people? What is his will for his church as revealed in his prayer?

He prays that the church may be characterized by four qualities.

The first is *truth* (v. 11, "Keep them in thy name").

The second is *holiness* (v. 15, "Keep them from the evil one" and v. 17, "Sanctify them through the truth").

The third is *unity* (vv. 22-23, "That they may be one . . . that they may become perfectly one").

The fourth is *mission* (v. 18, "I have sent them into the world" and vv. 21, 23, "that the world may believe").

Of these four, truth predominates, for it is the truth which both sanctifies and unifies and compels the church to evangelize. Holiness, unity and mission are all impossible without the truth.

So Christ's vision for the church is far more balanced and comprehensive than ours tends to be.

The greatest preoccupation of the contemporary church is its institutional or structural *unity*. This is (at least in some degree) a proper quest, but not in disregard of either the truth or the life which constitute the unity and are the means by which it grows.

Others are preoccupied with the *truth,* with doctrinal orthodoxy, and sometimes become barren, dry and self-satisfied, forgetting that truth is to be obeyed and propagated as well as believed.

Others are preoccupied with *holiness,* with the church's own interior life and communion with God, and withdraw into self-contained pietism, forgetting the church's mission to the world.

Yet others are preoccupied with this *mission* to the world and forget that the church cannot effectively serve others when its own life is in disorder, for the world will only believe when the church is preserved in truth, holiness and unity.

So truth, holiness, unity and mission belong together and cannot be separated.

These are the four so-called "marks" of the church, according to the Creed, namely, that the church is "one, holy, catholic [which means partly that it guards the whole truth] and apostolic [sent out into the world on a mission]."

All four are included in the prayer Jesus prayed. Most of the church's ills down the centuries and today are due to an unbalanced emphasis on one or some of these, to the neglect of others. Let's not put asunder what Christ has joined together. Let's rather pray for what he prayed and seek to secure what he prayed for—a church which guards the revelation once for all entrusted to it, a church which is sanctified and unified through this revelation which it preserves, and a church which, guarding this truth and exhibiting it in its own purity and unity, goes out on its mission to win the world for Christ.

Notes

[1]Calvin, p. 134.
[2]Marcus Rainsford, *Our Lord Prays for His Own* (Chicago: Moody Press, 1950 [First published as *Lectures on St. John 17* in 1873]).
[3]Calvin, p. 68.
[4]Thomas Manton, *An Exposition of John 17* (Marshallton, Del.: Sovereign Grace Book Club, 1958 [First published in 1620-77]), p. 92.
[5]Rainsford, p. 113.
[6]Michael Ramsay, *Image Old and New* (London: SPCK, 1963), p. 14.
[7]Manton, p. 9.
[8]Temple, p. 327.
[9]Plummer, p. 303.
[10]Bishop Stephen Neill, *Christian Faith Today* (Baltimore: Pelican, 1955), pp. 171, 174.
[11]Manton, p. 370.
[12]*Ibid.*, p. 405.

PART II

ISSUES IN WORLD EVANGELISM

WHAT IS EVANGELISM?

C. Peter Wagner

Strange as it may seem, the question, "What is evangelism?" has become a controversial issue in today's world.

Moreover, the answer you give to the question may make a difference in your life. People who define evangelism in a certain way will find themselves attracted to a certain mission board, to a certain field of service, to a certain type of campus evangelism, even to a certain circle of Christian friends.

Anyone who takes a serious interest in understanding the mission of the church in today's world does well to give top priority to developing crystal-clear thinking as to what evangelism really is. The mentality of a Christian worker at this point is almost as important as the acceptance or rejection of the germ theory of disease is to a physician, or selecting Adam Smith rather than Karl Marx as the point of departure for an economist.

You may have come here wondering where you yourself might

plug into the rather complex missionary enterprise of the Christian church today. If so, make it a point this week to reach some sort of conclusion as to what you believe evangelism to be. I have made my own decision, and I won't try to disguise it, because I feel quite excited about it. But at the same time I will attempt to present the alternatives fairly.

The thinking of some is foggy concerning the words *evangelism* and *missions.* For some time I tried to maintain separate files on the two subjects. But eventually, when I found that I was doing as much cross-filing as direct filing, I combined the two. They are intimately related. Some even consider them synonymous. Bishop Newbigin of India once defined missions as "the concern that in the places where there are no Christians there should be Christians." This is a simple phrase, but pregnant with meaning. It is a good definition not only of missions, but of evangelism as well. The one point of difference between the two might be that missions usually involves a cross-cultural element, whereas evangelism implies ministry within one culture only. This, however, is secondary. Both evangelism and missions are deeply concerned with making Christians of non-Christians.

Now this has been introductory. In the beginning I mentioned a choice which should be made. The choice is not between evangelism and missions. Neither can it be reduced to "What do you think of Billy Graham or Evangelism-in-Depth or Operation Mobilization?" Let's attempt to go a little deeper than our opinion of these things. Let's consider three basic styles of evangelism. To do so, I'm going to introduce a terminology which has recently been gaining increasing acceptance among missionaries. The three styles are known as presence evangelism, proclamation evangelism and persuasion evangelism.

The text I have chosen as a basis for this will anticipate my own choice. The Bible says in 2 Corinthians 5:11, "Knowing therefore the terror of the Lord, we *persuade* men," and further on, in verse 20, "Now then we are ambassadors for Christ, as though God did beseech you by us; we [*beg*] *you* in Christ's stead, be ye reconciled to God" (AV used throughout this section).

David Howard's talk brings us face to face with evangelistic *potentialities* in the student world. I want to focus on the definition of evangelistic *goals.* We can't deal with goals, however, if a personal commitment has not first taken place. What motives entice a Christian even to get interested in the question, "What is evangelism?" Before defining the three styles of evangelism, then, it would be well to take a moment to understand the two principal dimensions of missionary or evangelistic motivation.

The first is the inward and upward dimension. This reflects our own heart commitment produced by our vertical relationship to God. Paul sums it up in 1 Corinthians 4:1-2: "Let a man so account of us, as of the ministers of Christ, and stewards of the mysteries of God. Moreover it is required in stewards, that a man be found *faithful.*" Faithfulness is the key word. Faithfulness to God implies doing *his* thing, obeying the commands he gives us as Lord. That word *Lord* is no pious platitude extracted from children's prayers–it implies unbending allegiance to an absolute monarch. Sometimes we in the United States have difficulty in understanding it. Here, you can do *your own* thing if you decide to. But if you lived in old Babylon under Nebuchadnezzar or in new China under Mao, you wouldn't be able to. You could better understand what it means to be under a lord. God requires that kind of faithfulness of Christians–unbending obedience to his commandments.

The second dimension of motivation is outward and forward. In our text, we find Paul's words, "Knowing therefore the terror of the Lord. . . ." This expresses his motivation for persuading men that they must be reconciled to God. What did he mean? The word *therefore* refers us to the previous paragraph in 2 Corinthians 5 where Paul speaks about death–being absent from the body and present with the Lord. The very last sentence of that paragraph indicates what he means by the terror of the Lord–the final judgment. Contrasted to the benefits which death brings to believers, Paul mentions the distressing alternative of what awaits those who die without knowing Christ. This he describes as the "terror of the Lord." Such forward thinking, which theologians call eschatological, motivates Paul to reach outward to lost men, persuading them to become Christians before it is too late. Here is the outward and forward, or the horizontal, dimension. It complements the vertical one.

So much for the motivation. Now the definition.

The choice between the three definitions of evangelism is not so much a matter of black and white or right and wrong. It reminds me more of the Sears, Roebuck catalog and the days back on the farm when we looked at those sets of three pictures labeled good, better and best. Whenever we could, we ordered the best. Let's think of the three styles of evangelism in those terms.

Good–presence evangelism. The idea of presence evangelism was first popularized by the World Student Christian Federation back in 1964. In an excellent article on the subject, Leighton Ford traces the roots of the idea back to French Catholicism. The concern which produced the concept was a legitimate one. There was a widespread feeling that Christianity had become irrelevant in a rapidly secularizing world. The West was in full retreat; the age of colonialism was over. Would the retreat of the West mark the beginning of the downfall of Christianity? Many thought it would and began talking about a "post-Christian age." Pessimism reigned among church leaders. To some who had become involved in the new wave of left-wing revolutionary thought and action, the Christian message had never seemed so irrelevant. The World Student Christian Federation and others felt that the most appropriate action would be to secularize Christianity. As a part of this process, they would have to redefine the mission of the church.

Presence was therefore set in contrast to proclamation as the most desirable action of Christians in the world. It meant not only to be there in the world where the action is, but also to become involved in what (as they said) God was doing in the world–to campaign against all that dehumanizes man. Presence could be anonymous and silent; the name of Christ could or could not be mentioned, depending on the circumstances. Individual salvation, repentance, regeneration and the need for a conversion experience were called old-fashioned and gently pushed out of sight to make room for such activities as "redeeming social structures," "reconciling hostile men and nations," "arousing the oppressed to take arms against the oppressors" or "restoring manhood as reflected in Jesus."

This led to much confusion throughout the sixties about the mission of the church and the definition of evangelism. The word *missions* was changed by some to *mission* in order to provide an umbrella for everything good the church does. The mission of the church was seen primarily in terms of social action, over against an aggressive effort to bring those who did not know Christ into the kingdom of God. Attempts at gaining conversions were called "proselytism." Finally, evangelism itself came to be identified with social action. Harvey Cox, author of *The Secular City,* says, "Any distinction between social action and evangelism is mistaken." Australian theologian Colin Williams says, "The distinction between individual evangelism, and evangelism calling for [social] changes is a false one." Presence evangelism, then, is any effort made by a Christian to better society or help his fellowman.

We began by saying that this was good. By this we mean that helping the oppressed, feeding the hungry, caring for the aged, promoting civil rights, distributing contraceptives, eradicating malaria, teaching illiterates to read, building roads, denouncing social injustices–everything that can be done in the name of Christ to bring a better life to mankind is pleasing to God and should be a part of normal Christian activity. "Thou shalt love thy neighbor as thyself" is a binding commandment on all Christians. The real problem enters the picture when we begin to call all this "evangelism." This twists biblical priorities and places us in the dangerous position of obscuring the primary mission of the church. But I need not say more on this point since Samuel Escobar will develop this in the following message. Incidentally, I know of no one more eminently qualified to speak on the true balance between evangelism and social action.

Christian presence, Christian social action, silent witness or whatever you might call it is good–but please don't say it is evangelism.

Better–proclamation evangelism. There is a wide river of difference between presence evangelism and proclamation evangelism. The proportionate difference between the two is admittedly much greater than that between the quality of the good and better overalls in the Sears, Roebuck catalog. They represent two different philosophies, with two different starting points. Christian presence asks the *world* to set the agenda; proclamation takes its agenda from the *Word.* Presence sees the root of the problems of mankind in *society;* proclamation sees it in *sin.* Presence emphasizes the *horizontal* aspect of reconciliation, man with man; proclamation emphasizes the *vertical* aspect, man with God. Presence attempts to arouse a *social conscience;* proclamation attempts to arouse *spiritual conviction.*

The text for proclamation evangelism is most frequently Mark 16:15-16: "And he said unto them, Go ye into all the world, and preach the gospel to every creature. He that believeth and is baptized shall be saved; but he that believeth not shall be damned."

Many of the recent saturation evangelism movements have adopted a policy of proclamation evangelism. The official program of one states, "Our movement is biblical, based on the Great Commission as recorded in Mark 16:15-16, with emphasis on *every* creature." Those who strictly follow proclamation evangelism believe that the task of the evangelist has finished when the message is heard and understood by non-Christians. Whether the message is accepted or rejected is more the concern of God than the concern of the evangelist. "Eternity alone will reveal the results." The Bible says, "God gives the increase" and "My word shall not return unto me void."

In one of the most thoughtful studies of evangelism published in recent years, the author says, "To evangelize means 'to announce,' 'to proclaim,' 'to tell forth,' 'to bring good news.' . . . The important fact is that no evangelism has happened until the good news has been *told* . . . orally, intelligently, and understandingly communicated." This excellent statement of proclamation evangelism implies that when the gospel has been properly communicated, the evangelistic work as such has been accomplished. Among conservative evangelicals this undoubtedly has been the most commonly held point of view. (See, for example, J. I. Packer's *Evangelism and the Sovereignty of God* [Inter-Varsity Press, 1961], pp. 37-57.)

Proclamation is better, infinitely better, than trying to define evangelism as Christian presence. Yet the Sears customer is never satisfied with the better when he can afford the best.

Best–persuasion evangelism. If a wide river separates presence and proclamation, only a small stream flows between proclamation and persuasion. Yet, some small streams, like the one which separates Texas and Mexico, take on an importance disproportionate to their size. Those who hold this persuasion emphasis in evangelism admit that proclamation is an essential element in evangelism, but insist that it is not enough by itself. Proclamation is like the appetizer served in a fine restaurant: delicious, but not quite satisfying. The main course is the persuasion. Persuading men to become Christians is the main course, the true goal of evangelism. Proclamation is only a step in the right direction.

Persuasion advocates avoid as much as possible quoting Mark 16:15-16 in isolation from other texts, such as Matthew 28:19-20. The reason for this is not so much the textual question mark associated with the conclusion of the second gospel, but rather the danger of leaving the mistaken impression that by proclamation *alone* one can fulfill the Great Commission.

Take a close look at Matthew 28:19-20: "Go therefore and make disciples of all nations, baptizing them in the name of the Father and of the Son and of the Holy Spirit, teaching them to observe all things that I have commanded you . . ." (RSV). As Dave Howard has pointed out in his excellent new book, *Student Power in World Evangelism,* four verb forms combine to give a full view of what Christ wants his servants to do: *go, make disciples, baptize* and *teach.* Unfortunately in most English versions this is not fully evident, but in the original Greek three of these verbs are participles and only one imperative. *Making disciples* is the imperative. *Going, baptizing* and *teaching* are merely supporting activities, or means to the end. Proclamation is another means to the end.

Persuasion evangelism, then, sets as its goal nothing less than making disciples. Evangelistic strategy becomes geared not only to allow the most people to hear the gospel, but also to make the most disciples. Superficially the distinction may appear to be a slight one. But don't believe it. It is one of the most significant points of dialogue and strategy-planning in the world of evangelical missions today. Admittedly, Joe Bayly caricatures proclamation evangelism in his book *The Gospel Blimp,* but nevertheless he makes his point concerning some of today's frivolous goals in evangelism.

Look at it from another point of view. How can you measure success in evangelism? Of course, some people think it is unspiritual to measure success at all. They say, "Only God knows the results." I have a sneaking feeling, however, that this at times is just a pious smoke screen. If it were valid, it would make evangelists and missionaries about the most comfortable people in the world. At least they would be much more comfortable than others, such as businessmen who have to show profits in order to be considered successful, or surgeons who have to show recoveries, or pitchers who have to win baseball games or even students who have to pass final exams. Evangelists and missionaries would be comfortable because if you couldn't measure their success, neither could you measure their failure.

I don't believe it is any less spiritual to measure a missionary's success or failure than it is to measure the success or failure of, say, a church building fund. Honesty and realism should force us to do it if we haven't attempted it before. Let's try it now for our three styles of evangelism.

The success of presence evangelism can be measured in terms of how many people you help. Every wound that is bandaged, every broken heart that is comforted, every unjust social structure that is changed for the better are points in favor. As they say, all these things help to humanize man.

Proclamation evangelism measures success in terms of how many have heard the gospel and understood it. Some will accept and become disciples. Some will reject and remain pagans. But if all have understood, they have been successfully evangelized. Effective communication (even if it does not result in commitment) is the goal.

Persuasion evangelism is not satisfied with either. Ultimately, success can only be measured by counting up how many people outside of Christ have been born again by the Spirit of God, thus becoming faithful disciples of their Lord. The most objective test is whether they have united themselves to the visible church. Admittedly, this is a rather hard-headed and pragmatic way of looking at evangelism, but it is an attempt to take seriously the imperative of the Great Commission and the obligation that faithful Christians have to fulfill it. The Bible makes a special point of stating that heaven rejoices, not when ninety-nine people hear the gospel and *reject* it, but rather when one sinner *repents.* If a person whom God has called and gifted to be an evangelist takes count after a decade and finds he has won only a handful to Christ, he may deserve an "A" for evangelistic *effort,* but when measured against the imperative of the Great Commission, his evangelistic *results* have been somewhat less than successful. He may do well to stop and re-evaluate his ministry before beginning a new decade. Perhaps he will conclude he has been sowing good seed on barren soil. If he is convinced that God wants him to continue this, he should by all means do so. But also, he should consider the other possibility, that nearby he will find some fertile soil which God has prepared and which will yield fruit thirty, sixty and a hundred fold.

In closing, let me underscore once again the theological and spiritual basis for what I am saying: It is nothing less than faithfulness and obedience to God.

What is evangelism? Evangelism is where the real spiritual action is. It may be on the university campus. It may be in the black ghettos. It may be on the foreign mission field. Wherever it takes place, evangelism is seeking and finding the lost, effectively communicating the gospel to them and persuading them to become Christ's disciples, responsible members of his church.

SOCIAL CONCERN AND WORLD EVANGELISM

Samuel Escobar

I would like to start by telling you the story of Silvia. Silvia is a lay missionary in the north of Argentina. She asked to be sent as a teacher to an isolated little village, in order to be able to cooperate with the Anglican missionaries there. When she arrived at her post, she had to report to the military commander, who in that area, being close to the border, is also the civil, educational and political authority. She had to get approval from the commander for her teaching program as well as for some things she wanted to do in order to improve conditions in the school.

The presence of a big group of Indian children in the school caused some problems. (We have racial problems down there too.)

Silvia insisted on having an interview with the military chief. After some weeks of reluctance on his part she was able to see him. When she entered the room, the man had on his desk a file with Silvia's university record.

"I see you have a Jewish surname and you are interested in the Indians—too much interested. You must be a Communist."

Silvia was shocked but tried to be patient. Then she went on to explain why she was there. After a long talk the man was convinced. But his suspicion is a sad commentary on the state of the Christian church in some areas of the world.

Yes, in many countries where authorities are constantly telling us about their loyalty to the "Western and Christian way of life," if you are interested enough in the Indians, in the poor, in the one who suffers, to go and serve them in an isolated village, leaving behind a university career, you must be a Communist.

In some regions of the world Christianity has become synonymous with a gay, unconcerned and irrelevant selfishness and Communism synonymous with a committed, disciplined, sacrificial way of living. Our misunderstanding of the mission of the church accounts in part for this sad confusion. So it is a timely exercise to try to understand the mission of the church and the Christian in relation to the social needs and the trends of our day.

The fact that the most ardent defenders of evangelism have become at the same time so suspicious of social concern as to create the idea that one excludes the other can be explained by a variety of reasons. I will mention three.

First is a reactionary attitude against the movement called "the social gospel." This attitude has marked not only that distortion of orthodoxy called fundamentalism but also the evangelical approach to social responsibilities. The fear of forgetting the essential task of the church—proclamation of the good news—has produced a reluctance to deal with a most important aspect of the mission of the church. Biblical research, teaching and preaching about the subject are almost completely absent. There is no practical help available to the younger generation, which now finds itself like a helpless orphan at this point. Self-criticism should lead us to recognize the resultant defective character of an evangelism in which *ism* has been stressed more than *evangel,* thereby transforming it into a mere technique.

Second, the social origin of church membership, clergy and missionaries in evangelical churches accounts also for this failure. There is a "middle-class captivity" of the evangelical church which has determined a mentality reluctant to deal with social responsibility. The gospel has been transformed into a "middle-class gospel" and, immersed in her sociological condition, the church has been unable to see herself in perspective and to try to overcome the sociological conditioning of her life and message.

The prophet Amos preached against a society which was "at ease in Zion," having forgotten the evils of its material development and the situation of the poor. In the same way today, some aspects of prophetic teaching can awaken the church to her sociological captivity and lead her to rediscover the gospel for all.

Third, the virtues of the pietistic movement which were so important in the origins of the modern missionary movement have been carried to heretical extremes. Biblical separation has been identified with monasticism. But as time and developments bring social change, many contradictions appear. Politics is worldly, business is not. Active membership in a labor union is worldly, active membership in an association of real estate owners is not. Giving alms to the poor is acceptable, organizing them to fight the causes of poverty is not acceptable. So the Lordship of Christ, the consequences of the doctrine of creation and the activity of God's common grace have been covered under a heretical disguise which reduces the action of God to some aspects of the life of a group of people who are inside the so-called evangelical community.

As a result of all this, the gospel has lost its flavor and evangelism has become a technique for salesmanship and an effort to keep the image of the church. In days when concerned people in the world are desperately fighting to foster a change for the good, a change that will take us out of the critical dilemmas, evangelism, which was in the past an agent "of dynamical renewal in society, quite often serves now as a preserver of the status quo." No wonder that some people see the gospel we want to take to all the world, in obedience to our Lord, as nothing but the ideology of the Western, developed, white countries. Even worse, the rejection of this kind of gospel is seen as an apocalyptic sign in some books of eschatology in evangelical circles. As a result of the already mentioned causes and others similar to them, we have really changed the nature of the gospel so much that it is rejected not because of the scandal of the cross but because of the scandal of our distorted message.

The needed change cannot come from ourselves as self-critics nor from our outside critics. It has to come from the Word of God with the Spirit of God working through it. And my contention is that if we take seriously the message we say we proclaim, the consequence will be an involvement in all walks of life, a witness in all circumstances. Then we will see the gospel in action and the world, this Western world also, turned upside down.

We do not always realize the degree to which the proclamation of the gospel was in clear contrast with the dominant ideologies and ways of thinking in the world where it appeared. We do not realize the impact because we are accustomed to this "Christianized culture" which has traces of some of the Christian virtues. But if we rediscover the whole message in depth and wideness and if we proclaim it, it will challenge our society and our own values, it will be a headache for the powerful, it will call some men to commitment and service in areas where change is being prepared and promoted. The spiritual atmosphere of the world today is becoming increasingly similar to that of the first century. We need a reappraisal of the power of the contents of the message we proclaim and of the one who sends us to proclaim it.

To start with, our message is a message about God. We proclaim that there is a God–a holy, just, loving, powerful, personal God who made this world, who keeps it by his power and who loves the human race and wants the best for every man. He is a God who is against sin, a God who wants to reestablish the relationship of a father with the prodigal man who is lost in sin. As James Packer says in *Evangelism and the Sovereignty of God,* "These truths are the foundation of theistic religion, and until they are grasped the rest of the gospel message will seem neither cogent nor relevant. It is here, with the assertion of man's complete and constant dependence on his Creator, that the Christian story starts."

But we who proclaim this message must also live according to it. For ourselves this God is a father, a loving, just maker and keeper. Is he? A God who loves all men regardless of color, religion, race, political commitment. He is not the God of the white man or the God of the capitalist, or the God of the black and the God of black power. He is above all these differences. We pray every day, "Thy kingdom come," because we want his kingdom to be *the* kingdom.

And however patriotic we may be, we prefer his kingdom. Do we? What do our attitudes reveal about this?

When you speak as a missionary in a New York ghetto, a Peruvian slum or an African village, what does your God look like? We proclaim that this God wants the best for his creatures and we pray, "Thy will be done on earth." How can we be completely unconcerned then with the daily needs of our fellowmen? Is that his will according to his Word?

The will of God for the life of man has been revealed in his law to Israel and in his covenants with men. They reveal his character. As Carl Henry says, "The Christian because he knows the revealed commands of God, can and should contribute energetically to the debate over social justice. The Christian community as a whole, moreover, has its own special opportunity to appropriate and demonstrate it." We are not hearers, we are doers of the doctrine we proclaim. Are we? We are not like the demons. As James says, they believe and even tremble before God, but they do not turn his commands into actions.

In the second place, our message is a message about man. Man was created to be different, to have lordship over nature and create culture under God. But man is a fallen creature. He is alienated from God. He is not what he was created for. The evidences of this situation are seen in society around us.

This point may be where our middle-class captivity is more evident. Our notion of sin has been terribly impoverished. While those who do not accept sin are ably describing the depths of man's fallenness, we have reduced sin to those outward signs of antisocial behavior which are shocking to middle-class people. We are against the violence of an alcoholic who beats his wife or a terrorist who blasts a computer. But there is also the violence of those who do not need to act violently but pay and organize others to do so–those whose political life or business demands that type of violence. There is the injustice in relations of daily life which produces the soil where other sins appear. Marx and Marcuse describe adequately the way in which money, power or lust have spoiled our Western societies. They wouldn't call it sin. We *know* what it is. But they have detected the depths of injustice with far more realism and acuteness than the average preacher who should know more about it.

Recently a great French novelist, François Mauriac, died. He was able to bring back the discussion of sin in the literary world of the past decades in France. He could see sin in the lostness of the bourgeois—those well educated, virtuous, religious but lost. Mauriac did not care if his characters smoked, swore, danced or drank. He described sin where it was. Compare him with the average evangelical novelist, and you will realize how poor our concept of sin has become.

Renewal from the Word will teach us to preach again about sin with the precision, acuteness and courage of the prophets who pointed to sin expressed in social injustice and abuse. They pointed to sin where it was, even at the risk of being considered agitators, and were thus faithful to the whole counsel of God. It is at this point that the faithful preacher becomes a concerned critic of his society, of all social classes.

The following words from J. I. Packer have a social dimension as they show how evangelical preaching concentrates on the type of needs typical of people in the middle class:

> Nor should we be preaching the gospel (though we might imagine we were) if all that we did was to present Christ in terms of man's felt wants. (Are you happy? Are you satisfied? Do you want peace of mind? Do you feel that you have failed? Are you fed up with yourself? Do you want a friend? Then come to Christ; He will meet your every need . . . as if the Lord Jesus Christ were to be thought of as a fairy godmother or a super-psychiatrist.) No; we have to go deeper than this. To preach means, not to make capital out of people's felt frailties (the brainwasher's trick), but to measure their lives by the holy law of God.

And we can witness to the power of God to liberate us from sin, if we are able also to show by word and deed that we are being liberated from those sins of social injustice, social prejudice, abuse and selfish individualism which have brought our society to the mess in which it is. Can we measure the consequences of taking seriously the doctrine of sin which is part of the gospel we preach?

Third, the gospel is also a message about Christ and his saving work for men. It is a message about the incarnate Word, the crucified Messiah, the resurrected Lord and the way in which his work delivers man from the guilt and penalty and power of sin. There is a uniqueness in this work of Christ. The atoning work could be done only by him who was chosen by God himself to do it and who was the only just one who could die to save us from our injustice before God. God's work in those who trust in Christ sets them into a pattern of life, a new life which is an imitation of the life of Christ and the way in which he showed his concern for the whole of man with deep realism, sacrifice, self-denial.

Those who proclaim the crucified Savior are, as Paul said, "crucified with him." This is not only a mystical experience in the inner man; it is evidenced in the way those who preach regard their life, their career, their relationships with each other, their disposition to live truth and assume the consequences.

The elements of self-denial, poverty and sacrifice are completely absent from the Western capitalist society. They are virtues of those leaders like Che Guevara and Mao Tse-tung, virtues which give them followers among those who are fed up with wealth and affluence or who are victims of them. Unfortunately, evangelism has become a kind of successful business associated with conventions in luxurious hotels and trips by fast planes. In some of the underdeveloped countries I have seen eager status seekers who have forgotten the sacrificial aspect of their Christian life and have made "evangelism" a ladder to affluence and social success.

We accept the fact that Christ calls us to a life which includes a cross. We tend romantically to see that cross with more clearness in some men, like the five martyrs of the Aucas in Ecuador, or Dr. Carlson in the Congo. But I think we must come to the point where we also see the cross in Christians who for the sake of Christ and in obedience to him are ready to risk their lives in the hands of extremists of the right or the left, in Christians who try to be witnesses in the world of labor, politics, improvement of human relations, the fight for peace, and the fight for justice. These are laymen, and the fact that they are ready to suffer for Christ by living in the world of politics and civic affairs does not make them less than those who are engaged full-time in the communication of the gospel.

Even when we have clarified adequately the fact that Christ did not choose the way of a political Messiah, we cannot deduce from that that politics is no legitimate business for the Christian. We are all politic men because we live in the *polis*—in the city—and we should be concerned about what happens there. You cannot prove by the gospels that Christ was completely foreign to the politics of his day. He did not want to be a politician, but he touched with his presence and preaching every aspect of daily life. He did not hesitate to surround himself with activists from different groups. Even more, we cannot say that he was a representative of the status quo or the establishment. He was among the critics of the establishment. All that did not hinder him from doing what he came to do. Were he to come today to our situation, where would we find him? In what part of our city would he live? What church would he attend? For whom would be his hard words? With whom would he eat and drink?

Fourth, the message of the gospel is also a message that demands repentance and faith. It demands commitment. This means not only a refusal to trust your own justice before God, but a willingness to trust his promises. It also means a refusal "to set any limits to the claims Jesus makes on your life." There is a cost in following Christ, a cost which is such because it goes against our own dreams of greatness, our own plans for our lives, our own "way of life" be it American, Western, Eastern or nationalist in any nation. Counting this cost comes before commitment, and it means that we weigh carefully the consequences of identifying ourselves with a Lord whose worth was recognized but who was rejected, who gave himself and was killed. Faith in him is also faith in his provision of a transforming Holy Spirit who can help you in the daily fight. The daily fight is not only fought in the hothouse of a quiet middle-class life described in so many "victorious Christian life" handbooks. The Holy Spirit is able to assist you also in the hard life of a militant and to give you victory over the world, the flesh and the devil, whatever the circumstances of the life into which God calls you.

Can you see how this message of the gospel, this evangel, is relevant, exciting, dangerous? Can you see why evangelism cannot be divorced from social concern? And we have a great God, greater than the turmoil, revolution and crises of our day. Great is the privilege of his call to be his ambassadors today.

Indeed, this is a time of change and turmoil. Every value, every system and every doctrine is being questioned. This gives an open door to the gospel of Christ, who said, "I am making all things new!" Do we love this Lord? Do we recognize him as our Lord and Savior before whose name "every knee shall bow"? Then let us be obedient. Let us ask from him the courage to see the trembling world as a call to bold witness. Let us not try to save our status in this rotten affluent society which is coming to pieces! Let us leave behind the city of Ur if we are called to do so.

You might be called to be a missionary under a nationalist regime in Latin America and to teach God's Word there, where a new society is being born. Be ready to face difficulties. No success is guaranteed, but obedience is demanded. Won't you face difficulties for Christ? In some of these countries poverty has to be shared because there is not enough wealth to be shared. That also might be your lot. Will you go if Christ calls?

Recently a friend of mine received a letter from his father in a Latin American country where a socialist military government came to power: "There are new difficulties as banks and exchange are controlled by the government. We will have delays in changing our dollars and the government will check what we receive. But I do not consider that a reason to leave the country as so many missionaries are doing now." This is a form of loyalty to Christ's call and also of social concern.

You might be called to help national pastors who have had the courage to receive political activists who are believers among their young people. You might then have to spend hours of agony in prayer in order to counsel each one and not just repeat set phrases from a pastor's handbook.

You might be called to teach math or physics or linguistics to crowds of young people who ask you every morning your opinion about Cuba or your connections with the CIA. You will be suspected, and yet you will also have many open ears eager to hear about the radical change that Christ makes in lives. Will you face this for Christ? Do you really believe in his Lordship?

You might be called to be an agricultural expert to help people produce better food and to tell them about the one who created plants and controls day and night, rain and sun. You might be kidnapped and your family would suffer. Would you prefer then to stay in Ur?

You might be called to spend some years of single, unmarried life as a traveling staff member ministering the Word of God to students in Chile, Lebanon or Indonesia. You would have to live in poor boardinghouses like the students, eating what they eat, answering their questions about Marxism and the Old Testament prophets. You might even have to organize them for active social service in slums or rural areas. Of course, you might tell God that you prefer a new house, a nice wife and a new car every one or two years.

You might be called to be an active leader on your campus, a peacemaker in a tense situation where the older and the younger suspect your motives and where traditional Christians will call you pink, social gospeler, etc. Or you might be called, like some young people in the church of a friend from Colorado, to clean bathrooms, cook, nurse and minister God's Word to hundreds of hippies who have invaded a community that rejects them, gun in hand. One of these young Christians was stabbed by a drug addict. Did Christ fail? Are the peacemakers blessed? You can tell God you prefer to be an executive in an ecclesiastical machinery.

You might be called to protest, maybe to write poems which express your dreams of a new world or to write music to the powerful words of Isaiah, David or Amos. Inspiration, powerful inspiration for that, comes from a living contact with God's Word and also with God's world in need. You might be called to be the stoned prophet in a complacent Christian community which builds air-conditioned, carpeted sanctuaries close to areas of unemployment and gets impatient with the demands of grape pickers.

You have in your hands a message which is fire, dynamite. Let it change your mind and attitude, let it make you a good neighbor who goes around looking for evils to fight and good deeds to engage in. May he make us, wherever we are and go, the mysterious and powerful presence of the kingdom. May he let our hearts and lips be free to tell the world about the king.

RACIAL TENSIONS OVERSEAS AND WORLD EVANGELISM

George J. Taylor

When one thinks of racial tension, of racism, it is possible to believe that this is a problem only in the United States, South Africa, and England. The reason for this faulty thinking is that in these countries the mass media keep us informed, and we read about these problems immediately. I can assure you that all over the world people know what has taken place in Watts, in Alabama and in Harlem. And yet in other countries people do not hear about what takes place and what happens because they do not have the facilities to communicate that easily. Unfortunately one finds racial discrimination in many other countries, at times in very open ways, at other times in subtle ways, and at times through indifference. For instance, we find racial discrimination in Latin America, in the West Indies, and in Europe. Discrimination is sometimes against the blacks, sometimes against the Indians, other times against Orientals.

And we see discrimination in several areas of life—in housing, in social life, in marriage, in schools and in recreation. Here I will point to some examples of how race discrimination is manifested in Latin America. A little over three years ago a black teacher was invited to preach a sermon—just one sermon—on Easter Sunday in San Salvador, Central America. When the committee heard he was a black teacher, they immediately cabled: "Sorry, no visa for that preacher." The government would not grant it.

In Port Limon, Costa Rica, there is a special social club where one becomes a member only through invitation. But although the majority who live in that city are blacks, there is not one black who has received an invitation to become a member.

In the same city two couples, one couple black and the other couple white, wanted to spend a weekend in a hotel owned by North Americans in Port Limon. The desk clerk politely said to the two couples, "Sorry, we have only one room available," and he gave the key to the white couple. They refused it. And these people were South American.

In Ecuador, individuals born of Indian heritage and from the coast of this country are not accepted in the capital, Quito. Sometimes just the last name is sufficient for these people not to be employed in Quito. Unfortunately some mission boards are following the very same policy.

In Brazil where there are more blacks than in any other country in the Western hemisphere—close to 29 million black people live there—we also find racial discrimination.

In 1967, two Brazilians, a black and a white, conducted an experiment to prove what many people know and what very few people are willing to say: There is racial discrimination in Brazil. These two men, Narcisco Kalili (the white man) and Odaeir de Mattos (the black man) visited six major cities in twenty days in Brazil—Belem, Recife, Salvador, Rio, Sao Paolo and Porto Alegre. They had some very painful and striking experiences. They found out (1) that blacks could not enter certain hotels, (2) that black children could not enter schools in these cities, (3) that the people believe that a white man could not love a black woman but wanted her only for sexual relations, and (4) that the people believe that blacks are dirty, deceitful, and irresponsible.

These men did something very interesting. For instance, first, the black man pretended that he was sick and held on to a lightpost with his pockets out. People from all walks of life passed and looked at him. During a fifteen-minute test not even one person stopped to see what was wrong with this man. Ten minutes later, about six feet from where the black man had stood, the white man came and he began the very same test. He dressed the very same way and posed himself the very same way. Before five minutes were up many people had stopped to see what was wrong. They offered to call a doctor, but he declined the suggestion. They took him to a bar and bought mineral water for him and wouldn't allow him to pay for it.

In Brazil this whole attitude is paradoxical, since the most popular person in this country, the man who is considered to be a king–Edson Arantes Donasimento, "Pele"–is a black man. In the West Indies, countries like Jamaica, Barbados, there is not only white discrimination against blacks but something even worse–lighter-skinned blacks discriminating against darker-skinned blacks. This is repeated over and over in many countries in Europe, such as England, Italy, and Germany where at times the non-whites are only tolerated. It is difficult for non-whites to find employment and places to live in these countries.

I want you to ask yourself a question: How does this situation affect world evangelism? What meaning does it have for us who are called to proclaim the gospel of Jesus Christ? What implication for world missions?

First of all, we must realize that racism wherever we find it is a sin and it must be eradicated. This can only take place when the love of Jesus Christ is flooding the people's hearts. It is not by rules or laws that we can remove racism. It has to be something with force, with power. Jesus Christ can give it to us, and it can eradicate racism from the hearts of men. We cannot be indifferent either to the calling we have received as Christians or to the world situation.

I recognize a temptation. It is difficult for many black people from North America to consider missions in light of the many problems we are facing. Even if we were to remain at home either in the States or in whatever country you are from, we can imagine how few people know about Jesus Christ. But if the apostle Paul had remained in one country until all the problems were solved there, where would we have been today? If Christ had remained in one city during his life, how many people would never have heard of his gospel and would not have been touched by his power?

On the contrary, as Christians I feel we must accept this great challenge. Paul says in speaking to the Colossians, You have "put on the new nature which is being renewed in knowledge after the image of its creator. Here there cannot be Greek and Jew, circumcised and uncircumcised, barbarian, Scythian, slave, freeman [or white or black], but Christ is all and in all" (Col. 3:10-11). The world needs to see this, the gospel in action. This is really the hope for a better world, a world where men from all races can live together, work together, pray together; where the black men, the white men, the yellow men, can all come together. Why? Because Jesus Christ has filled their hearts and minds with love.

If the world sees this, we can expect a better world. We can expect the world to have a much more healthy mental concept of the gospel.

Second, I believe that we must try to remove the negative attitude toward many people in our countries. For instance, a couple of years ago it was very difficult for North Americans, for white people, to go to certain countries, especially in Latin America. People talked constantly of the ugly American. And yet after the Peace Corps began its work and members of this group went to several countries where they lived with people and worked with people, these young men and women very quietly removed the false image that so many had of the United States. And I feel that as Christians we are called to do the very same thing.

Third, there are several changes that must take place—primarily changes of attitude on the part of those who proclaim the gospel. When Jesus met the Samaritan woman, he did not let racial barriers interfere with his mission. The Samaritan woman said, "How is it that you would ask a drink of me, a woman of Samaria?" If Christ had given in to her argument, he would have left her. Yet Christ continued to minister unto her, and, because she received Christ, she was the instrument that God used to start a great revival in the country of Samaria. I don't think we have to evangelize more, although evangelism is necessary. I don't think we have to preach more, although we must preach. I think we must live together and show forth the love that Christ has for us.

When I was a little boy, about the first song I heard was the first chorus of the following: "Jesus loves the little children, all the children of the world. Red and yellow, black and white, they are precious in his sight." And yet over and over the question is asked, "If Jesus Christ loves the blacks, why are they absent in so many places in the world, especially on the mission field?" And then one says, "Maybe Christ loves me, but I wonder if the missionary really loves me." And we have to show people, crystal-clear, that we do love them.

Bill Pannell, while he was in Costa Rica, mentioned that Christ never said to anyone, "I love you." And he is right, for he gave such a powerful demonstration of love that it was not difficult for people to realize how much he loved them. It's not talking about love, it's living love.

This change of attitude must also be deep enough to remove stereotyped thinking. Dr. Alvin F. Poussaint, a black psychiatrist, says this: "In the legacy of our civilization the color black has been virtually synonymous with sin and bad. Witness such terms as black sheep, black magic, black list, blackguard, blackball, black light and many others. The word is associated with all the dirty, lowly, unintellectual functions in human life. The word white is usually invested with the opposite meaning. Americans have been conditioned to perceive black as inferior and white as superior."[1]

The change must be deep enough to remove these attitudes. Guy B. Johnson also zeroed in on this stereotyped thinking when he said:

> One might compile a catalogue of "What Every White Man Thinks He Knows about Negroes." Its main theme would be as follows: The Negro is lazy. He will not work if he can get out of it. He cannot manage complicated machinery because he cannot give it sustained attention and will fall asleep. He is dirty, "smelly," careless of his personal appearance. He is fond of loud colors and flashy clothing. He is less inhibited than the white man, is more given to loud laughter and boisterous talk. He is a natural-born clown and mimic. He is endowed with an inordinate sexual passion which overrides all considerations of modesty, chastity and marital fidelity. He has no sense of time; never gets anywhere on time. He does not know the value of a dollar and will spend his money on "foolishness"

> and then beg for the necessities of life. Even when he acquires property, he cannot take care of it. He is very gullible and is a great "joiner." He will join anything which promises a good time or a big noise or give him a chance to "show off." He is naturally religious, but his religion is all feeling, emotion, and superstition. He believes in ghosts, spirits, voodoo charms, and magic formulae. His mind works like a child's mind. His thoughts are shallow, his associations flimsy and superficial. His emotions are powerful but fickle. He is given to high criminality because he has no respect for life or property or morality and cannot control his impulses. He is incapable of appreciating the deeper values of white civilization, is incapable of self-government, and therefore must have the supervision and guidance of the white man.[2]

The danger about this is that many times white missionaries remove the word Negroes and think that Latins are lazy; they think the Indians are lazy, they think the Frenchmen are lazy. In other words any people are lazy except themselves.

Thus, a change of attitude is basic, because, even though we may pretend that we love, people can sense our attitude and it is difficult to win them for Christ.

Beside these things that I have mentioned already, there should also be a significant change in the proportion of blacks and other nonwhites willing to go as missionaries to other countries. I have lived in San Jose, Costa Rica, for more than twelve years. In the lovely city of San Jose, there is a Spanish language institute where the majority of mission boards send their candidates to learn the Spanish language. From 1958 to 1968 more than 117 agencies (denominations and the mission boards) sent 3,519 missionaries to prepare themselves for service in Latin America. Of this number less than seven were blacks, and I believe there were no more than five Orientals who attended the language institute during this period.

In the light of these numbers, one is faced with the following questions: (1) Does God call black missionaries and nonwhite missionaries? (2) Aren't white boards interested in sending nonwhite missionaries to other countries, especially Latin America?

I do not know how many nonwhite missionaries are in Europe or in the West Indies, but I do know there are very few nonwhite missionaries in Latin America today, and the majority of them are working with one or two or maybe three mission boards. Today if one could analyze all the mission boards in the world, he would be surprised to see the small number of nonwhite missionaries and executives of different countries serving in these agencies.

I would ask the foreign mission boards represented here, "How many nonwhites are being sent out by your board? How many blacks have been sent? How many nonwhites form part of your executive committees?" Today you find that the number of black Christians goes into the millions and yet very, very few are represented on the mission field.

Many mission boards are not willing to send nonwhite missionaries and many are not willing to let their missionaries marry nonwhite people. How many missionaries were sent home because they fell in love with "a native"? I am not minimizing the problem that there is in a racially- or culturally-mixed couple. We must admit that intermarriage is a problem. But the more important problem is that the mission boards do not stop to consider the intellectual, emotional, or spiritual maturity of the native. Just when it is discovered that a person is in love with a native, he is sent home immediately.

This change will also mean that more nonwhites will take an active part in the decision-making process concerning theological education for future missionaries. In most theological training centers black leaders shine by their absence, and yet the leaders are all over the place.

This will also call for a change in the local church. I have heard of so many churches, local churches with a great missionary program, that will send their money and people to help the poor Indians over there, the poor blacks over there, and yet these very same churches, with great missionary vision and great missionary resources find it difficult at times to admit one Indian or one black into their fellowship. The local church must change. There are black Christians who have been refused permission to enter a white church: What they have suffered has been intense. It is difficult for us to express all the negative feeling, to understand what these people have gone through in this country especially.

But I believe firmly that as Christians we have the potential in our lives to show the world what the gospel can do. It can remove hatred and replace it with love. The Holy Spirit can open a mind that is closed.

This also means that more blacks and black churches will be involved in the world mission. Black people will also give their money. This is what really counts. More black churches will begin to send more missionaries to other countries and develop various mission boards. I'm sure that we have leaders in these churches.

Perhaps today as Christians we would like to face this challenge. David Howard has reminded us of the great impact that students have made in world missions. I quote from *Student Power in World Evangelism*: "It is remarkable that students have played a decisive role in many of the greatest forward movements of the church in world evangelism. It has been through their vision and energy that the church has often been propelled into a new effort of outreach." And I think today we stand at a turning point where students once more can give the church this vision; they can help us recapture the need to go and tell others about Jesus Christ. If while we are at Urbana we can live together and we can talk together, and if we can minimize hatred and let the world see how we love each other, this will be a new day in missions.

Notes

[1] *TIME* (April 6, 1970), p. 55.
[2] Quoted by George Eaton Simpson and Milton Yinger in *Racial and Cultural Minorities* (New York: Harper and Row, 1958), pp. 165-66; the quotation originally appeared in Otto Klineberg, ed., *Characteristics of the American Negro*, p. 4.

REVOLUTION AND WORLD EVANGELISM

Myron S. Augsburger

It is my prayer that as I speak you may become aware not simply of the words that I say here but of the absolute sincerity of my commitment to Jesus Christ as Lord. It is a joy to be here and share. I know that all of us are influenced by revolution. One of the evidences that the revolution has affected the Mennonite church is that there are some fifty young people here from Eastern Mennonite College, and we are only one of a dozen colleges in our brotherhood.

I am thrilled with much that is happening in our time; I believe that this is one of the most opportune times to be alive and serve. As I enter the forties, I envy you who are just going into your twenties because of the tremendous opportunities that will be yours. I am not a pessimist about the world in which we live. In fact I believe that we are only one decade from an altogether different society. If the young people today who have developed a conviction about some of the great values that we have talked of in the past put them into practice when they enter into leadership in business and professional life, they can demonstrate that we have discovered how to be a different kind of people.

The theme given me is "Revolution and World Evangelism." Whether you are for the kinds of revolution you see or not, you are influenced by them. Even when a person reacts, he is complimenting that which he reacts against. He lets it shape his life. I want to discuss revolution from the standpoint of what it means for us in world evangelism.

Jesus Christ said, "I am come to send fire on the earth" (Lk. 12:49, AV). Now that is not the kind of statement that we often pay much attention to, but it is incisive for our meditation today. I am afraid, however, that many people in the church have plagiarized Jesus Christ, have cut him up into parts, and have accepted only the part of him that is palatable.

Most of Protestant American Christendom has wanted to accept Jesus as Savior in order to have a guarantee that they will get a free ticket to heaven and will miss hell, but then they say, "Stand back, Lord, now I want to run my own life."

The concept of Jesus Christ as King of kings and Lord of lords, of knowing what it is to live by his mandate, of being a genuine disciple, of being a member of the kingdom of heaven first and other kingdoms second–that concept is practically lost.

We are part of a twentieth-century Constantinianism: Our society assumes that it is Christian. This is one of the greatest problems we face in our society and in world evangelism. I would to God that we could really hear Jesus Christ as Lord. It would make a lot of difference. But too often we don't hear.

I am reminded of the story of two men who went up into the temple to pray, the one a businessman, the other a poor schoolteacher. The businessman stood and prayed thus within himself, "God, I thank thee that I am not as other men are, especially as this poor schoolteacher here. I serve on the board of trustees of the school where he teaches; I'm a member of the salary committee that determines his livelihood. In fact I pay half his salary myself." And the poor schoolteacher wouldn't so much as lift up his eyes to heaven, but he smote on his breast and said, "God, be merciful to me, I was that man's teacher."

One of our greatest problems, in American society, is that we are not honest; we are phonies. We don't level with ourselves or with God, let alone with one another. We haven't come to face seriously what it means to be Christians. If we would put into practice what our Christian faith provides, this would be revolutionary in itself. We should take seriously practicing the presence of God. To believe that Jesus Christ is a risen person and that you and I can walk in the Spirit—this is revolutionary. Try it, and talk about it with others. You will discover they can hardly understand it.

If the Christian church would get free from its apathy and indifference, refuse to be a part of the status quo of our society, dare to commit itself unreservedly to the Lordship of Jesus Christ, we would discover once again what it means to be the church militant. Then Tom Skinner's concept of being militant or aggressive would make sense to us. We are polarized between pietism on one side and activism on the other—and that polarization is present in groups much smaller than this 12,300. Because we are polarized, we have come to the place where the activist is limited because he can not back up his action with deep devotional commitment to Christ and the pietist is limited because he is insecure, ineffective and irrelevant when it comes to involvement in society. This theme of revolution should do something to shake us from our apathy and call us to a new kind of relevance.

The dynamic of revolution is that it always moves from the indicative to the imperative. It moves from what is to what ought to be. That is dynamic. That is why Marxism has outstripped much of professing Christendom in the last fifty years. That is why much of the revolutionary movement in our own time has rallied people with a new kind of enthusiasm. They have a cause to believe in and a program in which to be involved.

A Christian friend of mine came back from a trip to the Far East. He was impressed with the same thing that hit me when I was there. You can go into some of those areas and can find young people by the hundreds and thousands, who, if you ask them what they believe, will quote the sayings of Mao by the hour. If you ask them what their purpose is, they will tell you. Come back to the average American Christian community, ask them what they believe, and they can't even quote the Bible much less understand it. Ask them what the purpose of God is for their life and they don't know. Yet the spiritual man, wherever he has been awakened, has always been at work for change and renovation in society.

In his inimitable style Socrates said, "I love my city, but I shall not stop preaching that which is true; you may kill me, but I shall follow God rather than you." The words of Jesus are even more incisive: "I am the way, the truth, and the life: no man cometh unto the Father, but by me," or in my text, "I am come to send fire on the earth; and what will I, if it be already kindled?"

God grant us the ability to change the world through the power of the risen Christ; grant us the power to work out an authentic kind of a life in our personal experience. A demonstration from history shows that while Voltaire, the French atheist, was decrying belief in God, in England there was a man of political influence by the name of Wilberforce, converted under the impact of the preaching of John Wesley, who said, "God has laid upon me two convictions: first, the destruction of the slave trade and second, the correction and improvement of the morals of England." And he set about to do it.

In the days of the early church twelve disciples turned the world upside down. From Urbana, twelve thousand young people dedicated to the Lordship of Jesus Christ could turn this nation upside down. The question you and I face has not to do with whether we recognize a revolution, the question is which revolution.

I have deep affinity with the black revolution as my brothers are seeking for a great sense of the freedom and equality that is their right as human beings under the handiwork of God. I would identify, only I have the wrong color skin. But I identify deeply in my soul.

Yet when it comes to some other revolutions, as a Christian I have to draw lines of discernment. I stand alongside and share with Tom Skinner and others of you in the black community as best I can. But when it comes to standing alongside of Jerry Rubin, that's another matter. You only need to scan his book, *Do It,* to know that we don't need the revolution of vulgarity and violence that he outlines.

What we need in our society is something different—a kind of revolution that will bring Christian values to bear upon our society, that will elevate once again the value of persons, that will tackle basic problems of our society and undercut our ease with language about kill-ratio which forgets that persons in the Far East are our brothers.

This revolution calls us to an understanding that Christians need to sort out their priorities. We have given in to the materialism and the affluence of our society. We have gone along with the kind of status quo we have liked in America. We have acted as though we were here forever and that we could measure a man's worth by what he has in his pockets. In fact, the Christian church needs a revolution internally, within itself.

Call it what you will, we need it. It may be a revival, but it must be one at the gut level, and not merely a surface kind of pietistic renewal. It must be a call to a radical kind of discipleship, to an absolute unconditioned commitment of obedience to Jesus Christ. It is only when Christianity has been unshackled from the acculturation which domesticates it that it has ever demonstrated revolutionary power. Then men have beat their swords into plowshares and their spears into pruning hooks. Then men have gone into all the world and built hospitals and taken care of the ill and the needy, shared clothes and food, and shared above all Jesus Christ. The acculturated kind of Christianity that is all about us fails to demonstrate to our society the real essence of what Jesus Christ is all about.

I came back from India about eighteen months ago with a conviction in my heart that the God who shatters idols is going to shatter another one in our time. In many parts of the world Christianity and Americanism are looked at as almost synonymous. And God—who is a God who loves the world, a Christ who died for the world, a Holy Spirit who is out to reach the world—that God is not going to be put in a box by Americanized Christianity. He is raising up strong Christian leaders from the Third World to let people hear the gospel of Jesus Christ.

Most people really do not understand Jesus Christ in our society, because they have been given a perverted picture of Christ. Gandhi was turned off by the church in South Africa by being told that the church is not for the likes of you; it is for white Europeans. When he went back to India, what he rejected was not Jesus Christ as much as the perverted picture of Christ he was given. Furthermore he never did become a committed Christian because he understood Christianity to be synonymous with Western culture and he was first an Indian. Would to God that the Indian people of his day had understood what has been breaking through in our time, that Christianity is Indian, it is African, it is American, it is trans-cultural, because Jesus Christ transcends cultural levels and identifications.

The first-century church moved into society as a revolutionary force. They confronted Caesar's empire and brought it to its knees with the simple declaration, "Caesar is not lord; Jesus Christ is Lord."

When I say today that I believe in the priority of the kingdom of Christ, I want to say without any disrespect to my nation or its leaders or its President that I serve a King that makes him and his program look like a piker. I believe that the Christian church of America needs to face the judgment of Jesus Christ and recognize that it is time for us to affirm the primacy of the kingdom of Christ. Then I will know how to live in freedom, for then I can identify with the good things in my nation, I can remain free from the things that are contrary to the principles of Christ and I can live as a human brother amidst a fragmented and frustrated society.

In contrast to our society today, there is a kingdom of Jesus Christ. The early church knew it–that Christ is Lord, that discipleship is the order of life, that love, holiness and peace characterize the conduct of the believer, and that evangelism is the primary function of this kingdom. In fact, the believers knew that they were members of the kingdom of Christ here and now. This was no mere pietistic escape from real life, but it was actual participation in a new way of life. They gave supreme loyalty to one who is beyond history and yet at the same time who acts and lives within that history. This discipleship, this *koinonia,* this kind of brotherhood is a most dynamic quality of evangelism, and it is the potent force that needs to be rediscovered in our own time.

But in contrast to the rule of Christ stands the revolution of a mere secular approach. Some Christians follow this and relate obsolete and sub-Christian levels of change to the issues of our time. And I believe that one of the evidences of judgment of our own time is the carelessness with which Christians are involved in supporting the destruction of life in other parts of the world and justify it by certain patterns of rationalization. But the sin is now coming back to us, the chickens are coming home to roost. The same arguments of the just war theory are now being used to vindicate or validate violence and civil disobedience against the very persons who advocated violence for conquest in other territories. Such have themselves become the prey of this view in our own society.

But it does little good to curse the darkness; we need to light a candle. In a broken world we are called to be agents of reconciliation. I call on you this morning to outline in your own mind a strategy of operation for the next decade. This means to me, the strategy of a believing minority. We must discover what it is to accept this as a strategy. When my black brothers feel they are part of a minority movement, I want to identify by saying that as a believer I have joined a minority movement—a believing minority in a world where the Christian faith will always have to face this fact.

But it is not enough just to affirm a believing stance. One needs to understand what is happening in the world. It is highly important to understand what is happening in revolution. John F. Alexander, in an article in the magazine called *The Other Side,* says that the revolutionary mood of our time has four basic sources. One is the attack on authority from the nineteenth century to the present. A second is the overlapping and interchange of various cultural expressions. Third is the meaninglessness of affluence. This has given rise to a whole hippie culture, people dropping out from the meaningless affluent way of life. Fourth is the depersonalization of technology. Along this line, I suggest Alvin Toffler's *Future Shock* if you want to get an impression of what is hitting our society and an interpretation of what has helped shape young people, even beyond their conscious articulation.

I turn now to the impact of this revolution upon the Christian community. What is the stance of the Christian church amidst revolution? The answer which sounds simple but is quite profound is "Let the church be the church." But I mean by that not the institutional church that is structured inside of four walls: I mean God's church, for the church is people. Let the church actually be the church.

We are called to behave our beliefs. Paul writes that we should avoid letting the world squeeze us into its mold. This works both ways in our society: We are to have a holy discontent with the status quo and a loving and discerning spirit amidst revolution. As polarization takes place, the Christian avoids both extremes and does so not by simply trying to straddle the fence but by declaring his commitment to a higher loyalty or a higher standard. He marches to another beat; his Lord is altogether different from the voices that are around him.

But this does mean that we take the revolution with absolute seriousness. There are three things which I suggest with respect to this seriousness.

First, the impact of the revolution calls us to reassess our culture. There really is no Christian culture as such. There is Christian influence within a culture but no Christian culture as such. In a secularized culture we must prevent the secular from claiming wholeness for itself. Furthermore, we must expose the perversions in secular culture for the sake of its own correction and enrichment, and then avoid the danger of idolizing that culture by calling it Christian because we have corrected it in part.

Culture itself is a scene of conflict, a stage on which the drama of life is enacted. Culture is ubiquitous, varied, pliable, changing, perishable. A Christian is called to distinguish between those things that are purely cultural and secular and those which are centered in the worth of persons (as we learn it in Jesus Christ) with universal value.

Even Paul Tillich said, "The uniqueness of Christianity is that it is both concrete and universal at one and the same time." There are other religions today that are concrete, animistic, but not universal, and there are some that are universal but not concrete. But in Jesus Christ you have something that is both concrete and universal. I believe that this has implications for our relationship to society.

I would affirm that just as we call the church to be the church, we call the state to be the state. There are times the church needs to rap the state's fingers and say, "Stay out of our religious affairs." One can never correctly render to Caesar what is Caesar's unless he first of all renders to God what is God's.

In our society today we have tended to separate church and state superficially. We have not seen that the actual division comes in another pattern. We confess a loyalty to Jesus Christ and his kingdom which has priority. This places us in a position of freedom as well as of influence, as we try to bring Christian principles to bear on all levels of life. The god of power has become predominant, and we must expose this, face it realistically and demonstrate what it means to advance the kingdom of Christ above every other program.

For this reason I am a global citizen. On a matter like the war in Vietnam I am a dove, without any apology. Over and beyond that I believe that there is something more in the New Testament, that I have not fulfilled my mission until I let it be understood by my brothers or neighbors in Vietnam, North and South, that I want them to know Jesus Christ and become my brothers in Christ. And I can't do that standing at one end of a gun barrel and they at the other.

But this is a hopeless dilemma for modern man, a dilemma expressed in the poetic lines of Auden:

The expert designing the long range gun,
To exterminate everything under the sun;
Would like to get out but can only mutter,
What can I do? It's my bread and butter.[1]

A few years ago my wife and I stood at Dachau, a prison camp comparable to Auschwitz, where thousands of Jewish people were exterminated along with thousands of church leaders. I penned a few lines that express my concern:

I stood at Dachau in the rain,
and it was night.
The drops splashed in circles,
To widen and disappear
And then be replaced by others and still others.

I stood at Dachau and its night,
dropped 'round me. The faces were there without names.
They had come and gone,
destroyed by the tyranny of man.
To pass and make room for others.

Is Dachau a memory for our fate?

The hopelessness of our time has converged upon modern man until he is seeking to break out of the trap. That trap is not only the city ghetto; that trap is a mental and a spiritual ghetto as well. And I dare to say that the revolution needed within the church is a revolution calling us to break out of religious ghettos to meet our society with new changes and a new freshness.

Second, the impact of revolution challenges us to reactivate our thinking. Someone has said, "You could live your whole life in America and never find out whether you are a coward or not." But we can be involved with the frontier levels of thought, and there, on that thought level, we can call people to understand the Christian faith. The revolution has called us to actually look beyond ourselves, beyond our own needs to the needs of others in poverty and want, in ghettos and graft, in despair and escapism. It has forced us into shaping up on loving our neighbor, the black man across the street, not just the one across the seas. It has forced us to relate intelligently to the secularization process and to clarify the core of the gospel, not just to repeat naive fundamentalist clichés that do not interpret to a modern generation what the gospel is all about.

Third, the impact of revolution convicts us to reaffirm our communication. But in saying that, I would underscore that what we are communicating must be Jesus Christ and not just words about him. There is a difference. We must communicate Jesus Christ, that he is around, that he is alive, that he is real, that he is here, that we know him in personal experience. This kind of following of Jesus Christ is revolutionary.

David ben Gurion, when he was still at the helm of the state of Israel, asked a group of American missionaries and tour guides, "When are you Christians going to take the initiative in working for peace?" Our problems are not just in Vietnam, but in the Middle East, Latin America, all over the world and here at home.

Dr. Richard Halverson has said that if you described our world by one word it would be the word *rift.* There are two Germanies, two Koreas, two Chinas, two Vietnams, and a black and white America. I would like to say with him that if you describe the gospel by one word, it is the word *reconciliation.* You and I are called to be agents of reconciliation. That is the greatest revolutionary program we can be identified with and share in. And the Christian church can rise to this challenge if it will be honest and daring–daring to be disciples of Jesus Christ in a world that needs to know that he is not to be put in the box of acculturated religion. As King of kings and Lord of lords, he can stride into any culture and call men and women to himself, change their lives and make them able to regenerate and transform that society.

Let me conclude by borrowing from Martin Luther King to say, "I have a dream." I have a dream of a Christian fellowship that will cover the globe and, while transcending national lines, admit them in a way that calls us to brotherhood. I have a dream of Christians pledging their lives and material means to help one another in the fellowship of Christ, even to laying what I own on the line for my brother. I have a dream of believers who see each other in Christ rather than through denominational, ethnic, racial or cultural groupings. I have a dream of discipleship becoming a way of life for believers, making them become in society the evidence of people who bear the cross of Jesus Christ. I have a dream of the day when the options are once again clear as to who is Lord, Caesar or Jesus Christ. Evangelism can become–rather than an emotional, moral or religious coercion or manipulation–an intelligent, impassioned presentation of the option. Faith in Jesus Christ can actually become a clear option once again in our society.

Notes

[1]From "On This Island," Poem XVIII, *Masterpieces of Religious Verse* (New York: Harper, 1948), p. 472.

OPTIONS FOR OVERSEAS SERVICE IN WORLD EVANGELISM

Ted Ward

The lights were dim and the roar was muffled, but I couldn't sleep. It was my first nonstop flight directly into the heart of Africa and we were high over the mid-Atlantic. I needed a stretch. Coach seats can get pretty stiff after a while. I shuffled down the aisle to the front of the cabin, turned and started slowly back. Then it suddenly hit me. These hundred or more huddled sleepers were largely unknown to me—I only knew the name of one other—but suddenly these travelers took on a specific meaning. It wasn't the tourist season and, anyway, we were headed for destinations that are not very popular with the tourist trade. No, these travelers were a small sample of the international set—the employed jet-set, if you prefer: professional and technical workers of the world—families, businessmen, young couples who had looked so matter-of-fact as we had awaited departure at New York's Kennedy. A few were Africans headed home, but most were

Americans and Europeans moving back to assignments where they would be working shoulder to shoulder with Africans.

It had crossed my mind during cocktail time several hours earlier to glance around and try to spot the likely missionaries, using their abstinence as an oversimplified criterion. But even then it was clear that most of this sizable squad of travelers were part of the huge traffic of international workers. What really struck me was that this cavernous ship of the sky and dozens like it were plowing through the Atlantic horizon many times each week with just such loads as this. Indeed, working overseas involves thousands and thousands of Americans. Not only are regular missionaries considerably outnumbered by other overseas Americans, but in the last dozen or more years the rate of growth of nonmissionary overseas Americans has been greater than the rate of growth of the missionary population.

It is easy to misunderstand the implications of these facts. We must be careful to recognize overseas employment for what it is (a major way to enrich your cross-cultural experience while productively employed in your specialty) and not to glamorize it for what it is not (a substitute for organized missions and the mission society sort of approach to the outreach of the church). Indeed, there are some rather practical problems in being an independent "layman-missionary," and these problems are rather thoroughly and somewhat pessimistically reviewed in a little leaflet entitled "Don't Turn Off the Mission Boards," by Forsberg and Schwab. There are problems, for sure, but we ought to look into the matter anyway.

In order for you to see yourself and your career in a world perspective, the program of Urbana 70 is being broadened through this presentation–broadened in order to make you aware of the new role being played on the world scene by a swelling crowd of "internationalists." The internationalists are men and women of various occupations whose careers are played out across international boundaries–people from one country who are employed in a different country.

One of the eminent anthropologists of the white-collar international set is Dr. Ruth Useem, a colleague of mine at Michigan State University. She is convinced that the internationalists–expatriate professional workers–constitute a new and different cultural form. These people, native to one culture and voluntarily transplanted into another, Dr. Useem calls the people of the "third culture." Their life styles and values are drawn from the cultural systems of both their former and their present communities, and thus they conform to neither, but create new and unique patterns of life. I have served in this third culture myself. It is quite a stimulating experience. Getting free of some of the limitations of one's own culture is a great way to gain perspective and to develop new appreciations for people and for other ways of life.

The internationalist is quite often a professionally trained or executive-type person. He was successful and respected in his organization or institution at home–and thus he was offered an assignment overseas. He then became a branch manager, corporate representative, research coordinator, or consular person in some exotic place across an ocean. And, let's face it, for the American with wanderlust, almost anyplace is exotic–for a few weeks anyway! We Americans come from a tradition of exploring and wandering. Most of our great-great-grandfathers were adventurous travelers, and the tendency seems to be still in our genes. I am convinced that part of the reason Americans have been as useful as they have been in extending Christ's church overseas is that, in comparison with many others in the family of man, we are less community-centered, less family-oriented and less geographically limited. And, of course, Americans have had more money to use for long-distance wandering.

The number of Americans engaged in overseas work can be determined from the statistical review of the nation's work force provided by the Bureau of the Census.[1] It is perhaps hard to believe, but at the time of this study, a year ago, one out of every 140 Americans was overseas. Of the male labor force of the U.S. (51 million) there are 437,000 employed overseas; that represents nearly one man working overseas for each 117 men working in the States. (Please note that this indicates long-term employment, not just one- or two-year assignments; the U. S. armed forces personnel overseas are *not* included; further, the figures as given here are conservative, since they do not include nonemployed dependents; nor do they include tourists and short-term employed persons.) You can certainly get the point: For an American, working overseas is not at all uncommon.

The total U. S. work force overseas is almost as large as that of a major metropolitan labor center such as Atlanta or Dallas–much larger, for example, than the tri-state metropolitan region around Cincinnati. In fact, it is a quantity of workers greater than all the firemen and policemen of every city of the United States all put together. To personalize these data we can look more closely at your age brackets and educational categories.

You are soon to enter your prime years of employability. During these years, from 25 to 44, nearly 1.4 percent of the male American population is involved in long-term overseas experience. For these same years of prime employability the college-educated subgroup is employed overseas at a much higher rate: 2.1 percent. If we were to assume that you here at Urbana 70 are a random sample of American college students, we could predict that more than one of each fifty of you will spend a substantial amount of your career outside the U. S. But you are *not* a random group; you are much more attuned to international opportunities than is typical. That is why you are here. Your awareness and sensitivity to the overseas opportunities and needs places you in a group apart. This factor will have the effect, conservatively, of doubling the probability that you will go overseas to work. Add the fact that many of you are committed to the Christian proposition for worldwide evangelism, and it follows that you, or one of the people at no more than easy arm's reach from where you sit, will be an internationalist.

Opportunities for women and the demand for trained husband-and-wife teams are increasing. Thus we have reason to include the women here as well as the men. Just for fun, try to predict which of the people near you will be an internationalist. Reach out and touch his or her shoulder. Go ahead! The reactions likely vary from "Who, me?" to "Are you kidding?" But were we all to regather here ten years from now, your experiences would have very likely fulfilled these informal predictions.

Many of you will become missionaries in the classical sense; certainly the day of organized missions is far from over. But not all of you who become internationalists will be full-time missionaries. The number of Americans going overseas in nonmissionary roles is increasing at a higher rate than the missionary force. In the twenty years from 1949 to 1969, the number of Protestant–that is, denominational and independent–American missionaries rose from

16,000 to 33,289. A bit more than doubling. The total number of American civilians overseas during the same period went from 491,000 to 1,399,000–almost tripling. Unless our nation reverts to an isolationist stance, these trends are likely to continue. And you are likely to be part of the action, whether as missionary or as "American worker, expatriate."

What is the "American worker, expatriate"? First, he is an American; then he becomes a member of that growing community of internationalists, sharing his skills and abilities with the world community of man. His skills are particularly needed in the developing nations, where his emotional bias and his aspirations must be committed to "working himself out of a job"–training and helping workers to take their rightful places in their own emerging nations. But the beauty of all this is that an exciting career can be built around a series of "dig-in, help-others, get-out" experiences. There is only one sort of person who will be miserable in the role of the new internationalist–the person who wants to settle down and lock himself into one steady role and to protect his status quo for life. If you are this sort of person, turn off your hearing aid; I am not on your wavelength.

What does a career overseas look like? Although there are occasionally some wild and fascinating variations, ordinarily the American family overseas continues to be involved in an American-style community–far too often it is a ghetto of the elite–complete with chain-link fence and armed guards. Of course, there can be plenty of involvement with the foreign nationals, but there are also the American-type schools and even American-style friendship patterns. As a witness for Christ within this community, the opportunities are rather as they are at home in the States, neither distinctly better nor worse. Starry-eyed visions of becoming a part-time missionary are often unfulfilled.

Was it Shakespeare or Hezekiah who first said it? "Airplane riding doth not a missionary make." Isolation and loneliness can hit you pretty hard when you discover how much you need support and encouragement from fellow Christians, especially when you begin to sense the long and difficult task of establishing satisfying interaction with the national community.

It is difficult to find reliable data on the number of years spent in foreign service by the Americans overseas. My observations suggest that the average falls somewhere from eight to twelve. There seem to be three patterns: the *limited assignment,* from one to five years; the *career experience,* from eight to twenty years overseas; and the *lifetime* people—those who really cut their ties to America, taking satisfaction in the thought of being buried in the soil of their adopted and beloved country. These "lifetime" people are a minority, though their number is growing in such countries as Israel and, for a while at least, in Sweden and Canada.

Very few Americans, even those who are altruistic and highly motivated, are able to change their life styles enough to step down to the economic realities of "going on the local economy"—that is, learning to live on the salary that a local national person would be paid for doing the job that you are paid three to twenty times as much to do in the U. S.

You may prefer to think of yourself as a "career" or "limited-assignment" person. Most of the American community overseas are temporary residents. Most do not renounce their American citizenship; most return to the U. S. for a month or more of furlough or vacation at one- to four-year intervals. Most live at salary standards far above the local population. (In fact, many live like kings and are hated for it.) Most can save enough of their so-called "hardship allowance" while overseas to allow an improvement of their standard of living even after they return to the U. S. Many is the swimming pool that has been built on a hardship allowance!

Indeed, the American communities in Paris, in London, in Buenos Aires, in Berlin, Rome, Nairobi, Manila, Melbourne, Singapore, and New Delhi constitute large unevangelized fields in themselves—and these spiritually needy Americans are upper middle class and above in our terms, and upper class in local terms. There is a message here! Missions have tended to leave the rest of the American community alone. Although the primary justification of foreign missions is, of course, reaching the citizens of the host nation, the witness to and among overseas Americans should not be neglected. Careful reading of Acts 16 indicates that Paul, the first missionary to Europe, went first to relate to a person of his own religious and cultural background. Christian businessmen, engineers, teachers and government agents are needed to infiltrate this overseas community. And vital work for Christ needs to be done, in English, by wives of businessmen and government staff persons. Is this where God wants you? If so, there is a price to pay. You will have to be a missionary on an overtime basis. It is harder, and in some respects less productive, to be a self-supported missionary than to be a church-supported missionary.

Following are a few specific comments on overseas employment as it could affect you.

Business and industry constitute the largest category of employment overseas for Americans. Opportunities in this private sector typically involve considerable freedom and, in fact, free time to engage in outside activities of the sort that can make your "other career" as a missionary as extensive as you wish. There are some restrictive exceptions, particularly in the Arab countries.

Government service positions are a bit more strictly defined. Since the representative of the government is more or less "on display" most of the time, whether the occasions are formal or informal, there is some restriction on involvement in "sectarian ventures." But the occasions and the context for personal influence and private conversations about Christ can be both numerous and consequential. Think of the importance of sharing Christ with strategically placed people in other nations. There are people to be reached by laymen whom missionaries can not even get to. Ambassador John Gordin Mean, for one, found it possible to be both ambassador for the United States and ambassador for Christ at the same time. His assignment in Guatemala was shortened by an assassin's bullet but not before he had established in one more country that Americans can live and speak for the transforming power of the gospel of Christ.

And while on the subject of Guatemala, you should know that our current ambassador is an active member of a Spanish-language Protestant congregation of believers in the capital, a church that began as a mission church.

A wide array of positions is available in government service, from career posts in the diplomatic service to limited-term positions in civilian support system roles related to the armed forces. There are positions requiring various levels of education and various degrees of career commitment.

And rather than neglect them altogether, the Peace Corps and other quasi-governmental operations should be mentioned as one of the ways young Americans can give substantially of themselves for the sake of humanity. Like most experiences in life, a term in the Peace Corps can be as valuable or as trite as you make it. A really dedicated young man or woman can make a most worthy start toward a career as an internationalist through an assignment as a Peace Corps volunteer. A short-term mission assignment or even a summer overseas can serve the same purpose, though in general, the longer, the better.

The demand for professional workers overseas is very real. Since my own experiences are more in research and development than in industry or government, I am particularly aware of the huge American stake in overseas research and research on international affairs. Just one example: The Social Science Research Council and the American Council of Learned Societies recently counted a roster of 416 U. S. professors who are scholarly experts on Japan; they are located on 135 different campuses in the United States. These specialists were primarily responsible for the $15,000,000 spent on Japanese studies last year. This illustration deals with Japan alone, not even one of the so-called underdeveloped nations where an immense American involvement still continues despite war-economy cutbacks. These millions for research and training were spent by and through projects in which overseas Americans were involved.

Consider: Thousands of Americans are choosing international research as a career; is this for you?

Many of you intend to be teachers when you graduate. You have likely heard about the thousands of teachers engaged in the education of the dependents of overseas Americans, but there is an even more exciting job to do. Especially in the rapidly developing nations, education in the national schools and in the nonformal educational programs promises to continue to be a major employment field for overseas Americans. One major difficulty with this category of service is that teacher salaries in the local economies are often incredibly low. But many teaching positions are subsidized through USAID or American foundations. Several of my friends have taught in literacy programs, small-farm management, family nutrition and family planning. Not the typical subjects of the American curriculum, but American-trained teaching skills can be useful in a variety of subjects!

Yes, there are even opportunities for productive relationships between internationalists and traditional missionaries. Missionaries and Christian internationalists must learn to help each other. This sort of cooperation can be extremely important in strengthening, enriching and deepening the right sort of impact of missions on the local scene. There is a rub in all of this: Regardless of the way you go, the length of time you are there or the roles you play, you should plan to learn the language! Many Americans overseas fail to take the local languages seriously. Without a doubt our monolingual culture tends to make us linguistically handicapped. So when you add a bit of laziness to ineptness, it is not surprising that avoiding language learning is common.

English *is* a marvelously handy language and, in most cities of the world, it is possible to make your way rather well with nothing but English. Nevertheless, if you intend to double in missions you will need the local language. Knowing the language of the people is part of what it takes to be a beautiful American. And you have to want to get close to the people. You need to take a real interest in their condition–their needs, their hopes, their past and their beauty as people.

Why should we encourage American Christians to go overseas? We live in the reality of the one-world era. The involvement of *all* nations in the problems that affect any *one* nation is a matter both of atomic energy and of total ecology. From a pragmatic viewpoint, there is no feasibility in isolation. From a Christian viewpoint there is no feasibility in separateness. We are in the world. Christ is building his church in this world. We are partners in this singular venture. As American Christians the inordinate and imbalanced riches of our land and of ourselves–in the light of the impoverished majority of the world–make us even more profoundly debtors to all men. We have obligations. Christians must not be counted among the more selfish people of our nation. We should seek out many ways to share. Sharing is not just a matter of monetary wealth, but involves our *selves,* our *lives,* our *careers.* Americans are sharing–and they are sharing in all sorts of capacities and roles. Should you as *Christian*

Americans not be aware of your potentialities as internationalists even as you are aware of your opportunities in church-financed mission possibilities?

Another reason for Christians to be involved as members of the general American community overseas is the need to get a balance in the American image. If the only American Christians the non-American sees are church-supported missionaries, he can get the impression that all Christians drop out of everything else to be full-time employees of the church. He can also assume that the more prosperous Americans (whom he likely envies for their worldly goods) are rarely Christians—thus it seems that God doesn't prosper the very people who are called by his name.

Further, going overseas as a secular worker is one way to help enlighten the church of Jesus Christ in the U. S. Of all the supposedly sophisticated Christian groups of this world, the church in America is one of the most distinctly culture-bound. Overseas experience of American church members might do much to reduce the parochial and narrow views of how God works and what God wants in a life. Mission board members, pastors, deacons—as well as parishioners in general—need a high degree of cross-cultural sensitivity and profound Christian love for human variations. As we work together to reduce the Americanness of our Christianity and rely more on the scriptural models of faith and love, we have better claim on the orthodoxy of community and the orthodoxy of compassion that Francis Schaeffer talks about.

Cross-cultural communication and the methods of anthropology can make a constructive difference in the church at home. We can all work toward the day when a majority of church members have had some firsthand experience in productively relating to others whose cultural backgrounds are different. That will be a great day!

The gospel of Jesus Christ has a cross-cultural appeal—but most American Christianity does not. I am eager for the day when alumni of the Peace Corps and short-term missionary programs become deacons! And even better, what a great thing it would be for a local church to deliberately take on an overseas experience through the eyes of three or four families of internationalists.

In summary, here are several suggestions.

1. For those who are trying to select a major field of study:

Select a field that will prepare you for a versatile career—in the U.S. and the *world*!

2. For those who are planning on graduate school: Consider a graduate program that includes overseas learning experiences.

3. For those who are going to be college and university faculty members: Give special consideration to institutions that are involved in overseas contracts and will give you a chance to participate as part of your assignment now or later.

4. For all of you: Take some studies in cross-cultural understanding, area studies in geography, sociology and history of specific world regions, and also some basic anthropology courses.

5. One further suggestion: Get some cross-cultural experiences now by learning to work in an American subcultural setting somewhere where you live or go to school.

Americans are going overseas to carry on the business, research, training and cooperative development which is part of the world obligations of a profoundly indebted nation. Should Christians be among them? *Yes.*

Notes

[1] U. S. Bureau of the Census, Current Population Reports, Series P-20, No. 193, "Mobility of the Population of the United States: March 1968 to March 1969," U. S. Government Printing Office, Washington, D. C., 1969.

HOW TO PREPARE FOR A FOREIGN EXPERIENCE IN WORLD EVANGELISM

Warren W. Webster

I have in my hands a copy of what purports to be a very old, though possibly spurious, manuscript. It is addressed to:

The Rev. Paul, Apostle
Independent Missionary
Corinth, Greece

Dear Mr. Paul:

We recently received an application from you for service under our Board. We have made an exhaustive survey of your case and, frankly, we are surprised that you have been able to "pass" as a bona fide missionary.

1. In the first place we are told that you are afflicted with severe eye trouble which is almost certain to be an insuperable handicap to any effective ministry. We normally require 20/20 vision.

2. Secondly, we take a dim view of a full-time missionary doing part-time secular work, but we hear that you are making tents on the

side. You admitted in a letter to the church at Philippi that they are the only group supporting you. We wonder why this is.

3. Further, is it true that you have a jail record? Certain brethren report that you did two years' time at Caesarea and were also imprisoned in Rome.

4. Moreover, it is reported from Ephesus that you made so much trouble for the businessmen there that they refer to you as "the man who turned the world upside down." We feel such sensationalism has no place in missions. We also deplore the "over-the-wall-in-a-basket" episode at Damascus. We are appalled at your obvious lack of conciliatory behavior. Diplomatic men are not stoned or dragged out of the city gate or assaulted by furious mobs. Have you ever suspected that gentler words might gain you more friends? For your benefit we enclose a copy of Dalius Carnegus' book, *How to Win Jews and Influence Greeks.*

5. Frankly, Mr. Paul, there has been some criticism of your sermons as well. In a recent message you stated: "God forbid that I should glory save in the cross of Jesus Christ." It seems to us that you ought also to glory somewhat in our national heritage, our denominational program, the unified budget and our World Federation of Churches. Your sermons are repeatedly criticized as being much too long for the church-going public. We hear that at one place you spoke until after midnight and a young man was so sleepy that he fell out of the window and broke his neck. You should know that nobody is saved after the first twenty minutes. Our advice to speakers is: "Stand up, speak up and shut up."

6. Finally, Dr. Luke the physician reports that you are a thin little man, rather bald, frequently sick, and always so agitated over your churches that you sleep very poorly. He indicates that you pad around the house praying half the night. *Our* ideal for all applicants is a healthy mind in a robust body. We believe that a good night's sleep will give you zest and zip so that you wake up full of zing.

We hesitate to inform you, Brother Paul, but in all our experience we have never met a candidate so opposite to the requirements of our mission board. If we should accept you we would be breaking every principle of current missionary practice.

Most sincerely yours,

J. Flavius Fluffyhead, Secretary, Foreign Mission Board[1]

We hope that modern mission secretaries are more sensible and more spiritually sensitive than the purported author of this document, but one sometimes fears that modern methods of processing candidates are intended primarily to appoint harmonious, "well-rounded" individuals while screening out the potential Apostle Pauls. If, as I suppose, this picture is somewhat overdrawn it does, however, remind us that God uses all types of people, and that means he has a work and a place for you!

It is not my primary purpose to challenge you with commitment to Christ and his global mission. Many of you have already made this decision, and I assume that as committed Christians *all* of you are willing to consider the possibility of long- or short-term involvement abroad as the Lord may indicate.

Today we want to look at some of the factors involved in preparing for cross-cultural communication of the Good News. In some ways "preparing for a foreign experience" is like learning how to swim or how to parachute. You can be taught all the techniques and what to expect, but the moment of truth comes when you actually make the plunge–and nothing can fully prepare you for that, though training and counsel may provide some basis for courage and confidence if you remember what you learn.

The key words in preparing for overseas service must be "variety" and "flexibility." This is necessarily so because of (1) rapidly changing world conditions, (2) the vastness and diversity of human culture, (3) individual differences among those who go abroad and (4) the many different types of Christian witness overseas. Some of you will go in the name of Christ as international students, college professors, vocational witnesses and non-professional missionaries. Perhaps many more of you will go in connection with regular mission organizations in which there are many different types of missionary service: long-term, short-term, career, independent, denominational, general, technical, specialized.

Because of so many variants I cannot tell precisely how *you* should prepare, but I can suggest some basic elements of preparation that you should consider.

I. The primacy of spiritual preparation

1. Preparation begins with radical commitment to the Lordship

of Christ and involves counting the cost of discipleship. It also involves counting the cost of disobedience. How many of you are afraid to be outside the will of God? Only then are you in a position to count the cost of discipleship.

2. Spiritual preparation for your mission in life must place a high priority on knowing the Book of God and the God of the Book. Not simply the kind of biblical knowledge that comes from attending lectures and memorizing notes, but the experiential knowledge that comes through discovering its truths for yourself and integrating them into life. It is not so important *how* you gain this knowledge—whether through formal training or your own faithful study—but no one should presume to go abroad as a representative of Jesus Christ who has not demonstrated his ability to use the Bible effectively in teaching, preaching or witnessing at home. If a person cannot present the gospel scripturally and intelligently in his homeland, it is not likely that he will accomplish much under the more difficult and demanding conditions abroad.

3. Spiritual preparation for evangelism recognizes that the Spirit of God is the Great Persuader of men's hearts. What do you know personally of the Holy Spirit working in and through you? Learn from him to "walk in the light" with the roof off between you and God, and the walls down between you and your brothers. Learn to experience the healing that enters into fractured personal relations when you confess your failure and ask for prayer and forgiveness. Be prepared for such openness across national and racial lines as well. A medical doctor in Africa relates how, in a burst of anger over apparent dishonesty in the hospital, he dismissed several student nurses, at least one of whom was probably innocent. In any event he realized his anger and attitude did not commend the gospel, and after prayer he went to meet the Africans he had offended. He acknowledged his hastiness and harshness and asked their forgiveness. At first they listened sullenly and skeptically, until recognizing his evident sincerity one turned with a smile of reconciliation to say, "Doctor, this is the first time a white man ever apologized to us."[2] That too was a work of the Holy Spirit.

The goal of all spiritual preparation for evangelism is that we should be "approved by God" as fit "to be entrusted with the gospel" (1 Thess. 2:4). The very word "entrusted" implies a proven trustworthiness. The man or woman God uses abroad will normally have been proved and approved by the Holy Spirit in Christian witness and service at home before being sent to distant places. Workers approved as the result of being tested—that is the type of evangelist and missionary known to the New Testament. Let it be our standard as well, remembering the words of Paul to the young Timothy: "Do your best to present yourself to God as *one approved,* a workman who has no need to be ashamed, rightly handling the word of truth" (2 Tim. 2:15).

II. **Educational preparation**

While spiritual factors are basic to all Christian service, the educational side of preparation for overseas ministries should not be minimized, especially in a day when higher standards and a rising tide of educational expectancy characterize the aspirations of both developed and developing nations.

Once again generalization is difficult because of individual differences, but there are several types of educational training which may contribute to your preparation.

1. First comes basic preparation for life which for most of you is pursued at the college level and should include an understanding of the revolutionary forces at work in the twentieth century. Whether at a Christian or secular college this basic training may include some technical or specialized aspects, either as part of an undergraduate program in, for example, mass media and communications, journalism, science, engineering, education, nursing, etc. or through post-graduate study in areas such as medicine, linguistics or anthropology.

2. There is also need for some theological preparation—the type and amount of which should be suited to the needs of the individual and his intended ministry.

Theological training for some people may be self-acquired. More often it is undertaken as part of a course of study in a Christian college, or through 1-3 years of post-college study at a Bible institute or seminary. Most mission societies *recommend* theological training of some kind, and some *require* it—with considerable allowance made for short-term or highly specialized personnel. Obviously not everyone engaged in overseas evangelism requires a formal theological education, though everyone needs to know the Scriptures well. It is not likely that the pilot of a plane serving missionaries needs to be able to read the Bible in Hebrew and Greek, but the translator working in the village beneath him ought to be able to do so—and many others will profit from that thorough type of study. Some have tended to view seminary training as the burial ground of missionary vision, but this is not necessarily true. Today many evangelical seminaries are at the forefront of establishing schools or departments of world mission and regularly see 20-30% of their graduates going into overseas teaching and evangelistic ministries. For career missionaries the right kind of seminary training often gives a breadth and depth that contributes stability, effectiveness and satisfaction to a long-term ministry.

At the same time it must be admitted that seminary training sometimes puts more emphasis on the classical than the contemporary, and is largely oriented to the static situation in American Christianity rather than to the dynamic forces encountered in cross-cultural communication. No less a student of theology and church history than Stephen Neill reminds us that "No one has yet set to work to think out the theology of the Church in terms of that one thing for which it exists"—its mission.[3]

3. If you plan on living and working overseas your education should include some specific preparation for cross-cultural communication of the Christian message. The prospective overseas Christian witness, whether eventually planting churches, working with students or undertaking urban and industrial evangelism, needs an understanding of basic missionary principles with enough biblical and historical perspective to avoid the more common mistakes of past and present practice.

Equally important, anyone going abroad in Christian service should be able to understand and interpret at least three cultures:

In order to avoid many common errors of biblical interpretation, he needs a general understanding of biblical culture—both Semitic and Greek—during the period when God's Word was given to men.

He needs an understanding of his own culture—those forces, many of them unconscious, which shape his behavior and values—in order to distinguish clearly between the gospel and culture and, hopefully, to be freed from racial and cultural arrogance.

He also needs an understanding of the culture to which he is going in order to communicate effectively. A leading anthropologist observes that Americans "are apt to be guilty of great ethnocentrism. . . . We insist that everyone else do things our way. Consequently we manage to convey the impression that we simply regard foreign nationals as 'underdeveloped Americans.' Most of our behavior does not spring from malice but from ignorance, which is as grievous a sin in international relations. We are not only almost totally ignorant of what is expected in other countries, we are equally ignorant of what we are communicating to other people by our own normal behavior." He concludes: "We have to learn to take foreign culture seriously. The British are ahead of us on this, and the Russians are so far ahead it isn't even funny. We, in the United States, are in the stone age of human relations in the overseas fields."[4]

The understanding of culture—one's own as well as that of others—is a life-long process, but it needs to begin *before* going abroad with the gospel.

III. Practical preparation

There are some things that can be done to synthesize academic and spiritual preparation in real-life situations.

1. Gain experience in a skill or profession. Put your knowledge to work and acquire practical experience before going abroad to work. Government and commerce tend to offer overseas assignments to experienced men who are already successful and respected in their organization or institution. But mission societies have frequently sent out young, untested candidates, sometimes highly trained—in everything but experience. Knowledge is not enough. Today's world demands Christians with experience—both spiritual and professional. I read of a unique missionary orientation program in England which would not admit anyone for training until he had been earning a living in his own profession—for at least two years. Such a practice might go a long way toward reducing missionary wastage for both vocational and long-term career missionaries.[5]

2. Gain experience in evangelism here at home. Cultivate the habit of speaking naturally to as many people as possible about Jesus Christ. Spend more time with non-Christian friends in an effort to

introduce them to life in Christ. An excellent means of preparing for overseas evangelism might be to regularly lead a Bible class made up largely of interested non-Christians, including foreign students. If possible, study or take a trip abroad in order to break out of the mono-cultural box that blinds most Americans, or at least seek cross-cultural experience through learning to work in an American subculture in the inner city or elsewhere. Wherever you go, try to live so that people can see Christ in you and periodically ask yourself if men and women are finding him as a result of your life and witness.

3. Orient yourself toward people outside your ordinary circle of contacts. See if you have the adaptability to penetrate levels of society where you would not normally feel at home. Is there evidence that you can "bear the yoke"—working happily with, or under, people of other races and cultures? Do you have "staying power" in the face of danger, fear and stress? Learn to develop "coping strategies" for responding creatively to whatever cultural nuances may be encountered. These are among the qualities that mark an effective ambassador of Christ in today's world.

IV. **Linguistic preparation**

Almost without exception, anyone going abroad with an evangelistic purpose should expect to learn at least one language *well.* Efforts to acquire the national or local languages are appreciated by people everywhere. Language is "the shrine of a people's soul" and the doorway to deep cultural understanding and effective communication through identification.

Language learning is far more a matter of *attitude* than of *aptitude.* Anyone who has learned to speak his mother tongue can also learn to communicate in another language, and modern techniques help speed up the process. Learn to *love* the language you are learning. See it as an opportunity to understand the Scriptures in a new dimension, and value it as a living instrument for communicating the Word of God in the words of men.

It may seem that preparation for Christian service abroad is somewhat long and rigorous, but the Lord of the harvest has high standards. Whatever you do, don't cut your preparation short. Remember that Christ spent thirty years preparing for only three or four years of ministry. And even the Apostle Paul, though very well educated when he met Christ on the road to Damascus, had to spend another three years in Arabia preparing for his evangelistic task—and it was some fourteen years after his conversion before he undertook his first missionary journey.

Many centuries after the Apostle Paul, a similarly gifted and well-trained man named Adoniram Judson left the shores of the U.S. as the first American missionary to Asia. Judson was a brilliant young man who declined an appointment as tutor in Brown University and turned down a position in the largest church in Boston to lose himself in obedience to his Lord and ultimately to translate the Bible into Burmese by way of establishing the strong church found in Burma today in the midst of a socialist state.

Years later his son Edward wrote a book about his father in which he said that it is a mistake to think that a second-rate man is good enough to send to the non-Christian world. "The worst off," he wrote, "need the very best we have. God gave His best, even His only begotten Son, in order to redeem a lost world." He went on to point out that missions have made their greatest advances when some of the church's best men and most dedicated scholars have devoted their talents to the evangelization of the world. Then he concluded by observing, "It would be a sad day for American Christians if they should ever deserve Nehemiah's reproach: 'Their nobles put not their necks to the work of their Lord.' Christianity will advance over the earth with long, swift strides when the churches are ready to send their best men, and the best men are ready to go."[6]

God so loved the world that he *gave*—the *best* he had.
How much do *you* love?
What have you *given*?
What *more* can you do?
When will you begin?

Notes

[1] Adapted from an anonymous article (original source unknown).
[2] Arden Almquist, *Missionary, Come Back!* (New York: World Publishing Co., 1970), p. 14.
[3] Stephen Neill, *Creative Tension* (London: Edinburgh House Press, 1959), p. 111.
[4] Edward T. Hall, *The Silent Language* (Greenwich, Conn.: Fawcett Publications, 1959), p. 9 and back cover.
[5] A. Jack Dain, *The Screening of Missionary Candidates* (Washington, D. C.: Evangelical Foreign Missions Association, 1957), p. 20.
[6] Edward Judson, *The Life of Adoniram Judson* (Philadelphia: American Baptist Publication Society, 1883), p. 19.

THE LOCAL CHURCH AND WORLD EVANGELISM

Samuel Kamaleson

There are many experiences in life that a man can have and can enjoy in seeming solitude, but being a Christian is not one of them. Salvation, of which the good news speaks, is—as the very Word itself teaches—the summing up of all things in Christ: It embraces within its scope the restoration of harmony between man and God, between man and man, and between man and nature. Within a congregation or community of Christians is the basic relationship of the individual to that community.

The core of biblical history is the story of the calling of a visible community of men to be God's people. Through his deliberate, concrete acts of calling individuals, Jesus made this visible community take shape. Individuals were called into the visible fellowship in order to carry out God's will in the world. Although God's plan of salvation in Christ demands the calling of a visible community into existence, it is God's desire that all men should be saved and should come to the knowledge of the truth. This is implied in the account of the fishermen who were called into this visible community in order that they might be made fishers of men.

Some kind of structure is necessary for this community to function properly. But the essence is not the structure, the essence is the community. It is at this point that many of us have become confused, either denying the church or thinking of her as more than she rightly is. It is the community's task to obey Jesus Christ who will achieve God's purpose in the world with it and through it. This obedience is expressed corporately and individually, but never outside the consciousness of a community. The structure of this community is only for the achievement of God's purpose. Hence, when the structure hinders this achievement, that structure ought to change.

But the community goes on; it is indestructible. Known as the congregation or the community of God, she represents God's new humanity, defined very forcibly in Ephesians 2:1-22. She is called into being by hearing, believing and obeying the good news.

The basis of the unity within this community is not racial or national; it is not class consciousness, cultural consciousness, or linguistic consciousness. The basis of unity within this community is the one who called it into being and the obedience to this one's call.

Furthermore, this community finds continuity by participating in the sacraments. And then she functions properly because of the dynamic of the Holy Spirit who controls her and activates her. No individual can ever be part of the body of Christ without becoming part of this local community of Christians. This community is the functioning reality or the community of the Holy Spirit here among men.

We use the term *community of God.* Within this term the descriptive part is *community;* the operative part is *God* or Christ. Hence when individual Christians cite the sins of this community of Christians as a reason for not being part of the community of Christians, their argument is not operationally valid. For when Paul addresses the visible, sinful congregations in Corinth and Asia Minor by the words "body of Christ, bride of Christ, temple of God," he uses these words precisely in the context of the urgent need to correct the sins found in them.

And hence we sum up: As long as the congregation of Christians carries within itself the life and witness of the gospel of Jesus Christ, she has all that is necessary for her own repentance. And we also assert that no other institution contains within her heart such devastating possibilities of self-criticism without running the risk of self-destruction. It is all because of her Lord Jesus Christ.

Sometimes I think the modern Pharisee is to be found outside the church and not within it. The criticism with which the church is now criticized is often apt and right because it bears the categories that are suggested by the gospel itself: brotherhood, love, concern beyond one's own self, giving of oneself so that redemption can come to others. These are categories that the gospel suggests. And the church is constantly criticized on the basis of these categories. But I wonder: If criticism without reflective participation is the role of the critic, then does not he himself deserve the label, Pharisee, rather than the church that engages in reflective participation?

Since I came to the United States, I have entered into the cultural preoccupation with comic strips. One such comic strip is *Winnie the Pooh.* Not too long ago I heard Winnie suggest to his friend, Christopher Robin, that he would like to hear a story. Christopher Robin, being a congenial friend, turns to Winnie the Pooh and asks, "What would you really like to hear a story about?" And Winnie smiles and says, "Tell Winnie a story about Winnie. There is no story that Winnie likes better than stories about Winnie himself." I said to myself, how human can a bear get?

I find, strangely, within the caucus of so-called Western Christianity immeasurable possibilities for self-division. I find also within the caucus of this very aggressive community a desire to export self-division to the so-called mission field. There must be an enormous tariff exercised on such export commodities. This preoccupation is derived from the extreme individualism which is sometimes a plague on so-called Western Christianity. But divisiveness is not indigenous to the gospel; it is an occupational hazard of identification with local conditions.

Further, the good news of reconciliation can be communicated only by a reconciled community. The individual believer is sustained within a community which understands itself as dependent. She is not her own; she is her Lord's. To such a community Jesus said,

"Fear not, little flock, it is your Father's good pleasure to give you the kingdom."

This community finds itself among other communities in the expanding cycle of expanding communities. The believer not only finds that he is part of the community of God, but that he is also part of his family, his neighborhood, his local city, his state, national, and possibly international and world communities. Within such a consciousness, words like *individual, social, secular, sacred* are never mutually exclusive. Within such a consciousness, every human being has a status whether he is within Christ or not. And when the community seeks to communicate, she does so only with such an understanding.

How woefully one reflects when he hears about what Gandhi could have been if things had been different when he was seeking the message through the Christian church in another part of the world! A story is told about a person who was a driver of the limousine that carried a judge to a church in that very same part of the world where Gandhi first sought to become a Christian. The one who drove the limousine was a very colorful brother. The judge whom he drove to the services unfortunately was a colorless brother. On several occasions when he dropped the judge at the service, John (we will call the driver that) went in to worship in the same congregation. The congregation, unwilling to turn the judge out, wanted to diplomatically communicate to John that his place was elsewhere. So they asked him to pray about it. But every week even after praying John kept coming back. So one day they called him aside and said, "Did the Lord tell you anything in your prayer?" John said, "Yes, sir, he did. He told me, 'John, don't get discouraged. They have successfully kept me out also.' "

Such a community, I beg with you to understand, will never communicate. She is not the community of Christ, and she cannot have an evangelistic purpose wherever she may be existing. The communicating community transcends, as I said earlier, all man-made barriers. Among these is the so-called international barrier.

We have often called the church an international institution. We reduce her when we say that. She is not an organization but a supernatural organism: She feels, she throbs with vitality. In other words, when the church in the United States is pinched, the church in India must say, "Ah, that hurts!" If this is not what we have achieved, we have not heard the gospel properly, for this is the new humanity.

Although individual and corporate communication is possible, the total capacity of the entire communicating community of God is greater than the sum of the capacities of its individual members. This is always true. Simply consider a convert without a community wherein he can be nourished and made to grow. Consider the support that comes from people who are like-minded and have only one purpose in mind.

Let me cite one example that I know too well. We were working in India in an agricultural fellowship, seeking to produce better grain and better quality animals. We needed help from someone who knew the advanced technology of the West, but who had to identify with the East. We prayed as a community. And God strangely used a brother from the United States who was traveling through Paris, France. His car broke down. From the nearest house, a Frenchman came out to help get the car started. In broken English, he told the American brother that he was a believer and that he was an agriculturally trained university graduate who desired to go and serve the Lord in India. Seven years he had tried, but the doors were closed.

The American said, "I know of an Indian veterinarian who is a Methodist pastor who wanted someone like you. I don't know his exact address, but he lives in Madras. Would you like to go and find him?" And though there are 520 million people in India and he had only the name of the city, the Frenchman was still willing. The American, as God would have it, had in his car two obsolete TV movies which spoke about the Lord and in which I had appeared while here in the U.S. (Incidentally, it is a practice of my mission to send the obsolete stuff to the mission field once it becomes useless here. I think this is deplorable. It is not in my subject, but I inject it anyhow.)

In any case, the American said, "Why don't you take these movies and find him?" The Frenchman had the holy audacity to believe this was God's will, sold his property, bought a secondhand Peugeot, put in his one-year-old son, his wife and himself, drove down to Marseilles, bought a one-way ticket to Bombay, got only a three-month visa, drove to Madras, went to a Pentecostal congregation because they are the only ones who do not ask for any more credentials than a statement of faith (praise the Lord!), and screened the movie. While I was singing "His eye is on the sparrow," he said, "Do you know this man?" They said, "He's a local Methodist pastor." So at 10:30 one night he walked in with a full-grown Frenchman's beard and a tan for which my country is very famous, and he said, "I have come from Paris, France, to work with you, brother." I said, "Sit down and tell me more before I believe it." Three years have gone by. Christopher Dufer is still with us. Now he has a new baby girl whose name in translation means spotless purity.

This is the community I am talking about. When it comes to fulfilling the purposes of the kingdom of God, there are no restrictions whatsoever. If we do not go from Urbana with this consciousness, I would question how much we have heard here.

The communicating community must realize that she is distinctly separate and different from other human communities because of her origin and sustenance and goal. When she does, then in her association with other communities she knows very well where they itch. It is very, very trying when somebody tries to scratch you where you are not itching. The man in the street is not in the least concerned with some of the preoccupations and theological hangups in the so-called church. Living in a diversified human society, divided and hateful, he wants to know if the community of God has an answer for this hatred. And we would forever find reasons to hate each other on the basis of minute theological differences. God help us!

May I cite one more comic strip character? In the afternoon on Saturdays, my children sit glued to the TV—one of the cultural hazards one has to face when he comes to the United States. I want to be a father in a communicating relationship with my children, so I watch these characters over their shoulders. One show is *Stop the Pigeon*; it's about a guy called Dick Dastardly. Dick Dastardly has a very unusual crew. One of them develops a very unusual flying contraption, but he cannot communicate because he only speaks in an unintelligible technocratic language. So the other guy has to translate for him. But the third character, who is the most colorful one, is a dog named Muttley.

While the flying machine disintegrates in the air and the whole crew is falling free, Dick Dastardly turns to Muttley and says in desperation, "Muttley, do something." Muttley fortunately has a tail that can function as a rotor. So Dick Dastardly says, "Mutt, please do something. You can do something now. Turn your rotor on and save the whole group." And Muttley, still falling free, says, "Medal, medal, medal!" which we can translate as, "If I turn on my rotor, will you honor me with medals?" What a parable of modern Christendom!

In the eleventh hour, in a world going to pieces, the Master is turning to the community that he has left and says, "Do something. You have the power. You can save. You can turn loose and save the entire generation around you." And still we are stuck, caught up in the structural consciousness, saying, "Will somebody give me recognition? What type of medal will you pin on me?" There is no medal promised, except the assurance that you and I will be part of the greatest revolution ever, instituted by the greatest revolutionary, even Jesus Christ. Apart from this participating privilege, there is no other privilege guaranteed. Will we get in or will we get out?

THE NATIONAL CHURCH: DO THEY WANT US?

Byang H. Kato

I appreciate the privilege of being at Urbana, not just for the topic that is mine, but to be able to tell you that in spite of all the mistakes of mission boards and missionaries, missions as a whole have been a success. I stand as a living witness of what the Lord Jesus Christ has done not only through the Sudan Interior Mission, but through missions as a whole. There are many students here and a few of them overseas who have in one way or another been influenced by the work of missions overseas. And so, in spite of all the mistakes, and in spite of all the weaknesses of humanity, on behalf of Christians from overseas, I want to say to the congregation here, you from North America in particular, "Thank you very much for all that you have done over the years for missions."

The national church–does it want us? After so much has been said, I think as we speak about the national church our primary concern is with the church in Latin America, Africa and Asia. And I will focus mainly on those areas. But the church is the church universal. And so, when we speak of a church needing the ministry of another church, we should bear in mind that the church in North America needs the ministry of Christians from India, Congo, Brazil as much as the people in those countries require the services of Christians from North America.

As Christians, we need the services of one another. Every Christian—no matter how mature, no matter how well he can expound the Word of God—still needs and appreciates the services of Christians who have been gifted by the Spirit of God. And just as Christians need one another, so churches also need the services of one another. The Lord Jesus Christ in the parable of the seeds (Mt. 13) pointed out that the world is the field: North America is just as needy as Africa, Asia and India. Christians of every race and color need the services of one another.

I want to make an appeal to my black brethren. My heart has been saddened when I have heard some of my black brothers here in North America say that they are afraid they might not be accepted in Africa. You are very much needed; we regret your absence. Do you know that about a tenth of the African population now lives in North America? More than 20 million of the 200 million people of Africa live here in the United States. How many blacks do we have as missionaries working in Nigeria, Ghana and other parts of Africa? There are problems involved, and Tom Skinner has pointed them out. But we hope solutions will be found, and we plan to work together so that we will see more black faces as missionaries in Africa. There are cases where black missionaries have come and the way they have been received is just beyond description!

Before we deal with a missionary as a professional, we want to point out that there are endless opportunities today in many countries, especially in Africa, where a North American can witness without necessarily being directly involved in a missionary society. There is a need for born-again Christians as private businessmen, employees of oil and other companies, professors, Peace Corps workers and tourists. Such people can often go where personnel under missionary societies may not be welcome. People in such categories are appreciated by the church for their part in building up the kingdom of God at large. They can also make a direct contribution to the life of the church. They can supplement the work of missionary societies, provided that they appreciate the position of a missionary and see the validity of the existence of a local church.

We want to mention in passing that the ripened mission field of foreign students studying in North America should present a challenge to the Christians of this Christian-orientated continent. A foreign student influenced for Jesus Christ here will go back to his country someday as a missionary. Unfortunately, many students have been disillusioned because of their experience here. Hence, hospitality and college friendship can go a long way.

The General Director of The Evangelical Alliance Mission expressed the mind of most, if not all, evangelical mission societies and national churches when he said recently, "I sat with the Field Council on a number of occasions when the matter of placements was studied. Always the problem was the same–there were not enough missionaries to meet the urgent needs of the work." I myself have sat in a number of mission council meetings. In every one of them, the matter of stationings has been the longest on the agenda. Usually, an average missionary on the field has two or three possibilities for stationing. Being human, of course, he can be in only one place at a time. I have yet to meet a national church leader who can honestly say missionaries are no longer needed. Circumstances have curtailed the number of mission personnel in foreign countries. But the church of Jesus Christ has been helpless in many of these situations.

Although churches have been established with national leadership, there is still a tremendous need for mission personnel. The national leadership needs to be trained in the Scriptures, in the ministry of the Word, in administration and in technical skills of various kinds. For example, the ministry of teaching in government schools in some countries is an area which the national church cannot yet handle. In this case, finance and personnel are problems. Evangelism in the middle- and high-class community requires higher qualifications. The fact that the urban population of less developed regions of the world will increase 4.1 percent, compared with 1.9 percent in the more developed countries, according to a U.N. report, presents a challenge to the evangelical church. People with specialized training are much in need. The young church is not yet in a position to meet the demands.

The main concern today is the type of missionary wanted or not wanted. This has to be the question because of the tremendous change that has taken place in countries overseas. Not only civil rule has come of age, but the ecclesiastical voice should also be listened to. The grown-up son wants to be recognized as a partner in the business. Both the church and the mission need to recognize this fact. Theological problems are no longer the exclusive concern of the older churches. The full effect of Vatican II is yet to be felt, and it will be felt worldwide. For these and many other reasons we must give serious thought to the type of missionaries wanted today. No one person can speak for the whole world. But the following general principles should cover many situations.

Needless to say, the first basic requirement for a missionary is that he be rightly related to the Lord of the harvest both in salvation and in daily living. The young church has enough problems with her carnal Christians who do not live a dedicated life in the Lord. The missionary should be there to counsel and not to be counselled. This proper relationship includes the assurance of his call by the Lord of the harvest.

The national church is not interested in receiving a missionary who comes with a selfish motive. The sense of adventure, shelter from the complex life of the jet age and "the glory of the battlefield" may be some of the reasons for ruined mission stations which today stand as monuments to failure. One sometimes wonders if it is not this kind of selfish motive that underlies some of the so-called missionary deputation which usually consists of showing out-dated and irrelevant slides. To go because of a mere sense of sympathy for the physical needs of the people is not a good enough reason. Such a person would do better to go under a philanthropic organization. Anything less than the spiritual motive is a tool in the devil's hands.

Social work has already relegated the ministry of the pure gospel to the background in some missions work today. We should learn our lesson from the "social gospel" venom seen in advanced countries. The gospel truly is for the whole man. But man's greatest need is the salvation of his soul: "What will it profit a man, if he gains the whole world and forfeits his life?" (Mt. 16:26)

We are not minimizing the significance of providing for man's physical needs. Jesus Christ himself fed the hungry and cured the sick. But spiritual needs should be the basic concern of the church and the mission.

Educational and health services being provided with the help of the government of the countries concerned have often been criticized by new arrivals on the field. One needs to understand the situation overseas before becoming critical. In many cases it is absolutely necessary and has promoted the work of the gospel to have these amenities. But again, evangelism should be the hub of every activity of a missionary and a missionary society. Any program that does not help evangelize or promote church growth quantitatively and qualitatively should be carefully reviewed.

The national church is in search of a good example in administration, doctrine and practice. Unity both of purpose and of sound evangelical doctrine is required. If a new missionary cannot agree with the society that has brought the national church into being, his presence will be detrimental to the work of the church. Individual theological idiosyncrasies should not be allowed to cause division in the young church. "Think sessions" should have their place, but no one should try to win individual less-instructed believers into one's particular viewpoint against the general position of the national church. The spirit of dissension is condemned in the Word of God (I Cor. 3).

Positively, the national church is very much in need of a missionary who, under the guidance of the Holy Spirit, is led to "become all things to all men" (I Cor. 9:22). We need someone who is coming, not with the sense of superiority in race or education, wealth or culture, but a person coming as his Master came into the world, "not to be served, but to serve" (Mk. 10:45). This calls for humility and sacrifice without one's being aware that it is a sacrifice.

"What a waste!" has been the sort of attitude that people in the homeland have had regarding an educated person's going to the mission field. While it is true that some elites have defied the popular opinion and gone forth, the image of an average missionary has been a high school graduate who has also graduated from a one- or two-year Bible school. The Lord did use them and he is still using people of this caliber. They surely "served the Lord in their own generation." But it is the feeling of the church today that we need more educationally qualified missionaries. This is no reflection on present missionaries. Rev. Allen Thompson, Director of the West Indies Mission, underlined this point when he said recently, "In missions today we need men of theological orientation."

A missionary is usually looked upon as a genius with the final answers on every issue. The church is faced with such issues as church union, situational ethics, God-is-dead theology, church government, Bible translation and authority of the Scriptures. It is true that the degree of growth in churches overseas is not the same. But we cannot deny the fact that as the church has taken root, it is bound to tackle these and/or similar problems. The battle on the mission field will be theological within the next decade. A missionary going abroad should therefore be acquainted with major theological issues of the day. The manifestations of liberal tendencies may come in a different pattern in developing countries. But a well trained person can detect them and offer the corrective measures.

Secular qualification is also a requirement, on the part of both the church and the government, but more so in the case of the latter. To warrant his presence in the country, a missionary should possess knowledge that can contribute to the economic progress of a country. Possessing a college degree or a professional certificate is a status symbol and a key to many opportunities for witness. The days when just anything will do for the foreign field are past in many countries. Spirituality is no substitute for knowledge. The greatest missionary who ever lived was among the "Who's Who" in his days. Probably this is why more than half of the New Testament was written by the apostle Paul.

Our Lord was involved in the ordinary things of life in his days. He shared in people's joy (Jn. 2) as well as in their sorrow (Jn. 11). A missionary who would follow the steps of the Master in involvement is what we want. Circumstances may preclude his learning the local language. But where at all possible he should do so. Respect for other people's culture, even though it militates against good American or Canadian culture, will open many avenues for witness.

We want a missionary who will be involved in the life of the local church. In the involvement, the lesson of partnership needs to be learned by both the church and the missionary. The missionary should feel himself part of the church where he is serving. Some missionaries, however, have made the excuse that their home church wants them to maintain their membership at home *in absentia.* Churches in North America should be reminded that their many years of missionary service overseas have not been in vain. Since the Lord brought his church into being in Africa or Asia or Latin America, then everything should be done to support the church. There should be no strings attached if the offering has been made as unto the Lord.

The older churches should change the old philosophy of supporting the missionary rather than the mission. Supporting the missionary rather than the mission has caused suspicion within the national church. Why should the support be cut off as soon as a missionary is withdrawn from the field, even though a national is doing exactly the same ministry? This has allowed the accusation of colonialism to stand.

Although it is not the purpose of this paper to deal with the matter of finance, we want to digress a little bit. Where the national church is weak economically, financial support can be used effectively without weakening the church. There are cases where the national church could employ some nationals to do the job a missionary would do. But lack of funds has prohibited this. With support from overseas, carefully channelled through the right means, the Lord's work could see real progress.

Evangelicals are far behind in theological education. Just one example: In Nigeria where there are at least half a million evangelical Christians, there is only one seminary, belonging to one denomination, that offers a Th.B. degree. Nothing higher is available. Christians of other theological persuasions can offer Ph.D. degrees. Unless funds are made available from the older churches, the young church overseas stands in the danger of being overwhelmed by liberal theology. In Africa it is much easier to get a scholarship for liberal theological studies than for evangelical. In his evaluation of evangelical missions activity in Africa, Dr. George Peters of Dallas Seminary correctly pointed out, "It is evident that evangelical missions have not taken the ecumenical movement seriously enough. The evangelical younger churches as a whole are not able to withstand the pressures and the play on nationalism on the one hand and the promises and enticements on the other. Bold and tactful indoctrination, rather than cold denunciations, is urgently needed."

The problem of racism in North America is beginning to have its influence overseas. A church that hypocritically sends a missionary to evangelize Africa but shuts out Negroes from her precincts in North America may wake up someday to find her missionary returned with shame. We cannot wait for problems in North America to be completely settled before we face the urgent task of mission call; however, a would-be missionary should communicate his convictions to his home church first. The Lord of the harvest has outlined the program for us: "You shall be my witnesses in Jerusalem and in all Judea and Samaria and to the end of the earth" (Acts 1:8).

Does the national church want missionaries? The answer is emphatically positive. These are days of harvest in many fields. The net is breaking. We are beckoning to you to come and join us, draw the net. We are not inviting you to come and be the boss. Neither are we calling you to come and serve us. But we want you to come, realizing that our Lord Jesus Christ is the Master of the harvest. We are all going to be partners under the Lordship of Christ, for we are "workers together with him" (2 Cor. 6:1, AV).

PART III

THE CHALLENGE OF WORLD EVANGELISM

STUDENT POWER IN WORLD EVANGELISM

David M. Howard

World evangelism—Why? How? Who? These are the questions we are concerned with during Urbana 70. As we seek solutions, we will naturally be looking at the world around us and at the future that lies ahead. For unless we can understand the world we live in, we will be in a poor position to talk about evangelizing that world. By the same token, unless we can understand what produced the world we live in—that is, where we came from and why we stand at this particular juncture in history—we can scarcely hope to understand our present age.

I am well aware that it is in vogue today to call this the Now Generation. We are intensely concerned with the *here* and *now*. We want to be where the action is today, not where it was yesterday, nor where it will be tomorrow. Yesterday is gone forever, and who knows if tomorrow will ever come? So I can live only in and for today. From one standpoint, this is a noble aspiration. However, proper focus on the present requires a proper focus on the past from which we have come and on the future to which we are heading. A man is not only lost when he does not know where he is going; he is also lost when he does not know where he has come from.

The very mention of the word *history* may already have caused some of us to turn off our hearing aids. Perhaps we consider history as either a prison to chain us to the past or an irrelevant factor to be ignored. To be sure, history can serve as a prison binding us to traditions which may hinder our own creative growth. But let us not forget that history may also be a pedestal on which we may stand and launch out to new horizons. We can stand on the shoulders of our forebears and view more distant horizons with greater clarity. But if we choose to ignore the past, we lose the benefit of all that history can teach us. And we do well to recall the wise dictum, He who refuses to learn from history is condemned to repeat it. So we will attempt now to set in historical focus the present student generation and its relationship to world evangelism.

Where do we stand as students at Urbana 70 in relationship to God's plans for world evangelism?

Dr. Clarence Shedd of Yale University, in his definitive work entitled *Two Centuries of Student Christian Movements,* makes the following statement:

> In all ages the great creative religious ideas have been the achievement of the intellectual and spiritual insight of young men. . . . In literature, the arts, the sciences, many of the most revolutionary ideas have been worked out by young men under thirty and frequently by youth between 18 and 25. . . . Since Jesus' time numberless bands of Christian youth have turned the world upside down and thus led mankind forward in its struggle for freedom and deeper religious experience. The universities have always been breeding places for such groups.

(It is interesting to note that this was written in 1943 and not in 1970, as might be assumed.)

The university as we know it today did not exist during the early centuries of Christianity, nor during the so-called Dark Ages. Therefore, during that period there was no exact parallel to the students of today. However, it is significant that the only true missionary work which was carried out during the Dark Ages was led by the monks of the monastic movement. The monasteries of the day were academic as well as cultural and religious centers. It is, therefore, reasonable to say they represent the academic community of the day. And it was from this academic community that the gospel was spread to the pagan lands surrounding the civilized nations of the Roman and post-Roman Empires.

For example, Martin of Tours of the fourth century, patron saint of France and the monk for whom Martin Luther was named, has been described as "a true evangelist, who traveled far and wide, combatting paganism at every step, and bringing the gospel to bear on the life of the country folks in regions in which previously it had been limited to the cities."

Or consider Columba, the great Irish monk who lived A.D. 521 to 597. He founded a monastery on the island of Iona that became a center for the evangelization of Scotland. Indeed, it has been said by competent church historians that "monks were the missionaries of the medieval church. They went out as fearless soldiers of the Cross to found new monasteries, and these became centers from which whole tribes were won to Christianity."

Thus, even in the medieval period it was the academic community that led the way in the evangelization of the pagan world.

When we move into the period of the Renaissance and the Reformation, the university had already developed into a significant factor of life. As a matter of fact, the first universities in Europe actually grew out of the monasteries. In tracing the history of the modern missionary movement, it is remarkable that students have played a decisive role in most, if not all, of the greatest forward movements of the church in world evangelism. It has often been through their vision and energy that the church has been propelled into renewed efforts of outreach.

Thus, in our attempt to place this present student generation in historical focus, it is well to see the rich heritage left to us by former generations of students.

Probably the earliest traceable instance in which students had a part in promoting world outreach is found in Germany in the early seventeenth century. A group of seven young law students in Lübeck committed themselves to carry the gospel overseas. At least three of them sailed for Africa. Only the name of Peter Heiling has survived today. He went to Abyssinia in 1634. During some twenty years there he translated the Bible into the Amharic language and later died a martyr. No successors carried on his work, but the translation of the Scriptures was a significant contribution which unquestionably left results.

The name of Count Nicolaus Ludwig von Zinzendorf (1700-1760) stands high in the annals of missionary history as a leader of the great Moravian movement, one of the first, most effective and most enduring of missionary enterprises. Between the ages of ten and sixteen he studied in the pietistic Paedagogium in Halle, Germany, and personally knew both Spener and Francke, the founders of Pietism. While in this school he and five other young students formed The Order of the Grain of Mustard Seed, a spiritual secret society. They declared for themselves four purposes: to witness to the power of Jesus Christ, to draw together other Christians in fellowship regardless of ecclesiastical connection, to help those suffering for their faith and to carry the gospel of Christ to the heathen beyond the seas. Thus, it was as a student that Zinzendorf took his first steps toward a world outreach.

By 1732, Zinzendorf's burden for sharing the gospel had become so great that he became one of the leaders in founding Moravian missions. Their first two missionaries sailed for the West Indies in August, 1732.

Thus, the modern worldwide missionary movement (which traces part of its roots to the Moravians of 1732) was actually born in the hearts of a group of students at Halle who joined together to pray and work for world evangelism.

During this same period, God was at work in the hearts of two brothers in England–John and Charles Wesley. While John is known primarily as an evangelist and theologian and Charles as a hymn writer, they both began their remarkable careers as overseas missionaries. In 1735 they sailed to the colony of Georgia with General Oglethorpe with the specific purpose of evangelizing the Indians. But where had they received this vision? While they were students at Oxford University, they had banded together with like-minded students in a fellowship of prayer and Bible study. This group was dubbed by their contemporaries as the "Holy Club" and later, because of their methodical approach to life, the "Methodists." It was through this group that the Wesley brothers began to see their responsibility to share their faith with those who did not know Christ.

No summary of the movement of God among students in England would be complete without reference to Charles Simeon. As a fellow of King's College, Cambridge, his remarkable ministry spanned fifty-four years (1782-1836). The Inter-Varsity Fellowship of England (from which IVCF in the United States and Canada grew) traces its origins directly to the great work done by Simeon at Cambridge. Out of the small groups for Bible study and prayer which Simeon led came some of the great leaders of the church during the nineteenth century.

When David Livingstone visited Cambridge in 1857 on one of his returns from Africa, students in these groups that had been founded by Simeon were moved to form the Cambridge University Church Missionary Union to encourage a more active missionary spirit on that campus.

In 1882 the American evangelist D. L. Moody visited Cambridge. While his ministry caused a great impact in terms of evangelism, historian J. C. Pollock points out that "it was in the increase of missionary zeal that the impetus given by Moody was the most marked. . . . Many of Moody's converts were soon sensing a call to the foreign field."

One indication of this was that the following year at Cambridge seven of the outstanding student leaders applied to the China Inland Mission, recently founded by J. Hudson Taylor. These young men included such leaders as C. T. Studd, captain of the cricket team, and Stanley Smith, the stroke oar on the varsity crew. Following graduation from Cambridge the seven men decided to travel together throughout the British Isles for a few months to share with the churches and schools the burden for world evangelism which God had given to them. By the time they sailed for China in February, 1885, their brief tour had made such an abiding impact on the church of Britain that in subsequent years literally hundreds of young people volunteered for overseas service.

On the North American continent the beginnings of overseas interest on the part of the church can be traced directly to students, and, in particular, to one student, Samuel J. Mills, Jr. (1783-1818). Before his birth Samuel J. Mills' mother reportedly consecrated him to God for missionary service, a remarkable fact when one remembers that in those days there was no such thing as a mission board in North America. The church here apparently felt little or no obligation to evangelize beyond its own immediate borders.

Converted at the age of seventeen during the Great Awakening, Mills enrolled in Williams College in Massachusetts in 1806. Here it soon became his custom to spend Wednesday and Saturday afternoons in prayer with other students on the banks of the Hoosack River, which flowed near the campus. One Saturday afternoon in August, Mills and his companions were caught in a thunderstorm as they returned from their prayer meeting. They sought refuge under a haystack and spent their time in prayer as they waited out the storm. The focus of their prayer that day turned to the awakening of foreign missionary interest among their fellow students. One historian says of them, "Bowed in prayer, these first American student volunteers for foreign missions willed that God should have their lives for service wherever He needed them, and in that self-dedication really gave birth to the first student missionary society in America."

Returning to the campus, Mills and his friends formed The Society of the Brethren, whose members were bound together by oath to pray for one another that God would use them in spreading the gospel to other parts of the world. During the next four years, several of the members went on to other schools, where they formed new chapters of this society.

By 1810, these students had become so convinced that God wanted to send some of them overseas that they decided it was time to take steps in that direction. In June of that year, they went to the annual assembly of the Congregational Churches of Massachusetts with a petition for action. It requested that a foreign mission society be formed which would serve as the channel to send young people overseas. The petition was originally signed by six students, but not wishing to scare off their elders with too long a list, they eliminated two names, leaving only four.

An interesting facet of this story is the rapidity with which the church acted. The petition was presented on June 28, 1810. On June

29, 1810, the assembly voted to form the American Board of Commissioners for Foreign Missions—the first foreign missionary society in North America. By February, 1812, less than two years later, their first volunteers sailed for India. Among them was Adoniram Judson, who later persuaded the Baptists to form their own society, which, in turn, became the second mission board in North America.

Today it is popular to criticize the church for failure to be sufficiently concerned with the social and physical needs of people. However, anyone who studies the life of Samuel J. Mills will be impressed with the breadth of his concerns. For him there was no false dichotomy between "home" and "foreign" missions or between social concern and evangelism. He saw the world as a whole in need of Christ.

In addition to founding the Society of the Brethren and being instrumental in the founding of the first foreign missionary society, Mills participated in many other activities. He spent some of his summers in New York's urban slums, in what we call today the ghettos, ministering to the social, physical and spiritual needs of the poor. While there he saw the needs of seamen who came into the port of New York from around the world. He saw the potential also of putting the Word of God into their hands to be taken to other parts of the world. So he helped to found the Marine Bible Society, whose purpose was to evangelize the seamen in New York and then provide them with Bibles to be spread around the world.

In 1816, he also was a founding member of the American Bible Society, a group whose influence on world evangelism for a century and a half has been incalculable. He also helped to organize the Foreign Mission School at Cornwall, Connecticut, whose purpose was to train international students from overseas to return to their countries to evangelize.

Mills was also impressed with the needs of the American Indians. He made several trips to the Mississippi Valley and helped to organize home missions to these Indians.

While he desperately wanted to go overseas himself, he was persuaded by others to remain in the U.S. to help foment missionary concern among young people.

The crowning glory of Mills' work came through his keen insight.

He saw the needs of Africa, a continent as yet almost totally unevangelized. Then he looked at one of the glaring social ills of the United States at that time—slavery. This was an issue that was not as yet widely discussed in the early 1800s. Mills felt deeply concerned to evangelize and liberate these slaves. Putting together his concern for Africa and his desire to help the slaves, he conceived the idea of liberating these slaves and sending them back to Africa to evangelize their own people. In 1817, he participated in the founding of the American Colonization Society, whose purpose was to evangelize, liberate and repatriate slaves from North America to Africa.

In November, 1817, Mills went to Africa to survey lands—in what is now Liberia—to find a suitable place for this repatriation program. In June, 1818, while returning from Africa, he was taken ill and died at sea at the age of thirty-five. Less than twelve years had passed since this young man had knelt under a haystack with his companions near Williams College. Yet in that short span, he was instrumental in the founding of the Society of the Brethren, the American Board of Commissioners for Foreign Missions, and the Foreign Missions School, worked among the poverty-stricken in the ghettos of New York, helped form the Marine Bible Society, the American Bible Society, and home missions to the Indians of the Mississippi Valley and finally gave his life in the effort to break the chains of slavery and combine this with the evangelization of Africa. Not bad for a life span of thirty-five years!

During the next half-century, the Society of the Brethren expanded in its influence throughout the universities of the United States. Then, in 1851, a new society—the YMCA—came to the U.S. from England. The major emphasis of the YMCA was evangelistic, combined with efforts to meet the social and physical needs of young men. Within three years, there was a YMCA in nearly every major city of the United States. As early as 1856, YMCA's were beginning to appear on the campuses as well. At this time there was no movement working exclusively among the university students of the United States.

In 1877, the YMCA formally organized its collegiate division. Luther Wishard was named full-time secretary. He was the only such university worker in the world at that time. Wishard was a missionary candidate, and he considered his work on the campuses to be not only evangelism and social welfare, but also awakening missionary interest among students. In fact, he was so anxious to go overseas himself that it was a major spiritual struggle for him when the YMCA asked him to remain in the United States for an extended period of time to serve the students here. During his first year as YMCA secretary, Wishard visited Williams College and knelt at the monument on the site of the Haystack Prayer Meeting held in 1806 to commit himself anew to God and to the world outreach of his church, saying, "I am willing to go anywhere at any time to do anything for Jesus."

God was at work elsewhere during these years. In the early 1840s, a student named Royal Wilder was a member of the Society of the Brethren at Andover Seminary. In 1846, he sailed for India under the American Board of Commissioners. After serving there for thirty years, he was forced home in 1877 by poor health. Settling in Princeton, New Jersey, he founded a periodical, *The Missionary Review of the World.*

His son, Robert Wilder, enrolled in Princeton College in 1881, where he became greatly concerned that God would awaken students there to their responsibility to the rest of the world. On Sunday afternoons he would meet in his father's living room with other students to pray to this end. In 1883, they formed the Princeton Foreign Missionary Society.

Then God began to bring together some other strands. J.E.K. Studd, brother to C.T. Studd of the famous Cambridge Seven, came to the United States in 1885 to share with students here the vision which the Cambridge Seven had spread in England. While visiting Cornell University he was used of God to influence deeply the life of a young sophomore there named John R. Mott.

In the summer of 1885, God in his sovereignty brought together Luther Wishard of the YMCA, Robert Wilder of Princeton, John R. Mott of Cornell, and J.E.K. Studd of Cambridge—all of whom shared a mutual vision for awakening missionary interest among students. Strands which had begun eighty years earlier under the haystack were being formed into what has been called "the golden chain stretching from the Haystack Meeting to the greatest student uprising in all history." These young men were convinced that God wanted to do a great thing among students of their day. So they requested D. L. Moody, the evangelist, to sponsor a student Bible conference in the summer of 1886. He agreed and plans were under way.

In July, 1886, 251 students gathered at Mount Hermon, Massachusetts, at the conference grounds of D. L. Moody, for a month of fellowship, prayer and Bible study with Moody and A. T. Pierson, editor of *The Missionary Review of the World* and a renowned Bible teacher. Wilder and his sister, Grace, were praying that out of that conference God would call one hundred missionary volunteers.

During the month the Holy Spirit began to work in a quiet yet unmistakable way. After a powerful address by Dr. Pierson on "God's Providence in Modern Missions," most of the students spent the better part of the night in prayer. That address provided the seed thoughts for the watchword that became the cry of the students: "The evangelization of the world in this generation." By the last night of the conference, ninety-nine students had signed a declaration saying that they were willing and desirous to go to the unevangelized portions of the world. On that night one more student came to Robert Wilder to indicate a similar desire. Wilder's prayers were answered.

But the students were not willing to let this vision stop with the end of the conference. They requested Wilder and another Princeton student, John Forman, to travel during the coming year to other campuses to impart a similar vision to students around the United States and Canada. Wilder and Forman agreed. During the 1886-87 school year, they visited 162 schools and saw 2,106 students sign missionary volunteer declarations. Among these were some of the great missionary leaders of the next half-century, including Samuel Zwemer, a great apostle to the Muslims, and Robert E. Speer, an outstanding Presbyterian statesman.

The students also felt that some form of organization was needed to keep up their impetus. So they formed the Student Volunteer Movement for Foreign Missions, which was formally incorporated in 1888. John R. Mott was named chairman and Wilder traveling secretary. The cry, "The evangelization of the world in this generation" became their watchword. Mott in later life said, "I can truthfully answer that next to the decision to take Christ as the

Leader and Lord of my life, the watchword has had more influence than all other ideals and objectives combined to widen my horizon and enlarge my conception of the kingdom of God."

The growth of the SVM was phenomenal. In 1891 they sponsored the first student missionary convention. This subsequently became a quadrennial affair, held every four years. (IVCF readily acknowledges its debt to the SVM for the idea which lies behind this present Urbana convention.) For the next thirty years the conventions and the movement in general grew rapidly. By the post-World War I era, literally thousands of students had gone overseas as missionaries as a result of the influence of the SVM. The entire church of Christ in the United States and Canada was awakened to its worldwide responsibilities by the impact of this movement.

The first quadrennial convention following World War I was held at Des Moines, Iowa, in 1920. This was the SVM's peak year, statistically and in terms of influence. There were 6,890 people who attended the Des Moines Convention, and 2,783 students enrolled as missionary volunteers the following year. Less than twenty years later the entire enrollment of student volunteers for one year was 25. The quadrennial convention held at Toronto in 1940 was attended by only 465 delegates. What had happened to cause such a drastic change in so short a time?

Let me read from a report of that Convention:

> The Convention at Des Moines in 1920 was a revolt against older leadership. The . . . students who gathered there were not dominated by any great missionary purpose. . . . They rightly believed that selfishness and foolishness had involved the world in terrible war and bloodshed and they expressed their intention to take control of Church and State in an effort to bring about better conditions. . . . Many students were determined to work for reforms–either with or without the help of God.

Reports of the conventions for the next sixteen years indicate a veering away from the original purposes of SVM and a notable absence of the watchword. By 1936, at Indianapolis, it was stated that "the audience was the mission field rather than the missionary force."

Dr. William Beahm, in a doctoral dissertation written at the University of Chicago on the history of the SVM, states, "Their emphasis shifted away from Bible study, evangelism, lifework decision and foreign mission obligation on which the SVM had originally built. Instead they now emphasized new issues such as race relations, economic injustice and imperialism." In view of this Dr. Beahm states that "by 1940 it had almost ceased to be a decisive factor either in student religious life or in the promotion of the missionary program of the churches."

In 1959 the SVM merged with several other groups to form the National Student Christian Federation. This, in turn, merged in 1966 with the Roman Catholic Newman Student Federation and others to form the University Christian Movement. In 1969 the UCM quietly voted itself out of existence. At the time of this action one officer of the UCM declared, "We made some significant compromises in affirming our Christian identity. . . . We have failed in being self-consciously Christian," and attributed part of the demise of the movement to that failure. Thus, the final vestiges of the greatest student missionary movement in the history of the church were laid to rest, eighty-three years after the Spirit of God had moved so unmistakably upon the students at Mount Hermon.

Yet, God does not leave himself without a witness. By the middle thirties with the great decline in missionary interest, the Great Depression taking its toll, war clouds rising again in Europe and the liberal-fundamentalist controversy raging, the church was deeply discouraged. But once again God moved upon students who would not be deterred from fulfilling God's call in spite of surrounding circumstances.

In 1936, at Ben Lippen Bible Conference grounds in North Carolina, a group of students from Christian schools around the country shared their concern over the fact that the SVM seemed to have changed its original purposes and that the church in general seemed to be losing its missionary interest. Dr. Robert McQuilkin, founder of Columbia Bible College, counseled them as they sought God's will concerning what they should do. Finally, convinced that they could not sit idly by and watch the church give up its missionary outreach, they decided to act. The following week a delegation from Ben Lippen went to Keswick, New Jersey, to share with a similar conference of students there the burden God had given to them. After careful consultation with some SVM leaders, and feeling that their purposes were now different, they decided to form a new organization.

Thus, the Student Foreign Missions Fellowship was organized. In 1938, the SFMF was formally incorporated under student leadership, and chapters were formed throughout the country on college campuses. Rapid growth was experienced, and once again the church was awakened through students who refused to be daunted by the circumstances of their lives.

In 1939, IVCF came to the United States from Canada. It was soon evident that one of its purposes–fomenting missionary interest among students–overlapped directly with the purposes of SFMF. After several years of prayer and consultation both groups felt led of God to a merger, which was consummated in November, 1945, with the SFMF becoming the Missionary Department of IVCF.

In December, 1946, the newly merged SFMF and IVCF sponsored their first international missionary convention, held not at Urbana, but rather at the University of Toronto, under the direction of J. Christy Wilson. There 575 students from across Canada and the United States gathered to consider God's claims upon their lives. It was my privilege to attend that convention as a student. And I can honestly say that it was one of the factors which God used in ultimately leading me to serve him in Latin America. In 1948, the convention was moved to the University of Illinois, where it has been held every three years since that time.

Following World War II, there was a great upsurge of missionary concern. Veterans who had fought in the Pacific and European theatres of war returned to the campuses of the United States and Canada, deeply desirous to go back and share the gospel with the people who so recently had been their enemies and were now shattered in the aftermath of war. These veterans were older than the average student today. They had seen the world, life and death in a way few students before or since have seen it. And God used them to lead others into an understanding of our obligations to the world. From many campuses in the late 1940s and early 1950s, more students went overseas in missionary endeavor than at any other comparable period in history. Then came the Silent Fifties. The previous four decades had been incredible upheavals–World War I, the Roaring Twenties, the Great Depression of the thirties, World War II in the forties. Now it seemed as though the human race was begging for a breather. This general lull took its toll in missionary interest as well, and once again there was a decrease in the churches and among students.

Then in the early 1960s God again spoke to students, particularly at Columbia Bible College. Student leaders became concerned that there was a decrease in missionary interest and outreach. The SFMF of the IVCF movement seemed to have stagnated. But the activism so characteristic of students in the sixties was also at work among missionary-minded students. New life was poured into the SFMF. An Inter-regional Coordinating Committee, entirely composed of and engineered by students, began to work closely with the national office of SFMF. Student leaders began to reach out to their peers on their own campuses and beyond to help revitalize missionary concern elsewhere. As God had so often done in the past, once again he was laying his hand on students as his means of awakening others.

Yet in 1970 we stand at a crossroads similar to that at which the student movement of 1920 stood. At that time some said, "Let us forget evangelism, Bible study and foreign missions, and concentrate on the true issues of the day, such as race relations, economic injustice and imperialism." The issues, strangely enough, have not changed very much. But our response to those issues can determine the course which the church of Jesus Christ will take for the next generation. If we do not learn from history, we are condemned to repeat it. One of the great mistakes made in 1920 and subsequent years was a polarization of issues. It became an "either-or" situation–either social concern or world evangelism. Today we dare not ignore the burning issues of race relations, economic injustice and imperialism. Precisely for that reason we include these issues in our program here at Urbana with sessions on social concern, racism and revolution. By the same token we dare not ignore God's eternal and unchanging commands to his church to make the gospel of Jesus Christ, in all of its totality, available to all mankind. These commands will also be treated this week.

To be sure, missions in the past have made mistakes. The church has been guilty of a lack of social concern. We must confess to a long list of failures. But in so doing, let us not forget what God has done in a positive way through students and missionary leaders through the ages.

One of the most encouraging signs of God's continued work among students is to see the continuity of what he began a generation ago at Ben Lippen. The student chairman of that conference, Mr. Joseph McCullough, is today the General Director of the Andes Evangelical Mission in Bolivia and is seated behind me tonight on the platform. The first part-time student secretary of the SFMF, Dr. Wilbert Norton, served in Africa for many years and is now Professor of Missions at Wheaton College Graduate School of Theology. He, too, is on the platform with us. The first full-time secretary of the SFMF, Dr. Kenneth Hood, is not with us tonight because he is in Costa Rica where he has served for twenty-five years with the Latin America Mission. His successor, Mr. Neill Hawkins, is not with us because he is in Brazil as field leader of the Unevangelized Fields Mission, with whom he has served since 1942. The next secretary, Mr. Peter Stam, served in Africa and is now the Home Director for Canada of the Africa Inland Mission. He is with us tonight. His successor, Dr. Herbert Anderson, is today the General Director of the Conservative Baptist Foreign Mission Society and is also with us tonight. Dr. Christy Wilson, first Missionary Director of IVCF following the merger with SFMF and Director of the 1946 convention at Toronto, is in Afghanistan where he has lived and worked for over twenty years. Dr. Norton Sterrett, Director of the 1948 Urbana Convention, now serving under IFES in India, is also with us. Mr. Wesley Gustafson, former missionary to China and Director of the 1951 Urbana Convention, is now Personnel Secretary of the Evangelical Free Church Board of Foreign Missions. His successor, Mr. David Adeney, is in Singapore directing the Discipleship Training Center. Mr. Eric Fife, who directed the last three Urbana Conventions, is today actively involved in Christian outreach in Florida where he moved for reasons of health.

Thus, every former secretary of SFMF and Missionary Director of IVCF is still active and exercising a position of vital leadership in the world outreach of the church of Jesus Christ.

So, when we are tempted to disparage the past and claim that the failures of the church and of missions turn us off, let us remember that the sovereign God of history is still at work. Let us make history a pedestal and not a prison. Let us thank God for all that he has done in the past, and let us be sure that we become a part of all that he wants to do in the future, for we know that the kingdoms of this world shall become the kingdoms of our Lord and of his Christ, and he shall reign forever and ever.

You and I have the exciting possibility of becoming a part of God's program for world evangelism. This can begin right now, in our student years and on our own campuses. Let us ask him to make us a part of that great body of his people of whom the hymn writer speaks:

> A noble army, men and boys, the matron and the maid
> Around the Saviour's throne rejoice in robes of light arrayed.
> They climbed the steep ascent of heaven, through peril, toil,
> and pain;
> Oh God, to us may grace be given to follow in their train.

THE U.S. RACIAL CRISIS AND WORLD EVANGELISM

Tom Skinner

Any understanding of world evangelism and racism in our country must begin with an understanding of the history of racism. To understand why we are in the middle of a revolution in our time, to come to grips with what the black revolution is all about and to understand what the nature of racism in our society is, I must take you back approximately 350 years, when the early ships landed in this country in approximately 1619.

On those ships were approximately forty black people. Notable among them was a couple known as Isabel and Antony, who started the first black family on American soil in 1624. You see, one year before the Mayflower, 150 years before the Constitution or the Declaration of Independence was ever signed, black people had settled this country and were an integral part of this society.

Between the years of 1619 and 1660 there was relatively no race problem in our country. Our country had what was known as indentured servanthood. An indentured servant was a person who, coming from the Old World, could not afford to pay his passage to the New World and was brought out by someone of means. He came to this country and worked for that individual seven years, something like Jacob did for his father-in-law. At the end of that time he was set free to develop his own life.

Now keep in mind in that context: Those people who in the name of God think that America was founded on godly principles and that our country was started by God-fearing people deeply committed to the truths of God's Word must reexamine that idea in light of the fact that the jails of England were emptied in order to bring people to settle this continent.

The state of Georgia is a classic example of the kind of people who settled America. Georgia was first settled by prisoners from England whom the English wanted to get off their hands. The English sold them to wealthy people for whom they worked here for seven years and finally were set free.

So, if you have any illusions that America was founded on godly principles, reexamine them.

We must also recognize that between 1619 and 1660, black and white people worked together, black and white people were indentured servants, black and white people owned indentured servants, black and white people lived together, ate together, slept together, bought each other, killed each other, sued each other, married each other, took each other to court, murdered each other and pretty well lived together with each other.

But, in 1660, there arose a tremendous problem: that is, white indentured servants tended to run away. Of course, it was very difficult to recapture the white indentured servants because they could easily be assimilated into the majority society. But when black people ran away, it was very easy to recapture them because of their high degree of visibility. It was therefore decreed in 1660 that only black indentured servants would be used. And by 1702 slavery became a permanent way of life in American society.

Now, let us understand that slavery was upheld by three sectors of society: (1) the economic system, (2) the political system and (3) the religious system. It was upheld by the economic system because slavery was economically feasible. A good, healthy male slave could be bought for $600, a healthy female for $300. You made them cohabit and, within several years, you could breed a prosperous brood of slaves.

In our country what is upheld by the economic system is generally upheld by the political system because you must keep in mind that politics and economics in our country are synonymous, parallel to each other. What happens in the economic world affects the political world. If you check out the state of politics in our country previous to the 1968 election, you will notice that, when Richard Nixon was nominated at the Republican convention, the Dow Jones industrial average went up eleven points. The day before the election, when the polls showed that Mr. Humphrey was narrowing his margin on Mr. Nixon, the stock market reacted by backtracking. Things that happen in the political world affect the economic world.

You must keep in mind that in our country a mere 1% of the total population controls the entire economic system. One percent of all the companies in our country produce 70% of all the wealth. One percent of all the people in our country have 46% of all the outstanding cash. And no matter what they tell you about people's capitalism in our country, that everyone can have a piece of American society, it really boils down to the fact that 90% of all common stock in this country is controlled by 5% of all the stockholders. It is those 5% who make the political decisions. It is those people who, in the smoke-filled rooms of political conventions, nominate whom they want and at election time issue two of them to us to decide which one we like.

But the third sector of society that upheld slavery was the religious system. Numerous churches and denominations preached that slavery was a divine institution ordained by God. There were those who quoted a verse in the book of Genesis where Noah is supposed to have gone to bed drunk and naked one night. His son Canaan comes in and mocks his nakedness. The following morning, when Noah discovers what his son has done, he curses his son. A group of *ad hoc* biblical dispensationalists argued that Canaan was a descendant of Ham and the word *Ham* means black; therefore, God has cursed all black people and relegated them to conditions of servitude. And, incidentally, I can name to you right now at least five Christian colleges and at least a dozen Bible institutions in this country that still teach that in their classrooms today.

During slavery, the slavemaster allowed no marriages. There were only temporary arrangements, and they were usually pronounced with the words, "Do you promise to stay together until death or distance do you part?"

Rather, the slavemaster developed what was known as the stud system, in which a healthy male slave was forced to cohabit with a healthy female slave in order for her to bear healthy slave children. When the woman became pregnant, the male was moved to other quarters to do the same thing. And within the course of ten years he could have brought into the world a hundred children, never being allowed to father any of them. Very few children went around the plantation saying "Mommy" or "Daddy" because they did not know who they were.

Now keep in mind that numbers of slavemasters were also Christians. These same slavemasters–many of them deacons and elders in their own local churches–would have never tolerated sexual immorality in their own church, but found no difficulty in putting a black slave woman and a black slave man together under immoral conditions for the purpose of breeding slaves to maintain the economic system.

Slavery finally came to an end with the declaration that slaves were free–the Emancipation Proclamation. But keep in mind that all the Emancipation Proclamation said was that the person was no longer a slave. The proclamation never defined him as a man. It simply said, "He is not a slave."

Between the years of 1865 and 1877, the society then turned to the former slave and said, "Now that you are free, you are to settle down, become the husband of one wife, the father of your own children, and you are to assimilate yourself into American cultural society." And they expected this former slave to undo in one night what he had been taught to do another way for 250 years. And the amazing part about it was that he began to do it.

Between 1865 and 1877, numerous black people were elected to state legislatures–in South Carolina, Florida, Mississippi, Alabama, North Carolina and Louisiana. A black man was governor of the State of Louisiana in that period. The speakers of the house and the state legislatures in 1876 in South Carolina and Florida were black. Black politicians controlled numerous state legislatures throughout the South. Scores of them were elected to the United States Senate and House. And they began to make a tremendous upsurge in political power.

But, by 1877, cries were heard in certain sectors of society: "This former slave is moving too far too fast. He has only been free for twelve years. Does he expect to have all of his marbles in twelve years? He must learn that these things take time. He must learn to be patient. He cannot have everything at once."

Now that was 93 years ago. When was the last time you heard that statement?

In 1877, the United States presidential election was thrown into the House of Representatives. Mr. Hayes, in order to be elected, entered into a compromise with Southern politicians in which he promised that, if elected, he would withdraw troops from the South, end Reconstruction and allow white people to deal in their own way with black people.

It is ironic that that compromise was put in black and white and signed and sealed in the Alexander Hotel in Washington, D.C., which at that time was owned and operated by black men.

Mr. Hayes was elected. Troops were withdrawn from the South and white political leaders began to deal in their own way with black people. And, from 1877 to almost the present, there was a wave of lynchings and murders and drownings and disappearances of black people unequalled in the history of the Western world. Black people were lynched by the thousands, their homes burned, their women raped, their children beaten. They could not go to court or fight the issues. A black man was looked upon as property and not as a human being. He could be put to death for looking at a person too long, for being too familiar with a white person or wanting to do dumb, illegal things like vote.

World War I came in 1914, and the black man put on an American uniform and went off to defend America as "the land of the free and the home of the Boston Braves." As a result, he became stationed in the armed services in the northern metropolitan cities–Chicago, New York, Philadelphia–and word began to trickle back to the South (where 90% of the black population then lived) that if black people would migrate north they would find greater economic opportunity and social justice.

So between the years of 1920 and 1950, there was a mass movement of black people to northern cities. Songs like "So Long, Dixie" developed. The North became the promised land. By the thousands, blacks made their way to the northern cities in hope that there would be liberation.

But when they arrived in the North, they discovered that the patterns of segregation were no different than in the South: They were forced to live in certain communities; they could buy, sell or rent only in certain neighborhoods. They soon discovered that integration in the North was defined as that period between the time the first black family moves into a neighborhood and the last white family moves out.

You must keep in mind that, during this period of time, in general (there were some notable exceptions, but in general) the evangelical, Bible-believing, fundamental, orthodox, conservative church in this country was strangely silent. In fact, there were those people who during slavery argued, "It's not our business to become involved in slavery. That is a social issue. We have been called to preach the gospel. We must deliver the Word. We must save people's souls. We must not get involved in the issues of liberating people from the chains of slavery. If they accept Jesus Christ as their Savior, by and by they will be free–over there."

To a great extent the evangelical church in America supported the status quo. It supported slavery; it supported segregation; it preached against any attempt of the black man to stand on his own two feet. And those who sought to communicate the gospel to black people did it in a way to make sure that they stayed cool. "We will preach the gospel to those folks so they won't riot; we will preach the gospel to them so that we can keep the lid on the garbage pail." And so they were careful to point out such scriptures as, "Obey your masters," "Love your enemy," "Do good to them that hurt you." But no one ever talked about a message which would also speak to the oppressor.

It was during this period that my own parents found their way from Greenville, South Carolina, to the city of New York, where I was born and raised. I was born in a little community called Harlem, which is typical of most black communities throughout America. Harlem is a small, two-and-one-half square mile area with a population of almost one million people.

The social scientists tell us that if you took the entire population of the United States of America–all two hundred million Americans–and you forced every American citizen to live somewhere in New York, New York still would not get as congested as Harlem is right now.

It was in that community that I was born and raised in a fairly religious home, religious to the extent that my old man is a preacher, and that makes me a preacher's kid. But don't feel too bad about it–I got through it.

I went through the motions because it was expected of me. But I never bought any of it basically because, like a great number of black people, I could not reconcile Christianity with the kind of community that Harlem was. Harlem was more than 40% slums. Thousands of people lived in rat-infested, rundown, dilapidated apartments where landlords never came around to provide services.

It was not uncommon for some mother to wake up in the middle of the night and send a piercing scream through the community as she discovered that her two-week-old baby had been gnawed to death by a vicious rat. You could set your watches by the police who drove into the neighborhood to collect their bribes to keep the racketeering going.

Now, today, during this great upsurge in revolution and rebellion that has been going on, there have been great numbers of evangelical Christians who have joined the hoot and cry for law and order.

But how can you explain law and order to a mother who stands at the foot of her bed watching her baby lie in a blood bath, when she knows that that baby would never have been bitten by the rat in the first place, and the rat would never have been in the building, if the landlord to whom she had been paying high rent had been providing the kind of service she deserved for the kind of rent she was paying? How do you explain law and order to her when she knows the building code inspector, who represents the city administration, who is supposed to check out violations in buildings, came by that building the day before but was met at the front door by the landlord who palmed a hundred dollars in his hand, and sent the building code inspector on his way?

Now that is lawlessness.

But the point is: We never arrest the landlord. We never lock up the building code inspector. But I tell you who we do lock up: We lock up the frustrated, bitter, sixteen-year-old brother of that two-week-old sister who in his bitterness takes to the street and throws a brick at that building code inspector. We lock him up and say, "We gotta have law and order!"

And make no bones about it—the difficulty in coming to grips with the evangelical message of Jesus Christ in the black community is the fact that most evangelicals in this country who say that Christ is the answer also go back to their suburban communities and vote for law-and-order candidates who will keep the system the way it is.

So, if you are black and you live in the black community, you soon begin to learn that what they mean by law and order is, "All the order for us and all the law for them." You soon learn that the police in the black community are nothing more than the occupational force sent into the black community in order to maintain the interests of white society.

Now, you may not be able to understand that. But allow me to break it down for you. If you ever tour Chicago, you will run into a community there called the South Side of Chicago where there are several hundreds of thousands of black people. Black people make up 30% of the population of Chicago. To illustrate it in the words of Jesse Jackson: In Chicago these 30% live on 10% of the land. That is, there are thirty thousand black people per square mile in the black community and only three thousand people per square mile in the white community. What's happening is the same thing that would happen if you took a quarter and tried to fit it into the area of a dime. Over one-fourth of the city's population is asked to fit into 10% of the land and is expected to maintain order. No way.

There is a reason why in the black community emphasis is placed on property values, and in the white community the emphasis is on human life, a reason why Chicago's Mayor Daley can say, "Shoot the looters." He means, "We must protect property at any cost. We don't care about human life here. In the black community we will shoot people to maintain property."

But in the white community, because there are fewer people in proportion to property, the emphasis can be on human life and not on property values.

Dick Gregory says that when Mayor Daley said, "Shoot the looters," he agreed with him. In fact, he sent him a telegram to say, "I agree. We ought to make that retroactive 250 years and put the guns in the hands of the Indians."

In this context, the question then becomes: How in the world do you communicate the gospel—whatever that is? How do you go in and communicate the message of Jesus Christ to a society that has been cut off and oppressed by the rest of society, especially when those people who wish to proclaim Christ have participated in the oppression?

I could not put all this together as a teenager, so I rebelled against the concept of Jesus Christ having any relevance. At that time I put people in two basic extreme positions. (I think I still do.) On one extreme was what I called the *pseudoexistentialist.* Don't get excited by that word—the person in this position is better known as the beatnik or the hippie. He is the cat who looks at life and says, "Life is too mixed up to get involved." He withdraws, sits on a mountainside, creates his own world, establishes his own values and, in fact, becomes his own god.

But on the opposite extreme was another coward. He was what I called the *hyper-Christian.* He called himself, and I quote, "a Bible-believing, fundamental, orthodox, conservative, evangelical Christian," whatever that meant. He had half a dozen Bible verses for every social problem that existed. But, if you asked him to get involved, he couldn't do it. If you went to him and told him about the social ills of Harlem, he would come back with a typical cliché: "What those people down there need is a good dose of salvation." However, I never saw that cat in Harlem administering that dose.

"Christ is the answer," he would say. To be sure, Christ is the answer, but Christ has always been the answer through somebody. It has always been the will of God to saturate the common clay of a man's humanity and then to send that man in open display into a hostile world as a living testimony that it is possible for the invisible God to make himself visible in a man.

One must then come to grips with the fact that God is the great manager of all time: He gets his job done through people.

But, you see, it is unfortunate that God had to raise up other people, other witnesses because of the silence of the evangelical witness in the black community. This may be difficult again for us to understand. But allow me again to break it down for you.

Throughout the world it has unfortunately not been the evangelist's message which has liberated people. What I mean is this: Almost a hundred years ago today, a position paper was written entitled "The Social Gospel." It said that Christians must become involved in the issues of the day and make Christ relevant in those issues.

That position paper immediately produced a dichotomy. On one hand some said, "No, we are not called to be involved in social issues; we are called to preach the gospel." On the other hand, another group said, "No, our position is to feed hungry people, feed empty bellies, put clothes on people's backs." And the more the fundamentalists said, "Preach the gospel," the more the liberals said, "Feed people." And the more the liberals said, "Feed people," the more the fundamentalists said, "Preach the gospel."

The problem was that both positions were wrong. Both were extremes. Both compartmentalized me. One said, "Just give him a passport out of hell to heaven, get him saved, give him eternal life and never mind about his oppression. Never mind about the fact that he has to live with rats and roaches. Never mind that he's a fourth-class citizen. Never mind that he will be shot on sight. Never mind that there are places that he can't go."

On the other hand the liberal compartmentalized me because he wanted only to feed my belly. He did not see me as a total spiritual being.

Throughout the world we have developed the same problem. But, you see, God will not be without a witness, which is precisely why, when the evangelical church was silent on the issue of preaching the worth and the dignity of all men, God had to allow communism with its emphasis that the state is more important than the individual to sweep the world in the last fifty years. And because it overemphasized the state, there finally rose up people who began to reconsider the dignity and the worth of the individual.

Because the evangelical church was silent on the issue of humility, and we evangelicals went out and supported the industrial complex, we, too, began to preach technological efficiency. We lost all sense of spiritual life, humility and spiritual being. But God will not be without a witness. And this time he has raised up a great upsurge in the consideration of Eastern religions. Why do you think young people are caught up with mysticism, Buddhism and Hinduism? Simply because they want something that teaches humility, something that teaches spiritualism.

In the midst of all the technology and super-scientism that has engulfed our society, God will not be without a witness.

Understand that for those of us who live in the black community, it was not the evangelical who came and taught us our worth and dignity as black men. It was not the Bible-believing fundamentalist who stood up and told us that black was beautiful. It was not the evangelical who preached to us that we should stand on our two feet and be men, be proud that black was beautiful and that God could work his life out through our redeemed blackness.

Rather, it took Malcolm X, Stokely Carmichael, Rap Brown and the Brothers to declare to us our dignity. God will not be without a witness.

But the problem that we have is that we tend to think that truth can come only from those people we recognize to be anointed by God. That is the reason that when Martin Luther King came along and began to buck the system and do some things to help liberate black people, immediately the evangelicals wanted to know, "Is he born again? Does he preach the gospel?" Because, you see, we think that if we could just prove that Martin Luther King was not a Christian, if we could prove that he was not born again, if we could prove that he did not believe the Word of God, then we think we can dismiss what he said—we think we can dismiss the truth.

My friends, you must accept the fact that all truth is God's truth, no matter who it comes from.

Because the church I knew would not accept this fact, I wrote the church off. Now, like a great number of talented black young men and women, I was not a dumb kid. I was president of the student body at school. But, in my frustration and bitterness, I became a member of one of the leading gangs in Harlem. I will not go into detail, but the problem was that I wrote off any Christian message. I regarded it as the white man's attempt to subjugate me, to brainwash me.

Again you might say, "But, Tom, I don't understand. If you were a star student, if you were getting good marks, if you were president of the student body at school (I was also president of the young people's department in my church), how do you reconcile your life?" But your asking that question just proves that you believe what all of us believe: All you have to do is pull yourself up by the bootstraps and you, too, can succeed.

But, you see, this bootstrap theory is one of the most damnable lies being preached in America today. There is no such thing as pulling oneself up by the bootstraps. Nobody pulls himself up by the bootstraps. Any of us who are anything at all are what we are because somebody opened some doors, somebody gave us some breaks, somebody provided some opportunities. In the case of black people, it is difficult to pull yourself up by the bootstraps when somebody keeps cutting the straps.

My nationalist friends said to me, "Tom, it's a fine thing that you're a brilliant student. It's a fine thing that you show the brilliant qualifications of leadership. But if you've got any ideas of making it in our kind of society, you'd better think again." They said, "This is the white man's world, and in his world he controls things from the top to the bottom. He might allow you to be a jazz player, a rock-and-roll singer or the janitor in his building. But he will not allow you to compete with him on an open basis to make a tangible contribution to society. He does not consider you to be his equal. You may be able to make $30,000 a year and move into the best of communities, but as soon as you move out there, they're going to protest so loudly that you will never make it. If you do succeed in moving, 'For Sale' signs will go up. And among those people who will sell their homes and run will be those Bible-toting Christians who say Christ is the answer.

"If by some stretch of the imagination some of them stay, when you grow up and have kids and your kids go out in the street to play with their kids, they are going to call their kids into their homes because they don't want your kids to play with their kids. They're afraid that, playing together at six years of age, the kids might plan to intermarry or something.

"They believe, of course, that integration would lead to

intermarriage, and intermarriage would mongrelize the races and people would walk down the streets with black blotches on one side and white on the other."

Now please do not walk away saying Tom Skinner advocates racial intermarriage. I do not know where white people get the idea that they are so utterly attractive that black people are just dying to marry them.

But just to set the record straight, keep in mind that when black people were shipped here from Africa, they were pure Negroid. Today fewer than 6% of all black people in this country are now pure Negroid, which means that there is a dead cat on the line somewhere. You must keep in mind that the sexual aggression could not have taken place on the part of the black person, because he would have been lynched if he were the aggressor.

In the middle of all of this, one must come to grips with where racism really lies. And so I became very angry and very bitter. I could bust a bottle across a fellow's head, break the bottle in half and dig the glass in his face and not bat my eye. By the time I left the gang, I had twenty-two notches on the handle of my knife, which meant that my blade had gone into the bodies of twenty-two different people, and I didn't care. All that mattered to me was that Tom Skinner got what he wanted. How he got it made absolutely no difference.

Then one night I was mapping out strategy for what was to have been the largest-scale gang fight ever to take place in New York City. And for the first time the rock-and-roll radio show I was listening to was interrupted by a very simple program. A guy started talking from a message written in 2 Corinthians 5:17, which says, "Therefore if any man be in Christ, he is a new creature: old things are passed away; behold, all things are become new" (AV).

For the first time something came through. For the first time I was told that what makes a person a sinner is the fact that he is born into the human race without the life of God. And that it is the absence of God's life in a man which causes a man to be what the Bible defines as a sinner. Now, up to this point, in what few gospel messages I did get from the evangelical crowd, I always heard that sin was a long list of no-no's: no smoking, no drinking, no night clubs, no miniskirts, no no, no no. And I soon got the impression that being Christian meant that you carried around in your inside pocket a bunch of rules and regulations which said, "Don't do this, stay away from that, don't touch that, and, for God's sake, don't look at that."

But that night for the first time I was told that what made a man a sinner was the fact that he does not have God's life in him. And I was told that the whole reason that God became a man in Jesus Christ was for the purpose of taking me in my human depravation, my oppression, my mental and spiritual slavery, and taking God in his liberation and bringing us together.

But I had a problem with this guy Jesus: Everything that I had ever been told about Jesus Christ gave me the impression that he was some kind of softie, some kind of effeminate. Christ was always pictured as an Anglo-Saxon, middle-class, Protestant Republican. He had those nice soft hands that looked as if they had just been washed in Dove. And I said, "There's no way that I can relate to that kind of Christ." I said, "He doesn't look like he'd survive in my neighborhood. We would do him in on any street corner—and we wouldn't have to wait until after dark."

Then I discovered that the Christ who leaped out of the pages of the New Testament was nobody's sissy, nobody's effeminate. Rather he was a gutsy, contemporary, radical revolutionary, with hair on his chest and dirt under his fingernails.

Perhaps one of the great debates going on today is being pushed by those people who resist the idea that Jesus was a revolutionary. But let us come to grips with what the Word of God says.

First, let us consider the definition of a revolution. You take an existing situation which has proved unworkable, archaic, impractical and you seek to destroy it, to overthrow it and to replace it with a system that works. Now, the whole premise of the Scripture is that the human order is archaic, impractical, no good, infested with demonic power, with sin, racism, hate, envy, jealousy, pride, war, militarism. The biblical position is that the whole existing human order is infested with ungodliness. And the whole purpose of Christ's coming into the world was to overthrow the demonic human system and to establish his own kingdom in the hearts of men.

Allow me to quote for you 1 Corinthians 1:28: "He has chosen things low and contemptible, mere nothings, to overthrow the existing order" (NEB). That is the Word of God.

But, of course, the moment you hear that you immediately think of SDS, Black Panthers, Communists, running through the streets with machine guns to overthrow the order. But that is not what God has in mind. And the thing that you have got to understand is this: What made Jesus Christ so utterly radical, so utterly different, was that he was the only man who ever walked the face of the earth who never did anything. How does that grab you? Jesus never did anything. He never healed the sick; he never raised the dead; he never gave sight to the blind; he never performed any miracles.

You cry, "Tom, heresy! I can buy a lot of that militant stuff you're saying up there. But now you're telling me Christ never did anything. We all know he was miraculous."

Let me explain. Jesus never did anything. His Father did it. Jesus never once made a move on his own. Jesus himself said, "That which I do my Father does it in me. I do only those things which please my Father." He even said to his disciples, "I don't want you to believe me because you see me healing the sick, raising the dead and giving sight to the blind. I want you to believe me because the works I do my Father is doing them in me. And if you ever see me doing something that my Father is not doing in me, then you have the right not to believe me. But as long as I'm doing what my Father tells me to do, you'd better believe me."

Now, what made Jesus radical was that he could walk into a temple, the house of his Father, which people had desecrated, and knock over the money changers and drive them out of the temple in a holy furor. And when they came to ask him, "By what authority do you perform such a radical act?" his answer was, "My Father."

But we must also understand something else: who the real oppressor is. And this is very important, especially for those of us as black students–to come to grips with where real oppression lies. It was Dick Gregory who put me on to this (again, not noted to be an evangelical, but nevertheless a prophet). Dick Gregory said, "We get angry at that policeman who busts our heads in the black community. But many of us never really understand that the policeman in the black community is the real nigger. Why? Because he, too, is oppressed. He's only taking orders."

So then when I find out who is oppressing that policeman, then I must find out who is oppressing the man who is oppressing the policeman. I keep going until I get on a higher plane. Then I begin to understand what Paul means when he says, "We wrestle not against flesh and blood, but against principalities and powers, against the rulers of darkness, against spiritual wickedness in high places."

We as Christians must understand who really runs this world—in whose hands the world really belongs.

One of the reasons we have a problem with this is because of some of our hymnology—songs like "This Is My Father's World." When you read the Scriptures, you discover the Bible says that Satan is the prince and power of the air, he is the prince of this world and has not been removed from that position. That is why, when Satan took Jesus on a high mountain and showed him all the kingdoms of the world and said, "I will deliver them to you if you will bow down and worship me," Jesus refused.

Many theologians say the reason Jesus refused was that he already owned the kingdoms. That was not true. If Christ already possessed the kingdoms of the world, then what Satan offered him would not have been a real temptation. The temptation lay in the fact that Satan did have the power to deliver to Jesus the kingdoms of this world.

If, then, the kingdoms of this world belong to Satan, then what you and I as evangelical Christians must become is infiltrators, fifth columnists in Satan's world for the purpose of preaching liberation to an oppressed people.

That is why, just as the Indian Christians had to renounce the British Empire, I as a black Christian have to renounce Americanism. I have to renounce any attempt to wed Jesus Christ to the American system. I disassociate myself from any argument that says a vote for America is a vote for God. I disassociate myself from any argument that says God is on our side. I disassociate myself from any argument which says that God sends troops to Asia, that God is a capitalist, that God is a militarist, that God is the worker behind our system.

The thing you must recognize is that Jesus Christ is no more a capitalist than he is a socialist or a communist. He is no more a Democrat than he is a Republican. He is no more the president of the New York Stock Exchange than he is the head of the Socialist

Party. He is neither. He is the Lord of heaven and earth. And if you are going to respond to Jesus Christ, you must respond to him as Lord.

Let me conclude my thinking then. There is no possible way you can talk about preaching the gospel if you do not want to deal with the issues that bind people. If your gospel is an "either-or" gospel, I must reject it. Any gospel that does not talk about delivering to man a personal Savior who will free him from the personal bondage of sin and grant him eternal life and does not at the same time speak to the issue of enslavement, the issue of injustice, the issue of inequality–any gospel that does not want to go where people are hungry and poverty-stricken and set them free in the name of Jesus Christ–is not the gospel.

Allow me to conclude with this illustration. The thing that turned me on to Jesus was the fact that in his day there was a system working just like today. The Romans were oppressing the Jews. And there arose in the hills of Jerusalem a fellow by the name of Barabbas. Barabbas said to his people, "There is only one way to get that Roman honky off your back, and that's to burn him out." And Barabbas went through the hills and suburbia burning those nice Roman suburban homes.

The Romans finally caught up with Barabbas and arrested him and charged him with anarchy, insurrection and murder.

But out in those same hills was another radical. His name was Jesus. He had no guns, no tanks, no ammunition. And, of all the dumb things, he went around preaching a thing called the kingdom of God.

But some things started happening. Blind people started to see. Lame people started to get up and walk. People started to get liberated mentally and physically. Homes started to be put back together. And from miles around people came to sit at the feet of this man who had this strong rap, this tremendous taste for the kingdom of God.

He began to point out some things. And some people started to get themselves together. But some people also began to get disturbed, because Jesus made the tragic mistake of hanging out with the wrong people. The accusation brought against Jesus was, "This man eats and drinks with sinners."

If Jesus had chosen to walk the streets of our ghetto today, you could see him walking down Lenox Avenue and 125th Street. And there is a little short brother who can not see Jesus, so he climbs up on the fire escape to get a view. And just then Jesus spots him and says, "Hey, Zack, what're you doing up there? Come on down, because today I've got to abide in your house."

And I can see those Bible-believing fundamentalist Christians standing in the background, saying: "But, Lord, you can't go to his house. You might lose your testimony."

But you see, Jesus lost his testimony every day because he rubbed shoulders with people. And I challenge you that if you are talking about evangelism and about missions, you have got to be talking about going into the world. And the world is where the action is. Get away from this business of "full-time Christian work" and recognize that every last one of us is called to a mission.

You may be called to be a business executive. Study, get your management principles down and infiltrate the business world for Jesus. You may be called to be an athlete. Get out on the field and become the kind of athlete that can cause you to have an effective witness in the sports world, for that is your mission field. If you are called to be a secretary, get it together, work your way up, become a sharp secretary to a top executive in this country. Secretaries influence executives. You can influence America from those offices. That is where the mission field is.

Some of you will be called to a life style of militancy. Get away from this business that to be militant is to be anti-God. I am a militant; make no bones about it. Jesus was militant. And some of us will be called to adopt the militant life style. But keep in mind that militancy and radicalism must be disciplined and controlled by the Word of God and by the Holy Spirit.

Let me hasten to conclude. Jesus was turning the whole thing upside-down. So they finally had to arrest him too, because, you see, Jesus was dangerous. He was dangerous because he was changing the system. The whole Roman Empire was shaking—no shots were being fired, no fire bombs were being thrown—but the whole Roman Empire was rocking. Because, you see, anybody who changes the system is dangerous.

Remember Chicago? Remember those 15,000 kids that went to

Chicago for the Democratic Convention in '68? Why did people get disturbed because those kids went? Was it because they threw urine at the police? Because they cursed the police? Because they were lawless? No. They were mad because the kids went to change the system.

Now, I am not saying that I agree with what they did. What I am saying is that their motive was to change the system. Six weeks before the Democratic Convention, the Shriners met in Chicago–30,000 of them had their convention in Chicago. And it is a fact that when the Shriners met in Chicago more booze and prostitution flowed in the streets of Chicago than in any other given period in that city. Prostitutes were brought in from Illinois, Michigan, Indiana and from all around to meet the needs of those men. But you never read about it, because those Shriners did not come to Chicago to change anything. They came to buy something. And as long as you are buying and not changing, you are safe.

But Jesus came to change the system. And so they had to arrest him too. Now, Jesus would not have disagreed with Barabbas' diagnosis of the human system. Barabbas said, "The Roman system stinks, it's militaristic, it's oppressive." And Jesus would have agreed. The difference between Jesus and Barabbas was in their different solutions.

And so the Romans have two revolutionaries locked up. It is around festivity time. And Pilate stands out before the Jews with these two prisoners–potential radicals. And Pilate says, "You know, around this time of year, I get very gracious. I want you to know that I love all you dear Jewish people. Why, some of my best friends are Jews. Now, I'm going to release one of these men to you, and I want you to tell me which one you want. Over here I've got Jesus Barabbas (that was Barabbas' full name), and, here, just plain Jesus. So you've got two Jesuses on your hands."

So it is not a question as to whether there is going to be a revolution. It is which revolution.

Pilate went on: "Over here I've got Barabbas. Barabbas has been burning the system down, killing people. Do you want him? And over here I've got Jesus, who claims to be the son of God. I've interrogated him, and I can't find anything wrong with him, other than the fact that some dead people are alive because of him, some blind people have seen, some deaf people are hearing and, by the way, he did feed a few thousand people with a welfare give-away program, but other than that I can't find anything wrong with him. So which one do you want? Jesus or Barabbas?"

And with one voice they cried out, "Give us Barabbas!"

The question is: Why Barabbas and not Jesus? Barabbas is the cat burning the system down, he is killing people. Why him instead of Jesus? Very simple. If you let Barabbas go, you can always stop him. The most Barabbas will do is go out, round up another bunch of guerrillas and start another riot. And you can always stop him by rolling your tanks into his neighborhood, bringing out the National Guard and putting down his riot. Find out where he is keeping his ammunition. Raid his apartment without a search warrant and shoot him while he is still asleep. You can stop Barabbas.

But how do you stop Jesus?

They nailed him to a cross. But they did not realize that, in nailing Jesus to the cross, they were putting up on that cross the sinful nature of all humanity.

Christ, nailed to the cross, was more than just a political radical dying; he was God's answer to the human dilemma. On that cross Christ was bearing my sins in his own body, and he was proclaiming my liberation on that cross. He shed his blood to cleanse me of all my sin, to set me free.

Then they buried him, rolled a stone over his grave, wiped their hands and said, "There is one radical who will never disturb us again. We have gotten rid of him. We will never hear any more of his words of revolution."

Three days later Jesus Christ pulled off one of the greatest political coups of all time: He got up out of the grave. When he arose from the dead, the Bible now calls him the second man, the new man, the leader of a new creation—a Christ who has overthrown the existing order and established a new order that is not built on man. Keep in mind, my friend, with all your militancy and radicalism, that all the systems of men are doomed to destruction. All the systems of men will crumble and, finally, only God's kingdom and his righteousness will prevail.

You will never be radical until you become part of that new order and then go into a world that is enslaved, a world that is filled with hunger and poverty and racism and all those things of the work of the devil. Proclaim liberation to the captives, preach sight to the blind, set at liberty them that are bruised, go into the world and tell men that are bound mentally, spiritually and physically, "*The liberator has come!*"

GOD'S WILL FOR ME AND WORLD EVANGELISM*

Paul E. Little

Suppose the Lord Jesus Christ were here at Urbana tonight in person, that he were sitting here in the front row, and that you could ask him one question—any question you wanted to ask. You would know that the answer you got would be from the Creator of the universe. What would that question be?

If you are like other groups in which I have actually conducted this experiment, the vast majority of you would ask a question related in some way to how you could know God's will for your life. Now this figures, because to a committed Christian this is really the only thing that counts. Peace and satisfaction depend on knowing that God is guiding us. And the absence of that certainty leaves us fearful and restless. It may be that some of you are in fear and

*This address is also available from Inter-Varsity Press in a fifteen-cent booklet entitled *Affirming the Will of God.*

uncertainty because you are not clear about God's guiding in your life.

Part of the problem lies in the confusion of knowing what the will of God is in the first place. And unless we are clear about that, we really cannot make much other progress. When most people speak of God's will, they mean something you have or don't have. "Have you discovered God's will for your life?" they ask each other. What they usually mean is, "Have you discovered God's blueprint for your life?" But the fact is that God seldom reveals an entire blueprint. Those of you who have come to Urbana looking for that blueprint in its entirety are likely to be disappointed. What God does reveal most frequently, however, is the next step in his will for a person. But this leads us into the fuller question of what exactly God's will is.

It is very important to understand at the outset that God has a plan and purpose for your life. To me, this is one of the sensational aspects of being a Christian. To know that your life can be tied into God's plan and purpose not only for time but for eternity as well. Paul, in writing to the Ephesians, speaks of God: "For we are his workmanship, created in Christ Jesus for good works, which God prepared beforehand, that we should walk in them" (Eph. 2:10). David, in Psalm 37:23, says, "The steps of a man are from the Lord, and he establishes him in whose way he delights." And in Acts 13:2, we read: "While they were worshiping the Lord and fasting, the Holy Spirit said, 'Set apart for me Barnabas and Saul for the work to which I have called them.' "

Not only does God have a plan for us, but he has promised to reveal it to us. In Psalm 73:24, David says of God: "Thou dost guide me with thy counsel, and afterward thou wilt receive me to glory." In Psalm 32:8, God promises, "I will instruct you and teach you the way you should go; I will counsel [or guide] you with my eye upon you."

Finally, those classic verses, Proverbs 3:5-6, two of the most compact verses on guidance in the whole Bible, say: "Trust in the Lord with all thine heart; and lean not unto thine own understanding. In all thy ways acknowledge him, and he shall direct thy paths" (AV).

Just what is God's will in the first place? It is important to realize that there are two aspects to it. The first is that aspect of his will and his plan which has already been revealed in his Word and which applies to every Christian. Has it ever struck you that the vast majority of the will of God for your life has already been revealed in the Bible? That is a remarkable and crucial thing to get hold of.

There are many positive commands. For instance, we are commanded by our Lord to go into all the world and preach the gospel to every creature. We know it is the will of God (from Romans 8:29) that we are to be conformed to the image of Christ. Do you want to know the will of God for your life? Read the book of James and list all the specific commands and you will have a good start on the will of God for your life.

Also, there is a whole series of negative commands in Scripture. God tells us in unmistakable terms in 2 Corinthians 6:14 that we are not to be unequally yoked together with unbelievers, which means, among other things, that a Christian is never to marry an unbeliever. Are any of you praying for guidance about whether you should marry a non-Christian? Save your breath.

The late A. W. Tozer pointed out that we should never seek guidance on what is forbidden, where God has said No. Nor should we ever seek guidance in the areas where he has said Yes, where there is a command. He then pointed out that in most other things God has no preference.

God really does not have a great preference whether you have steak or chicken. He is not desperately concerned about whether you wear a green shirt or a blue shirt. In many areas of life, using Tozer's phrase, God invites us to consult our own sanctified preferences. When we are pleased, God is pleased. That is a wonderful thing to know, isn't it?

Then Tozer points out that there are areas in which we need special guidance and that God has promised us special guidance in those areas. The Lord spoke to the prophet Isaiah: "I am the Lord your God, who teaches you to profit, who leads you in the way you should go" (Is. 48:17). These are the areas of life where there is no specific statement like, "Thou, John Jones, shalt be an engineer in Cincinnati," or, "Thou, Mary Smith, shalt marry Fred Grottenheimer." There are no specific verses in the Bible that will give you that kind of detail in your life.

When we recognize that there are two aspects to the will of God, namely, what is already specifically revealed in his Word and what is not, we get away from the static concept represented by the blueprint idea.

The will of God is not like a magic package let down out of heaven by a string, a package we grope after in desperation and hope sometime in the future to clasp to our hearts. Rather the will of God is more like a scroll that unrolls every day. In other words, God has a will for you and me today and tomorrow and the next day and the day after that. Now it may well be that a decision you or I make this week or next week will commit us to a certain thing for three months, or two years, or five or ten years, or for a lifetime. But the fact still remains that the will of God is something to be discerned and to be lived out each day of our lives, not something to be grasped as a package once for all. Then also, when we realize that our call is basically not to a plan or blueprint, or even to a place or work, but to follow the Lord Jesus Christ, we will sense something of the dynamic of it as well.

Now, after understanding something of what the will of God is in its two dimensions, we need to understand something of the prerequisites for knowing the will of God in these unspecified areas of our lives.

One prerequisite is to be a child of God. One day some people asked Jesus directly, "What must we do, to be doing the works of God?" And Jesus answered specifically and clearly, "This is the work [or the will] of God, that you believe in him whom he has sent" (Jn. 6:29). We must first come to Jesus in a commitment of faith to him as Savior and Lord. Then, since we are God's children, we can be guided by him as our Father. The Lord said in John 10:3, "He calls his own sheep by name and leads them out."

The second prerequisite is to obey, at least in the desire of our hearts, the will of God in those areas in which we know his will. What is the point of God's guiding us in areas in which he has not been specific when we are apparently unconcerned about areas in which he is specific? Mark Twain once wryly observed, "It's not the parts of the Bible I don't understand that bother me, it's the parts I do understand." Perhaps this is the problem for some of us now. We need to begin to obey in those specific areas.

We know, for example, that we ought to be meeting with the Lord every day in prayer. "But," you say, "you don't know my schedule. I've got a heavy course load this year. And yatita, yatita." All of us have twenty-four hours equally. It is merely a matter of setting priorities. If you are going to meet with God every day, it means you decide when you are going to bed, when you will get up and what you are going to study. You may have vaguely always wanted to witness to that fellow or girl down the hall. Then you must decide when you are going to do it. You must attempt to make some contact with that friend to see if there is any openness to the gospel. What are the areas of the will of God that you know already to be his will? To what extent are you acting on them?

The third prerequisite, and I think the most crucial, is that we must be willing to accept the will of God in these unspecified areas of our lives before knowing what it is, accepting it in advance, in other words. And for most of us, I suspect, this is where the real problem lies. If we are really honest, most of us would have to admit that our attitude is, "Lord show me what your will is so I can decide whether it fits in with what I have in mind." In essence we are saying, "Just lift the curtain a minute and let me see. I'd like to see it so I can decide whether I want to do it or not. Show me whether I'm to be married or not. Show me where in the world you want me to be and what you want me to do. If it's Palm Beach, or Laguna Beach, or Honolulu or some wonderful place like that, then maybe I'll consider it a little more seriously."

Now if we stop to reflect and we analyze this attitude, we will be shocked to realize that what we are, in fact, doing is insulting God. What we are really saying is, "I think I know better than you, God, what will make me happy. I don't trust you. If I let you run my life, you're going to short-change me." Have you ever felt that? It is a solemn thing to realize.

Now the tragic, mistaken idea most of us have is that our choice is between doing what we want to do and being happy, and doing what God wants us to do and being miserable. We think that the will of God is some miserable thing which he sort of shoves under our nose and demands, "All right! Are you willing, are you willing?" And suddenly we must decide there and then whether we are going to be miserable for the rest of our lives, whereas, if we could just get out from under his clammy hands, we could really swing. That is the implication of the attitude which is so common to many of us.

Nothing could be further from the truth. Such notions are a slur on the character of God. So many of us have gotten the idea that God is a kind of celestial Scrooge who peers over the balcony of heaven trying to find anybody who is enjoying life. And when he spots a happy person, he yells, "Now cut that out!" And if he ever got his hands on us, all enjoyment and happiness would be down the tube. That should make us stagger and shudder because it's blasphemous!

We need to have deeply planted in our hearts the tremendous truth of Romans 8:32: "He that spared not his own Son, but delivered him up for us all, how shall he not with him also freely give us all things?" If you can get hold of that verse, memorize it, meditate on it and allow it to get hold of you, you will have solved 90% of your problem with desire for the will of God, because you will realize the God who loved us enough to die for us when we did not care that much for him is not about to short-change us in life when we come to him and give him our lives. As Oswald Hoffman of the Lutheran Hour has put it, "Having given us the package, do you think God will deny us the ribbon?"

Think of it in human terms for a moment. Think of a father and his children. I have two children. A girl Debbie, and a son Paul. (We call him Small Paul, Small Paul Little. When you realize that in Greek *paulos* means small, it is the ultimate in redundancy.) When my children come to me and say, "Daddy, I love you," do you think I respond by saying, "Ah, children, that's just what I've been waiting to hear. Into the closet for three weeks. Bread and water. I've just been waiting for you to tell me you love me so I can make your life miserable!" Do you think that is the way I respond? Of course not. They could get anything they wanted out of me at that point.

And do you think that God is less loving than a human father? Rather, God's love far transcends any love that we as humans express. The Bible is constantly drawing contrasts between human love and activity and our heavenly Father's love. "If you then, who are evil," Jesus says in Luke 11:13, "know how to give good gifts to your children, how much more will the heavenly Father give the Holy Spirit to those who ask him!"

When we come to God and say, "I love you, and I'm prepared to do your will whatever you want me to do," we can be sure that God is not going to make us miserable. Rather he rejoices and fits our lives into his pattern for us, into that place where he, in his omniscience and love, knows we will fit hand in glove. The one who is our Creator, who made us, who knows us better than we will ever know ourselves, is the one we are talking to. He knows the end from the beginning.

I love the third verse of the hymn, "Still Will We Trust":

Choose for us, God, nor let our weak preferring
Cheat us of good Thou hast for us designed:
Choose for us, God; Thy wisdom is unerring.
And we are fools and blind.

God's will is not loathesome. It is the greatest thing in all of life to get hold of. There is no greater joy or satisfaction in all of life than to be in the center of the will of God and know it. Jim Elliot, one of the martyrs in Ecuador in 1954, wrote of the sheer joy of doing the will of God, as recorded in his biography, *Shadow of the Almighty.*

In the light of the character of God and considering the experience of people who have known him, I dislike intensely the phrase, "surrender to the will of God." To me, that implies kicking, struggling, screaming. It is like saying, "There is no other way out. I'm running, but I'm caught. I've got to collapse and surrender. It's all over. I give up."

Instead, I far prefer the term "affirm the will of God." If we had the sense we were born with, every one of us would affirm God's will with confidence and with joy and with deep satisfaction.

This is a very crucial prerequisite. It will involve eliminating areas of hold-out in your life—a relationship, an ambition, a qualification. No more saying, "I'll go anywhere, Lord, but . . ." or "I'll go and do anything, but it's got to be with so-and-so." Rather we will say, "Lord, you've created me and I belong to you by creation. Even when I was a rebel against you, you loved me enough to die for me. Everything I am and have belongs to you. I'm not my own, I'm bought with a price—the precious blood of Christ—and I consciously and joyfully commit myself to you for you to do with me as you choose." And when we come to that place, we will be able to say with Paul, and mean in the depths of our hearts, "To me to live is

Christ."

We must first, then, understand what the will of God is. Then we must be prepared to accept the prerequisites for knowing it in those areas about which the Bible is not specific. And in the third place we need to understand how, in fact, God guides in the areas where he has not been specific.

First, as we have already seen, God frequently guides through his Word, through specific commands. In addition to these commands there are principles in the Word of God which may have implications for our situation. And if we can understand their teaching and apply them to the circumstances of our lives, they can give us specific, practical guidance in specific situations.

Let me give you a negative example. Several years ago in the spring a person signed a contract to teach. In August, she received another offer from a school closer to where she wanted to live. So she broke the original contract. Now she was familiar with the biblical principle in Psalm 15:4, where God says that he is pleased with a person who swears to his own hurt and does not change, a person whose word is his bond, who accepts responsibility and can be counted on. The department chairman who told me about the Christian girl's action said her justification was, "I have a peace about it," and he commented rather sardonically, "Isn't that lovely. She's got the peace and I've got the pieces." You can imagine what it is like to get a teacher in August to teach in September. I believe that girl missed the will of God because she violated a principle which, if she had been alert and had applied it to her situation, would have given her very clear guidance in this specific detail of her life. God guides, then, through his Word and its principles.

In the second place, God guides us in prayer as we ask him to show us his will. I can well remember the Urbana Convention in 1948. Dr. Norton Sterrett, who spoke the last evening, asked, "How many of you who are concerned about the will of God spend even five minutes a day asking him to show you his will?" It was as if somebody had grabbed me by the throat. At that time I was an undergraduate, concerned about what I should do when I graduated from the university. I was running around like a chicken with its head cut off, going to this meeting, reading that book, trying to find somebody's little formula–1, 2, 3, 4 and a little bell rings–and I was frustrated out of my mind trying to figure out what the will of God was. I was doing everything but getting into the presence of God and asking him to show me.

May I ask you the same question: You who are concerned about the will of God for your life, do you spend even five minutes a day specifically asking God to show you?

As we pray, God often gives us a conviction by the Holy Spirit which deepens, despite new information, to an increasing sense of rightness or oughtness about a course of action. This is quite different from the "gung ho" emotion which prods us today to get on a plane to Hong Kong, and tomorrow to move into Chicago, and the next day to paddle a canoe up the Amazon, and each day after to go in a different direction. When the Holy Spirit in answer to prayer begins to move in our hearts, one conviction deepens and, while we recognize other situations, we have a sense of rightness or oughtness that this is the will of God for us.

Third, he guides and directs us through circumstances. Here, however, we must be particularly on guard. Most of us tend to make circumstances 99% of the guidance. But they are only one of the factors in guidance. Furthermore, we must view circumstances from God's perspective and values; they may be more of a guide negatively than positively.

For instance, if you think that God is leading you to go to graduate school in engineering, but you cannot get into any school in this country or abroad, it may be fairly clear and evident that God does not want you in engineering school. On the other hand, the fact that you are accepted into three engineering schools does not necessarily mean that God wants you to go into engineering. There may be other factors to consider.

You may graduate from the university and have fifteen job offers (although with the recession that is not quite as likely as it was a few years ago), but that does not necessarily mean that God wants you to stay in this country. He may have a prior claim on your life that will involve going into a far corner of the earth. And if you view the circumstances from God's point of view, you may be called of God to do something that the average non-Christian, who sees nothing but the visible world bounded by the cradle and the grave, would consider foolish, a tragic waste of time and talent.

One of the circumstances that God may use to show you your place in the world in evangelism may be this conference. Here you have a unique opportunity to get information about situations and circumstances all over the world. I hope none of you will miss the opportunity to talk personally with the missionaries here, to get pertinent books and to pursue this information by talking to missionaries from your church, in addition to asking God to guide you.

God may use a summer trip abroad to show you whether and where he wants you to go overseas. And it seems to me that in this jet age every one of us as students ought to consider the possibility of a semester or summer abroad in some other culture as part of our educational experience—not to speak of our Christian education and of our allowing ourselves to be open to where God might want us to be. On the other hand, as a result of study and circumstances, God might confirm a call to you here in the States to serve his program in some crucial way.

Familiarize yourself with the needs of the world. While it is quite true that the need in itself is not a call, that there are enormous, overwhelming needs everywhere and we can never meet them all, still needs cannot be ignored. The old illustration of a log carried by nine men on one end and three women on the other end may be trite and corny, but nevertheless it has a profound point. The question is: If you want to help, to which end of the log will you go? It is a fact that 90% of full-time Christian workers are in parts of the world which have 10% of the world's population and only 10% of them are in population centers comprising 90% of the world's population. Surely this is not the will of God since he has already told us in his Word that his desire is that every person hear the gospel. There are still millions of people who have never heard it for the first time.

David Howard has a real point in his leaflet "Don't Wait for the Macedonians" when he asks, "Why should anyone seek more specific direction to serve the Lord overseas than he does to serve in any other capacity or location? It may well be that we should make every effort to go overseas unless God clearly calls us to stay home, rather than the reverse. And as you make the effort, as you begin to move, God will guide. God can close doors very easily. But, as the old saying goes, you can't steer a parked car; you can't pilot a moored ship."

Another very crucial way you can know God's guidance through circumstances is to get involved in the work of evangelism where you are. It is foolish to think of traveling to some other part of the world if God has not already put his hand on you so that there is spiritual blessing in the people with whom you are already associated on campus. And please do not overlook the opportunities for personal witness to the hundreds of students who are living on this Urbana campus during this week but are not part of the convention. Be alert to them. Talk to them. They know something is going on although they do not quite understand it. Share what is happening with them.

Look out for international students on your campus, talk to them and see how God might lead you. Trust God to give you a solid friendship with at least one person from overseas. Ask God to enable you to share with that person the greatest thing in all of life—the love of Jesus—and to articulate the gospel to him. If you are able to get through to American, Canadian and international students on your own campus, God may then put a fire in your bones that will move you to some other part of the world.

Fourth, God guides us through the counsel of other Christians who are fully committed to the will of God and who know us well. Personally, I think that this is one of the most neglected dimensions of guidance in the lives of many Christians today.

I am always suspicious of a person who implies that he has a *personal* pipeline to God, even though saying "God led me" sounds very spiritual. And when no one else senses that what the person suggests is, in fact, the will of God, then we had better be very careful. God has been blamed for the most outlandish things by people who have confused their own inverted pride with God's will.

Occasionally I hear of a guy who, in the name of spiritual guidance, rushes up to a girl and says, "Susie, God has told me you're to marry me." I have news for him. If that is the will of God, then Susie is going to get the message, too. And if she does not, somebody's radar is jammed.

Are you wondering about marriage? Do you wonder what your gifts are? Do you wonder whether God might use you in an overseas situation in some capacity? Talk to some of your mature Christian friends, your pastor, elders in your assembly and others who know you and are concerned for the will of God for themselves and you. Their counsel may well be invaluable. Although it is true that sometimes we get mixed counsel from Christian friends, still their advice is frequently helpful. Remember, Acts 15 records, "It has seemed good to the Holy Spirit and to us. . . ." And I believe God usually guides in that way—a personal conviction corroborated by friends' opinions. Do not be afraid to talk to people whom you think might give you advice you do not want to hear. It may be you are too emotionally involved in a situation to see it objectively. Then you need somebody to talk really straight to you so that you can be realistic in your assessments.

Now when all four of these factors—the Word of God, conviction that he gives us in prayer, circumstances and the counsel of mature Christian friends—converge, it is usually a sign that God is leading and guiding us.

Lastly, I want to consider with you some serious mistakes to avoid in our thinking about the will of God for you in the area of world evangelism. First, we must not think that because we want to do something, it cannot possibly be God's will. Some of you may have wanted very badly to come to Urbana, and you might have thought to yourself, "Boy, this can't be God's will because I want it so badly. I wonder if that means I should give up going to Urbana?" But when we have that attitude, we display a distorted concept of the character of God. We really think he is a celestial killjoy. We need to recognize and have again ingrained in our being the wonderful truth of Psalm 37:4 where David says, "Delight thyself also in the Lord; and he shall give thee the desires of thine heart" (AV). Now David does not mean, "Delight thyself also in the Lord and he shall give thee a Sting Ray, a Cadillac, a Phi Beta Kappa key and the whole business." What he means is that as we delight ourselves in the Lord, we come, as the hymn says, "to will with him one will." As I delight myself in the Lord, my will and God's will come to coincide. And that is a most wonderful experience. The greatest joy in all of our lives is to do what the Lord wants us to do and to know we are doing it. Then we can say, as our Lord said in those tremendous words in John 4:34, "My food is to do the will of him who sent me." Now, admittedly, we must be on guard constantly against self-deception, but when we really want to do the will of God and do it, we have deep joy and satisfaction.

Second, we must guard very carefully against the idea that every decision we make must have a subjective confirmation. I have known people who have been paralyzed, can't act at all and don't know what to do because they did not have some kind of electrifying liver shiver about the whole thing.

If you are facing an important decision in which God has not given you specific guidance, postpone the decision, if you can, until the way seems clear. But, on the other hand, if you must decide by next Saturday and next Saturday comes and you still have not gotten any clear guidance about it, as far as you know, then you must make the decision. You must trust that God will guide you in the decision. After assessing all the factors, you launch out in faith, saying, "Lord, as I see it, there are four equally valid possibilities in front of me. I see no particular advantage or disadvantage in any of these options. So I am going to go down route 3 unless you close the door. And I trust that you won't let me make a crucial mistake."

And we can go joyfully, believing God did guide us, without spending the next twenty-four years second-guessing ourselves as to whether we are in the will of God. God does not play the game of mousetrap with us. He does not say, "Ha, ha. You thought that was the right lane, but it wasn't. Back to the start and better luck next time." That is not the way God operates. We must get rid of these distorted concepts of God's character. Rather, the God who loved you and me enough to die for us is not going to play games with our lives. We mean too much to him. We can come back to those words we have already quoted, "Trust in the Lord with all thine heart; and lean not unto thine own understanding. In all thy ways acknowledge him, and he shall direct thy paths."

Third, we must realize that there are often logical implications involved in the will of God. If some things are the will of God, then a whole series of other things are automatically the will of God and we do not have to pray about them. For example, if God leads you to get married, you do not have to spend hours in prayer agonizing over whether or not it is the will of God that you should support your wife. Now I would think that this is painfully self-evident, and yet I have met so many people who do not seem to have grasped it. I once loaned a guy ten dollars, and he is still praying about whether he ought to pay me back.

Fourth, we must not think that God's will is necessarily some wild and bizarre thing. There are many people who are afraid of using their reason in determining God's will. But we must recognize that God is not the author of confusion. When the Scripture says "Lean not to your own understanding," it does not mean "Kiss your brains goodby. If it makes any sense at all, it couldn't be the will of God." Rather, the Holy Spirit illumines us and then guides our enlightened reason. It may be that he will lead us to do something that is contrary to our unenlightened reason, but the idea that his will is frequently bizarre is a very dangerous assumption.

Fifth, we must guard very carefully against the subtle temptation to decide what we are going to do for God. This mistake is really critical and I would like you to consider it carefully. There is a vast difference between saying, "Lord, I'm going to be a businessman (or missionary or whatever) for you," and asking, "Lord, what will you have me to do?" It sounds very spiritual to say, "I'm going to be a businessman for the Lord and make money and give it to the Lord's work." Or, "I'll be a missionary for the Lord." But the Lord has not asked you to decide whether you are going to be a missionary, or a businessman, or whatever, for him. Rather, he has invited you to be a recruit and say to the Commander-in-Chief, "Here I am. Where in the battle line do you want me?"

In this connection, be careful you are not tied too closely to your background so that you think God can use you only in the context of the training you have. God may likely, and probably will, lead you in the area of your training, but as George Cowan says in the booklet *Your Training or You?* God wants you more than he wants your training. I took my training in accounting and business administration, but God never led me into that field. I have been in student work since I graduated.

Then, too, we must guard against the temptation to take Bible verses out of context to get God's will. Some people seem to think that the Bible is a magic book. You have probably heard of the fellow who, trying to get guidance, opened the Bible and put his finger down on the phrase, "Judas went out and hanged himself." That did not comfort him very much, so he tried again. And his finger fell on the verse, "Go thou and do likewise." That shook him terribly, so he tried it one more time, and the verse he hit on was "And what thou doest, do quickly."

On rare occasions, God will take a verse which has no specific application to you and give you a message through it, but this is the exception rather than the rule. And because of the violation of the basic biblical principle of interpreting and understanding the Bible in context, God has been blamed for all kinds of things which were merely human stupidity. I remember a British girl several years ago working with the organization that I was with at the time. She was sure God was going to give her a visa for the States because a Bible verse (Is. 41:2) said something about God raising up a righteous man from the east. That was guidance. I said, "What about the rest of the verse that says God is going to use him to destroy people with the sword?" The truth of the matter was she didn't get a visa. God didn't fail. She did–because she violated this principle. Be careful not to do this.

Seventh, you must avoid the mistake of thinking that you can be sure you are in the will of God if everything is moonlight and roses, if you have no problems or stress. Frequently it is when we have just taken a step of obedience that the bottom falls out of everything. Then only the confidence that we are in the will of God keeps us going.

Never forget the incident recorded in Mark 4. The disciples, at the Lord's specific command, had gotten into a boat to head across the Sea of Galilee. After they took this step in obedience to the Lord, the storm broke loose and they thought they were going to lose their lives. But Jesus said to them, "Don't be faithless, but believing."

In Mark 5 Jairus came to our Lord saying, "My daughter's sick. Will you come heal her?" The Lord said he would, and Jairus' spirit soared. But on the way to the home, some lady, who had had a medical problem for twelve years and who surely could have waited another two hours, interrupted them. Jesus got involved in talking and working with her. Jairus' servants came and said "Look, don't bother him any longer. Your daughter has died." And Jairus, who had done what was right–had gotten the answer from the Lord, had followed his will and obeyed–must have been crushed in bitter despair as seeming disaster had taken place. Our Lord's words to him come to us as well in similar circumstances, "Do not fear. Only believe." The test of whether you are in the will of God is not how rosy your circumstances are, but whether you are obeying him.

And then, in the eighth place, it is crucial to avoid the mistake of thinking that a call to world evangelism or missionary service is any different from a call to anything else. Dr. Norton Sterrett, in his helpful booklet *Called by God and Sure of It*, points out that every Christian, whether a wife, an electrician, a lawyer, a teacher or a cabinet maker, has both the privilege and the responsibility to know that he is called by God. And he also has the privilege and responsibility to know whether he is to serve in Cairo or Chicago. You don't get three more spiritual points in God's book for going overseas rather than staying in America, for being in "the ministry" rather than in some other form of endeavor. We have a false sense of spiritual hierarchical values which is not biblical at all. There are some people overseas who ought to be home, and there are many people at home who ought to be overseas. The crucial question each of us must ask himself is, "Am I in the will of God and sure of it?" It is not a question of fastening our spiritual seat belts and hoping we will not be swept by some emotion out of our seats into overseas service. It is not a question of taking our chances with the draft and if by some miracle it misses us, saying, "Phew, it got by me. I survived Urbana, man, O man, and now I can do as I please." Each of us has the privilege of discovering what God wants us to do.

Finally, I want to suggest that each of us should avoid the mistake of thinking that if we have ever knowingly and deliberately disobeyed the Lord, we are forever thrown on the ash heap, can never do the Lord's will and are doomed to "second best." God has the most wonderful ways of reweaving the strands of our lives. He takes us where we are when we come to him in confession and repentance and uses us fully again. Our disobedience did not take him by surprise, and his grace reaches right to us.

John Mark is a good example. He seemed to have blown it when he started out on a missionary trip with Paul. At the first stop he left and headed back for Jerusalem. You will remember that Paul and Barnabas had such a hassel over whether John Mark should go with them again on the next trip that Paul and Barnabas separated. But it seems that Mark was redeemed by God and redeemed himself and later had a full and fruitful ministry which Paul commended.

When you are feeling bad and know you have blown it in sin, remember Peter, too. He denied the Lord. But our Lord took hold of him and restored him to be a great apostle who has given us a part of the Word of God.

What is God's will for you in world evangelism? Realize, first, that God's will in most of its aspects is already fully revealed. Be sure you are familiar with it in the Word of God. In those areas about which he has not been specific, be assured God will guide you through his Word and its principles as you seek his face in prayer, as you view the circumstances from his point of view and as you seek the counsel of other Christians. Then, when you can say, "Lord, I want to do your will more than anything else in life," and as you avoid some of the mistakes which are often based on a distortion of the character of God, you will know where in the world and how in the world God wants you to serve him. He will show you what his will for you is today, and the next day, and the day after that.

Have you ever affirmed the will of God in your life personally? Paul, in Romans 12, invites you, "Therefore, my brothers, I implore you by God's mercy to offer your very selves to him: a living sacrifice, dedicated and fit for his acceptance, the worship offered by mind and heart. Adapt yourselves no longer to the pattern of this present world, but let your minds be remade and your whole nature thus transformed. Then you will be able to discern the will of God, and to know what is good, acceptable, and perfect" (NEB).

IS MAN REALLY LOST?

Leighton Ford

A few months ago Apollo 13 was launched toward the moon. At 10:08 p.m. (EST) on April 13, 1970, an explosion took place. And suddenly the routine was broken by a terse announcement from Jim Lovell: "Houston, we've got a problem." It quickly became apparent that the astronauts were in serious difficulty. "Lost in space" was no longer a fictional concept for a TV plot. National resources were mobilized for the rescue attempt and from all over the world messages offering help poured in. When the astronauts finally got back, John Swigert was asked if he prayed. "I sure did," he replied, "and I believe the prayers of a lot of people around the world had a lot to do with bringing us back."

If the whole world can be moved to concern for three men lost in space, how much more ought we upon whom Jesus Christ has laid his hand be motivated to rescue millions from spiritual disaster!

Once upon a time a great conviction gripped the Christian movement. It may have been put naively or even crudely sometimes, but the conviction was this: If man has a soul, and if that soul can be saved or lost eternally, then the greatest thing in the world is to bring men to salvation in Christ.

But today that conviction suffers from tired blood.

Many of us as Christians today are embarrassed to talk about the "soul" or "eternity" or being "lost." And even those of us who subscribe to the ideas expressed in those words don't seem very fired up about them.

When our daughter, Debbie Jean, was six, she disappeared one day. We searched everywhere for her—the other houses nearby, the shopping center, the schoolyard. I remember walking up and down a little dirt road calling, "Debbie Jean," and fearing the silence. Two hours later she showed up and told us she had gone with a friend to a candy store and then on to the friend's house. After the thunder, lightning and tears had passed, I reflected: During those two hours that my little girl was missing, there were books that I had to read, letters I had to answer, telephone calls I had to make, planning I had to do—but I could think of only one thing: My little girl was lost. I had only one prayer and I prayed it a thousand times, "God, help me to find her." But how often, I asked myself, had I felt the same terrible urgency about men who are lost from God?

What led Jesus to weep over Jerusalem? Or Paul to cry, "Woe is me if I preach not the gospel"? Or John Knox to pray, "Give me Scotland or I die"? Or Henry Martyn to land in India saying, "Here let me burn out for God"? Or George Whitefield to cross the Atlantic thirteen times in a small boat to preach in the American colonies? Or the aristocratic Lady Donnithorne of our own generation to go into the forbidden precincts of Hong Kong's "walled city" to bring the healing of the gospel to the pimps and prostitutes? Or Jim Elliot and his friends to stain a river in Ecuador with their blood to reach an obscure Indian tribe?

They were gripped with a tremendous conviction that without Christ men really were lost in a deep and eternal way.

But for many today to be "lost" seems to mean that you merely fly to heaven tourist-class, not first-class.

The belief that man is lost is far from the only motive for

evangelism. A thousand and one positive reasons exist for winning men to Christ. Yet there is this one great negative: that men *should not perish.* Take that away, and you will cut the nerve cord of concern. Trace the history of the movements which have brought great numbers to Christ, and at the heart you will find men who have prayed, planned, worked and witnessed with a great burden for the lost.

What dulls the knife edge of our concern?

For one thing, the general mind-set of our day isn't geared to the idea of dividing men into categories of "lost" and "saved." But Jesus talked about these categories. He said that men were building on one of two foundations, going into one of two doors, traveling one of two roads, serving one of two masters, heading toward one of two destinies. But we are not comfortable with that "either-or" kind of talk; tolerance is our great contemporary idol. The modern mind has shifted into neutral, disliking the pain of distinguishing right from wrong, or truth from falsehood. In philosophy, morals and everyday life we are told: *do your own thing.* The revolt against authority has left us with no binding standard. We call this being "liberated," yet fail to recognize the danger of a broad-mindedness that has no moorings. Tolerance divorced from truth very easily leads to totalitarianism.

Because we have become so permissive in our own lives, we have also become permissive about God. The belief that men are lost does not jibe with the idea of God as our "buddy" in heaven. So a new wave of universalism is abroad—the idea that everyone is doomed to be saved. Universalism began in the Garden when the serpent told Adam and Eve, "You shall not surely die," and it has often reappeared.

The older universalism told us either that men were too good to be damned or that God was too good to damn men. The "new universalism" is more subtle. It tells us that men are damned and need to be saved, but Christ has already saved them! To oversimplify, historic evangelism has said to men, "Believe on the Lord Jesus Christ and you will be saved." The so-called "new evangelism" says to men, "You're already saved. Believe it!" This is a sure way to short-circuit evangelistic urgency. If all men are "doomed to be saved," then there are many better ways to serve your neighbor than to try to save his soul.

Searing social problems also stab our consciences and demand first call on our energies. The Secretary-General of the United Nations, Mr. U Thant, warns that the members of the United Nations have only ten years to launch a global partnership to curb the arms race, improve the environment and defuse the population explosion. Human society today is like the chartered plane that carried the Wichita State football team to its death. Just as that plane couldn't climb over the Continental Divide, our problems seem insurmountable. Our leaders, like the pilot of that plane, are desperately trying to change direction.

What are we to do? Should we try to help the pilot change course or talk to him about his soul? When we see a man sitting with starving babies in his arms, a nuclear bomb over his head and pollution poisoning the air around him, we are tempted to say, "First, let's change the earth, then we can talk to him about heaven." So the church is polarizing into two camps: the "soul savers" and the "social reformers." But the core issue is this: Can we change the world without saving souls? And can men really be saved without becoming involved in the effort to change the world?

Then too, a new sense of honesty and realism has humbled our self-righteousness. No longer can we think of a "missionary" as a superior soul from Canada the Good or America the Beautiful going to set the poor heathen right. The events of the past few years have forced us to face our own shortcomings. We have seen the burned-out ghettos, the rural slums, the bodies at Kent State, the stupidity and greed that have killed Lake Erie. No longer can we live with the illusion that God is our "Great White Father" and that Jesus wears red, white and blue.

And if we have examined our own Christian experience candidly, we have had to admit that believing in Jesus has not made all our hangups disappear. Even though he may have profoundly changed our lives, we still fail and fall. So when someone says, "Jesus is your trip, LSD is mine," I may be tempted to ask, "Who am I to tell this guy where it's at?"

Add to this the fact that not too many people we meet today seem over anxious about getting "saved," at least in the traditional sense. James Boswell records a conversation between Dr. Samuel

Johnson and Sir Joshua Reynolds about Johnson's fear of death. "What are you afraid of?" asked Reynolds. "Damnation, sir," replied Johnson, "damnation." Now, unless I miss my guess, not too many people on your floor have said that to you this past semester.

What do you give the man who has everything? How do you relate Jesus Christ to the playboy who couldn't care less? to the friendly Hindu student down the hall? to the agnostic with the social conscience? to the engineering student who believes that, given enough time, man can solve all problems? How concerned can you be about people who don't feel "lost"?

Has the age when man really needed God faded into the age when man has everything and can do everything himself? Or have we been taken in by the image-makers? Which is the true-to-life picture: the man of distinction and the God who is dead? or the man who is alienated and the God who is really there?

Let us see how Jesus related in a similar situation to Zacchaeus, the old-time IRS tax official. Zacchaeus didn't seem to need God. He was a comfortable materialist, a "successful sinner" who had disregarded traditional moral codes and religious customs and had made it. To most of his contemporaries Zacchaeus did not seem very "lost."

Then along came Jesus, bringing his religious crusade to Jerusalem and on the way passing through Jericho where Zacchaeus lived. And a strange thing happened. Driven by longings no one suspected were there, the man "who had everything" runs out of his office, rushes to the main street, tries to elbow his way through the crowd and finally, forgetting his dignity, climbs a tree with the little urchins off the street—to see who this Jesus is.

Luke records that when Jesus came by, he looked up at Zacchaeus and called him by name. "Zacchaeus," he said, "Quick! Come down! For I am going to be a guest in your home today!" Zacchaeus scrambles down and takes Jesus to his house in great excitement and joy. There he says to Jesus, "Sir, from now on I will give half my wealth to the poor, and if I find I have overcharged anyone on his taxes, I will give him back four times as much!" And Jesus told him, "Salvation has come to this home today. This man was one of the lost sons of Abraham and I, the Son of man, have come to search for and to save the lost."

The key to this encounter is in the way Jesus saw Zacchaeus. He didn't view Zacchaeus superficially. Because Jesus knew God and knew he was on a mission from God, he had a deep view of Zacchaeus. And because he was in contact with both God and Zacchaeus, he could sense the gap between God and this man. I believe our sense of man's lostness will be in direct proportion to the quality of our relationship with God and with others. Evangelistic concern is born when, like Jesus, we walk with God among men. Break either of these contacts and we grow cold. We cannot conjure up a concern for others by withdrawing and praying, "God, give me a concern." As we get close to both men and God, God fans up the concern in our hearts.

It is important to note also that Jesus didn't go out of his way to find Zacchaeus. Jesus was focusing on God's will when he became aware of the need of this man along the way. To me, this suggests that Christian witnessing is more a way of life than a program. And it suggests that the way to get a concern for others is not by trying to carry the whole world's burdens, but by sighting in on one person.

Remember when you were a child how your parents would try to shame you into cleaning your plate by telling you about the starving people on the other side of the world? Somehow that never reached me. I could not see how finishing my spinach would help that boy in China.

Maybe this is part of our problem in developing a passion for the lost. We try to bear the burden of millions without Christ, and our emotions will not take it. We are not big enough. Only God can carry the burden of the world. He asks us simply to start with what is on our plate. Of course, we need to build a world concern, but we start with the one Zacchaeus we meet, perhaps even here at Urbana.

How did Jesus sense Zacchaeus' need? Had someone told him about Zacchaeus? Had he met him before? Or was it just his divine intuition? I don't know. But I do believe we, as Jesus' followers, can discern people's needs if *we are willing to listen.* All around us in our huge, lonely cities, on our vast campuses, in our affluent, empty homes people are crying, "Won't someone please listen to me!" Are we close enough to hear the "soul English" in their cries?

When I hear people say, "Modern man isn't concerned about

salvation," I feel like saying, "Don't talk nonsense! Even though people may not talk about damnation, if we care enough to really listen we'll find that most of what they're saying is about being lost and saved!"

Listen to the songs people are singing. In "Woodstock" Joni Mitchell writes, "We are starlight, we are golden, and we've got to get ourselves back to the garden." There, in almost biblical words, is the significance and the lostness of man.

Read what the social critics are saying. In *The Making of a Counter Culture* Theodore Roszak has given a devastating analysis of our dead-end technocratic society. He closes his introduction with this paragraph:

> . . . I find myself unable to see anything at the end of the road we are following with such self-assured momentum but Samuel Beckett's two sad tramps forever waiting under that wilted tree for their lives to begin. Except that I think the tree isn't even going to be real, but a plastic counterfeit. In fact, even the tramps may turn out to be automatons . . . though of course there will be great, programmed grins on their faces.

Roszak is saying, "Of course, man is lost. Are you too blind to see it? Can't you see that history as we know it has no purpose? that nature has no reality? that man has no significance?"

It is just not true to say that men have no needs and fears. Even those who deny God cannot escape from guilt. Even though they don't take it to a clergyman, they do take it to a psychiatrist. Our mental hospitals are half-full of patients suffering not from organic troubles but from deep emotional ones and especially guilt complexes. Before this school year is over, one thousand college students in America will commit suicide–many because they cannot escape the haunting sense of failure. They have never learned one of the great things about Jesus Christ–that he makes us free to fail.

People who don't see themselves as lost from God will freely admit they are lost in the sense that they have found no meaning, no direction for their lives. The longing for significance expresses itself most clearly in the fear of death. Note the obsession with death in movies like *Easy Rider* or *Love Story.* Neil Simon, who wrote *The Odd Couple* and *Barefoot in the Park,* was asked on the Dick Cavett Show whether making a lot of money concerned him. The studio went dead silent when Simon answered, "No, . . . what does concern me is the fear of dying."

How many live with a terrible sense of loneliness, when even in a crowd no one seems real? How many others are gripped by despair about the world situation? One student, when asked why he was on drugs, said, "Because I know the wrong finger on the right trigger will end the world, and I live for today because tomorrow may never come."

Get behind the mask, as Jesus did with Zacchaeus, and you will find the misery. And one of the best ways to get behind that mask is to listen with real interest. As someone has said, when as a Christian you listen with love it's like putting your hand into the other's life and feeling gently along the rim of his soul until you come to a crack, a frustration, a fear or longing that he may or may not be conscious of.

The question is: How deep is that crack? And what will it take to fix it?

People today realize a crack exists. They're crying, "Of course we've lost our way." Writing in *Harper's,* John Fischer envisioned a new university, across which he would emblazon the motto: "What must we do to be saved?" The old optimism is gone. Secular prophets have ripped the band-aids off humanity's hide and exposed the fatal wounds.

It is obvious that we have lost our way. We have lost our way internationally. The walls that divide men are higher than ever before. We have a 38th parallel, a 17th parallel, a Jordan River, a Suez Canal, a wall between East and West Berlin. We have lost our way racially. A decade ago it seemed that the end of racial segregation might be just around the corner. Now the question is: Can we avert racial war and suicide? We have lost our way morally. There have always been people who have broken the rules, but now they are saying, "There are no rules, there are no absolutes." We have lost our way ecologically. The new Jeremiahs of our day are the ecologists who are pronouncing woe and doom on a technological society gone mad with greed.

Of course we have lost our way. Man is alienated from himself, from his fellow man and from his world.

Yet our cures for the crack, for the alienation, fail because our diagnosis is too shallow. Many people might have looked at Zacchaeus and agreed that he needed a psychological salvation from his hangups and a sociological salvation from his hostilities. But when Jesus looked at Zacchaeus, he saw a man who was lost because he was alienated from God.

Let me illustrate this deeper spiritual alienation. A friend of mine was going fishing with another fellow early one morning. They stopped to drink coffee in the other fellow's house. While they were sitting at the kitchen table, his buddy's little girl came into the room crying. During the night there had been a thunderstorm and because she had become frightened her parents had taken her into their bed. They had gotten up early and left her in their room. Now she was sobbing and said, "Mommy, I looked in your bed and you were gone, and I looked in Daddy's bed and he was gone, and I looked in my bed and I was gone!" When she lost her relationship with her parents, she lost herself.

Similarly, but in a far more profound way, when we lose touch with God, we lose ourselves and our other relationships go wrong. The salvation we need is one that deals with our basic lostness from God and also begins to heal all these other alienations. And this is precisely what Christ offers!

If we really were gripped with the stupendous adequacy of our gospel, we would identify with Paul who wrote to the Romans, "I'm not ashamed of the gospel of Christ. It's the power of God to put men right with God and with themselves and with their fellow men and with their world. It is for all of men and for all of life."

"I'm not afraid to come to Rome," says Paul, "and to speak of Christ. This gospel will stand up in the marketplace of ideas and the pressures of real life. It's not puny and irrelevant. It's stupendous! It works!"

Universalism, in the sense that all men will be finally saved, is unbiblical. But there is another universalism which the Bible does teach.

The Bible teaches that (1) all men have been given life by God, (2) all men have rejected that life, (3) all men are offered, as a gift, new life in Christ.

Do we believe this universalism enough to put our lives on the line? All men, all men, all men.

I'll never forget once when I preached about Zacchaeus in a church in the United States. After I had finished my sermon, I found out that that morning a young black soldier on his way to Vietnam had been refused admission to the service because they said he was coming as a demonstrator. Afterwards I wrote a letter and publicly declared, "I will never preach in any place representing Jesus Christ where anyone is barred like that."

And when a friend of mine was going on a special mission to Vietnam, I had him make a point of looking up this young man and taking to him my personal apologies and regrets and witnessing to him about the Christ who died for all men, not just white men.

The message of the Bible is a universal message, that God has given life to all men.

The God of the Bible is not a cold, impersonal formula or power. Rather, he is personally interested in man, he wants us really to live–to know and enjoy him forever. As Jesus put it, "I have come that you might have life more abundantly."

God made man to have the highest destiny among created beings. You and I were made like God. The Creator said, "Let us make man in our image." This means that man has a soul–the capacity to have a unique relationship with God. "Life" as God planned it is much more than biological existence. It has a spiritual and moral dimension to it. "This is life . . . eternal life . . . to know the only true God," said Jesus (Jn. 17:3). And when we are in harmony with God, we really have abundant life.

God planned to build a wonderful world with man. He made man to live in peace and dignity and love with a real purpose. Instead, what do we see? Restlessness, war, prejudice, hatred, despair. What has happened?

The biblical diagnosis is that man has rejected life. The root cause of our human predicament is spiritual rebellion. The Bible's verdict is that "we have turned to our own way." "All have sinned." We have chosen to say No to God's design and to run our own lives.

When we say *sin,* most people think right away of sexual immorality or some terrible crime. But basically sin is pride, egotism, self-centeredness. Sin means that we deny the true God and we try to play God for ourselves. The "sins" men commit–for example, stealing, lying, hating–are the result of pushing God to the edge of our lives or ignoring him altogether.

The result of sin is spiritual death: "The wages of sin is death." Man may be mentally, physically and socially alive, alert, vigorous and successful, but still he can be spiritually dead. Like a flower cut off from its root, his contact with his Maker has been broken and that is why man is bored, lonely, guilty, restless, afraid. And the end result is eternal banishment from the presence and fellowship of a just and holy God.

But, someone may object, doesn't the Bible teach that "God is love"? Would a loving God punish and banish man from his presence? But the Bible also tells us that "God is a consuming fire" (Heb. 12:29), and that "God is light and in him is no darkness at all" (1 Jn. 1:5). Just as light and darkness cannot abide together, so a holy God cannot tolerate sin.

That is why when Paul says, "The gospel is the power of God unto salvation," he immediately goes on to say in Romans 1:18 that "the wrath of God is revealed from heaven against all ungodliness and wickedness of men who by their wickedness suppress the truth." Otherwise, men might shrug it off and say, "Who needs salvation?" or else, "O.K., you've got Jesus for your hangups; I've got pills for mine."

"Hold it," says Paul, "I'll tell you why you need salvation: It's because you're guilty, under the wrath of a holy God and you need Christ to set you right."

From the biblical perspective, all of man's alienations come because man is under the wrath of God. Master the first three chapters of Genesis and you will grasp the biblical view of man. Man is significant (made in "the image of God"). But man rebels against God. So what happens? Man is separated from God, expelled from the Garden–spiritual alienation. As a result, something dies inside man–psychological alienation begins. Cain kills Abel–sociological alienation begins. The ground is cursed because of man's fall–ecological alienation begins.

The reality of God's wrath is as much a part of the biblical message as is God's grace. "He who believes in the Son has eternal life; he who does not obey the Son shall not see life, but the wrath of God rests upon him," says John 3:36. Yet the concept of God's wrath is hard to take in. Why? Perhaps because our own anger is so often selfish and mean. I get frustrated, I blow my stack. I'm tired, I punish my children before I get all the facts and I have to tell them I'm sorry.

But God's wrath is not like mine, just as God's love is different from mine. Where my love is often fickle, God's love is faithful. And where my anger is often petty, God's wrath is pure. Where I "fly off the handle," God is "slow to anger" (Ex. 34:6). God's wrath is his settled opposition to sin. It is not vindictive; it is vindicative. It is the active, resolute action of God to vindicate his justice, uphold the moral law of the universe and punish sin.

We need to be clear that while God's blessing is eternal life, his wrath is eternal death. Where sin comes, death follows (Rom. 5:12). Death means that we lose something essential to the kind of life we were made for. In the Bible life means more than physical life–it is a relationship with God. And thus death means more than physical dissolution–it is a loss of that fellowship with God–here and now, and hereafter in hell.

Does the thought of hell seem to you to belong to the Dark Ages? Let me read a comment from Leslie Weatherhead, a liberal theologian:

> Sin is a terrible thing in the universe. Let us never forget that though the idea of hell has been caricatured as a fantastic vulgarity by the generation of our great-grandfathers, we are doing our generation a greater disservice if we make light of sin and pretend that it does not matter and that you are all going to the same place and that God will pat everyone on the head and say, "There, there, it doesn't matter. I'm sure you didn't mean it. Come now and enjoy yourselves." We need to remember that the most terrible things ever said were spoken by the most wonderful person who ever lived.

Never forget that the talk about outer darkness, the closed door, the weeping and gnashing of teeth and the lake of fire came from the lips of the most compassionate person who ever lived. Jesus, who died to save us from hell, had the most to say about it!

Many things we do not know about hell. But Jesus and the New Testament writers use every image in their power to tell us that hell is real, terrible, something to be feared and avoided at all costs. In his parable of the last judgment Jesus taught that some would go to eternal punishment, some to eternal life (Mt. 25:46). In other words, hell will be as real and as lasting as heaven.

The horror of hell is not physical pain. After all, the Bible tells us hell was prepared for "the devil and his angels," and they are not physical beings. Rather the "fire" and "outer darkness" and "thirst" depict spiritual separation from God, moral remorse, the consciousness that one deserves what he is getting.

Hell is the end result of selfishness–an eternal sentence to exist with self as our god. Hell is disintegration–the eternal loss of being a real person.

Hell is eternal desire–eternally unfulfilled. In hell the mathematician who lived for his science endlessly totals a column of figures, but can't add two and two. There the concert pianist who worshiped himself through his art can't play a simple scale. The man who lived for sex lives in eternal lust with no body to exploit. The woman who made fashion her god has a thousand wigs but no mirror!

But there is another side. G. K. Chesterton once remarked, "Hell is the greatest compliment God has ever paid to the dignity of human freedom."

Hell–a compliment?

Yes, because God is saying to us, "You are significant. I take you seriously. Choose to reject me–choose hell–if you will. I will let you go."

Hell is God's final monument to human freedom. After all, no one ever thought of a dog going to hell.

Incidentally, if we really grasp the biblical view of man–sinful but significant–then we won't get caught in the artificial hangup between social action and evangelistic concern. Because man is lost but of great value, the two belong together. To bring a man the Bible for his soul but ignore his need of bread is mockery. If we really believe man has a soul worth saving, then we will be committed to offer that man eternal life and also to see that he receives economic and social justice in this life.

On the other hand, if a man does not have a soul, then compassion is pointless and absurd. Why care, if man is a chance chemical accident? Man is valuable because he is significant. He is significant because he is morally and spiritually responsible. And because he is responsible, he is really lost. That is why our practical concern for man's earthly welfare must grow out of an overarching concern for man's eternal destiny.

Does the biblical teaching about God's judgment and man's lostness repulse you? Does it seem to degrade God into a monster and man into a puppet?

As Francis Schaeffer points out in *Death in the City,* the only way we can get rid of the lostness of man is to do away with either the holiness of God or the significance of man. Says Schaeffer:

> . . . If you give up the holiness of God, there are no absolutes and morality becomes a zero; if you give up the significance of man, man becomes a zero. If you want a significant man, with absolutes, morality and meaning, then you must have what the Bible insists upon—that God will judge men justly.

In the final analysis history is the record of man under judgment, man trying to get back to God and failing. We try to fill that God-shaped vacuum in our lives—by business, by pleasure, by possessions, by philosophy, even by religion and a good life—but we can't cross the gap that sin has made.

You and I cannot get back to God but he can come to us. In spite of our rebellion, God kept on loving us. And this great, holy, loving God in his mercy invaded history in the person of Jesus Christ to provide a solution. He paid a personal visit to our planet to repair that broken contact. "God was in Christ reconciling the world unto himself" (2 Cor. 5:19).

Two thousand years ago God gave us a personal demonstration of his love in the life of Jesus Christ who was God in human form. Jesus came to bring us back to God at the cost of his own life. He said, "I came to give my life a ransom for many." He committed no sin, but in his own person he carried our sins to the cross: "He, the just, suffered for the unjust to bring us to God."

Thus, Jesus Christ is the bridge by which we can come back into personal contact with God. He said, "I am the way . . . no one comes to the Father, but by me" (Jn. 14:6). Note that Jesus did not say, "You can't *believe* in God but by me." Rather, he said, "You can't *come* to the Father [that is, come into a living personal relationship with God] but by me."

It may sound like sheer arrogance for Christians to say, "There is only 'one way,' and we've found that way." It would be arrogance if salvation were a matter of attainment. But it is not. Salvation is a matter of obtainment. "The *gift* of God is eternal life through Christ." We are all in the same fix–Jew, Christian, Hindu, agnostic–we have all failed by our own moral standards. Even when we have done our best, our bridges do not reach to God. That is why God had to reach to us.

But what of those who have not heard of Jesus? Is it fair and just for God to judge them?

The first answer to the problem of those who haven't heard the gospel is to realize that if you are concerned about the fairness of the situation, God is more concerned. "Shall not the judge of all the earth do right?" asks the Scripture (Gen. 18:25). God is just and we can believe he will do right.

The second answer is to recognize that God will judge men on the basis of their knowledge, not their ignorance. Paul makes this clear in Romans 1 and 2. He points out that the wrath of God is revealed against men who "by their wickedness suppress the truth" (Rom. 1:18). He is referring here not to Jews, but to Gentiles, to men who do not have the Bible. And, says Paul, the truth they suppress falls into two parts. One part is the truth of God's power written into the order of nature (Rom. 1:19-20). The other is the truth of God's moral law written into their hearts (Rom. 2:14-15). So, says Paul, men are "without excuse." Even men without the Bible have consciences that make moral judgments and on the day when God calls men to account, the record of conscience will bear witness and "accuse or perhaps excuse" men.

To use Francis Schaeffer's illustration in *Death in the City,* it is as if each person had a tape recorder built into his conscience that registers every moral judgment made during that person's lifetime. At the last day God will play back the tape and every man will hear his own voice saying, "That's right. That's wrong. You shouldn't have done that. You should have done this." And then God will say, "Have you lived by your own moral standards?" And there will be an unearthly silence as every mouth will be stopped. Every man will have to plead guilty because he will have been judged not by what he hadn't known, but by what he had known and hadn't kept.

The third answer to this problem is that God has promised that those who seek him sincerely will find him (see Jeremiah 29:13 and Matthew 7:7). In Acts we read of Cornelius, a Roman army officer who, though not a Christian, was a God-fearing man. He earnestly sought God, according to the light he had. And God responded by sending to him Peter, who told Cornelius how his sins could be forgiven through Jesus Christ. When Cornelius heard, he believed. It was not Cornelius' good works that saved him. Like all other men he had sinned. But when he sincerely sought God by the light he had, God sent him further light. We must be careful how we interpret this story. It does not teach that any religion can save a man if he is sincere. It does suggest that God will in some way respond to anyone of any background who diligently seeks him, sending him the word of Jesus Christ.

And that is the fourth part of the answer. God sent Peter to Cornelius. If you are concerned about those who have not heard of Jesus, perhaps God is saying: *You go tell them!* "How can they hear without a preacher . . . ?"

Love for lost men led God to send his Son. Love for lost men led Jesus to seek and save them at the cost of his life.

What does love lead me to do?

If I have bread, another man is hungry, and I don't share, do I love him? If I know Christ, another man is lost, and I don't share, do I know love?

We do not evangelize from a superiority complex. We do not go in an attitude of condemning others. We must not say, "You're all wet and I've got all the answers." As D. T. Niles said, "We're beggars telling other beggars where to find bread." We go saying, "Brother, we're in the same boat. I identify with you. We've both failed. But Jesus Christ has enabled me to take my mask off and to face myself and admit my failures and prejudices. He's given me the way out, the exit. And this Jesus Christ can do the same for you. I'm not what I should be. I'm not what I'm going to be. But because of him I'm not what I used to be!"

That's witnessing! And we are witnesses, not judges. It is my responsibility to witness; it's God's responsibility to judge. Only God is good enough and knowledgeable enough to be the judge.

We are witnesses, not condemners. Jesus did not condemn Zacchaeus. He did not walk up to him and say, "Hey, you dirty sinner. You're going to hell." Jesus knew that Zacchaeus was lost, but he merely said, "I want to stay at your house." And faced with the love and acceptance of Jesus Christ, Zacchaeus could face himself and could find salvation.

We have been considering the question: Is man really lost? Maybe the question should have been, Am I . . . are you . . . really saved?

For if man is lost, and if Jesus Christ is God's stupendous answer to that lostness and if I don't care about sharing him, then something must be wrong with my relationship to God.

If I do not have that concern, either I do not know God or I have grown cold and have forgotten what Jesus Christ has done for me. Maybe I want so much to be popular that I will not pay the price of genuine love: to tell it like it is and face others with the finality of Christ. Maybe the problem is not my belief, but my obedience. Jesus could not save Zacchaeus and save himself too. Saving the lost is a costly business–spiritually, materially, emotionally. Maybe the price seems too great.

I suspect that the reason Zacchaeus trusted Jesus was because he sensed, "Here is a man who really cares about me." In fact, this man was ready to die for him. And I suspect that men will believe what we say about Jesus when they see that we really care, that we are willing, in some sense, to die for him and them.

Maybe the world does not believe because it does not believe the believers believe.

Last September, a black brother, a member of the Billy Graham Team, came to my room. The night before he had met until 1:30 with black students at a Pennsylvania university. "They are committed to revolution," he told me. "They are ready to die for it. They threw my words back in my teeth and said to me, 'Your Jesus is powerless, your Jesus is irrelevant in our situation.' I wanted to reach them, but I couldn't. I failed." And as he told me, he broke down in my arms and cried like a baby, a strong man racked with sobs.

Two days later I got word from the person who arranged that meeting. He said, "That was the most significant meeting we have ever had on this campus." He did get through. The next Sunday when he spoke in a church in that college town, thirty students, black and white, committed their lives to Christ.

And then I learned what had gotten through–what had really reached them.

At the end of that late night session my brother had looked at the students and said, "O.K., you say you're ready to die. Well, I want you to know I'm ready to die, too. And you can kill me right here if it will make you feel any better. But I want you to know this. If you die, you die for nothing. If I die, I die for something."

Is man really lost?

Don't answer too glibly.

For if we say yes, then Jesus may say, "Come with me, disciple–to Jericho, to Jerusalem, to Calvary, back to your home, back to your campus and to the ends of the world."

WHERE DO WE GO FROM HERE?

John W. Alexander

Where do we go from here? I am not focusing my attention now on that long-range future, that distant day when some of us will step ashore on a foreign land. The span I am concerned with is the short-range future—when some of us will be at school, some of us at work in the office and the factory.

What will happen when there is no more great convention singing, no more missionaries crowded into the armory, no more moving speeches from the platform, no more workshops, no more Bible studies, no more prayer cells and no more of the excitement of living with 12,000 fellow disciples of Jesus Christ? What will happen when we are in the old humdrum routine with the old familiar faces and the old familiar places? The emotional letdown is going to be terrific. So let's brace ourselves for it.

The issue is not at all what God has done in our emotions these last few days. More important, what has he done in our minds, in our intellects? And more important than that, what has he done in our wills? A brief comment, perhaps, about that ride home tomorrow. As we travel in that automobile, some of us half asleep, or fly, or take a train, would this suggestion be in order? While this convention is fresh in our intellects and memory why not review and express to one another what God has done in us, what God has done to us. And here we run into one of the major principles of learning, namely this, that expression deepens impression. We have had many an impression in our intellects these past four and a half days, but if we will express them tomorrow and the next few days, those impressions will grow deeper. I think it might be one of those days, at least in the early morning, when it would be good to keep the car radio off so that we can share with one another, pray together, and go over what we have learned here.

Where do we go from this point? What I am trying to do is reach back four and a half days and draw out what have seemed to be the main themes of this convention. I would like to weave them together, if possible, and then look into that short-range future. These strands have come to me from listening to the speakers here and from conversations with you–listening to you express your opinions and tell what God has done in your life. And I am trying to integrate what my impressions are under God. As I have prayed, I have sensed his leading that he would have us look into Scripture as a great reservoir, a quarry of granite. May I ask you, then, to go with me into this great quarry and dig out twelve massive chunks of granite of God's truth for us. As we go into the future, we can build and continue to build our lives on these foundation rocks, these massive portions that can be quarried from God's written Word. Let us look briefly at each of the twelve.

The first foundation truth is in Deuteronomy 8:11-20. Moses is poised on the bank of the Jordan River. The Israelites are ready to go into their future. Where do they go from there? Moses reminds them:

> Take heed lest you forget the Lord your God, by not keeping his commandments and his ordinances and his statutes, which I command you this day: lest, when you have eaten and are full, and have built goodly houses and live in them, and when

> your herds and flocks multiply, and your silver and gold is multiplied, and all that you have is multiplied, then your heart be lifted up, and you forget the Lord your God, who brought you out of the land of Egypt, out of the house of bondage, who led you through the great and terrible wilderness, with its fiery serpents and scorpions and thirsty ground where there was no water, who brought you water out of the flinty rock, who fed you in the wilderness with manna which your fathers did not know, that he might humble you and test you, to do you good in the end. Beware lest you say in your heart, "*My* power and the might of *my* hand have gotten me this wealth." You shall remember the Lord your God, for it is he who gives you power to get wealth; that he may confirm his covenant which he swore to your fathers, as at this day. And if you forget the Lord your God and go after other gods and serve them and worship them, I solemnly warn you this day that you shall surely perish. Like the nations that the Lord makes to perish before you, so shall you perish, because you would not obey the voice of the Lord your God.

I take this to be a warning which is appropriate today on at least three scales. First of all, to those nations who say they are God-fearing this indeed is a warning. I believe the older generation in the United States has forgotten God. May the youth of today not repeat the mistake of that older generation! I am more optimistic about this young generation after meeting with you here for the last four and a half days. God can use you Canadian and United States citizens to infiltrate, to penetrate as salt in a saltless society, as reminders in a nation which has forgotten God.

But I think that this passage of Scripture also applies to the church. Too much of the church has forgotten God. I am rather glad in some instances that the leadership of the church is passing into your hands. I am convinced that under the leadership of the youth today, the church of tomorrow is going to be different. But I have a reservation because it can turn out differently without being better. And I pray that the Holy Spirit working in you will make the church of tomorrow better.

Then this passage can apply on a third scale—not only to the nation, not only to the church, but also to movements such as

Inter-Varsity Christian Fellowship.

There is one thing which worries me about Inter-Varsity in light of this Deuteronomy warning against forgetting God: that Inter-Varsity will become infested with sophistry. Understand that I am all for loving the Lord with all of our mind. We are to think highly, sharply, acutely, and anybody who knows me knows that I am not willing to settle for anything less than excellence in academic activity. But it is possible to get so sharp in our brain and cold in our heart that we lose our cutting efficiency for the Lord Jesus Christ. And I pray that as we try to live highly and purely and excellently with our minds, we will keep that burning heart with our feet anchored on God's truth and keep walking close to him.

The second portion of God's truth that I would like to consider is the very brief statement in 2 Chronicles 7:14:

> If [a conditional, if] my people who are called by my name humble themselves, and pray and seek my face, and turn from their wicked ways, then I will hear from heaven, and will forgive their sin and heal their land.

Here is the remedy for a nation or a church or a movement which has forgotten God. But a mighty big if is involved: *If* my people . . . turn from their wicked ways.

Wicked ways? I find this easy to apply when I hear a speaker eloquently pointing out the weaknesses in somebody else. But this verse is talking about me. Could it also be talking about you?

We must turn from our wicked ways–our lying, for example. Are you distressed at how prone we Christians are to tell lies? I am troubled at how frequently within myself there bubbles up that tendency not to tell an outright falsehood, but to amend the truth just enough so that even though technically what I say is correct, the message I know my friend has picked up is not the truth. That temptation is awfully strong in all of us.

Jealousy? Envy? Aren't we all infected with this disease of "me first"? Or this tendency to cut down the other fellow, to gossip behind his back, to say things which are true–absolutely true, no falsehood involved–but unnecessary, communicating statements that nobody needs to hear, passing on information that nobody needs to possess? This puts the spotlight on my sin–not the sin of my brother, or my parents, or the pastor, or the "fighting fundies" or the "cold liberals"—but on you and me, we who are called by his name.

As I look at this passage from Chronicles, I feel a deep need for holy living in my own life. I am concerned when I hear that passage in Leviticus, "Be holy for I am holy," and when I hear Christ's words in the Sermon on the Mount saying, "Look, the standard is 100% perfection. Be perfect." I really want to be holy and perfect. I am concerned about that. I think we all should be more concerned about a holy life—true holiness, scriptural holiness—not the kind of holiness that somebody else can concoct, not the kind that some organization might promulgate, but biblical purity of life.

And pride is the big stumbling block, isn't it? We think we know better than the other fellow. Some of us think we know better than Scripture. We think we are better than others. It's that "me first" again. The passage says, "If my people . . . humble themselves." There is the great remedial treatment for pride.

I think of a quotation in this connection that comes from the biography of George Mueller, the famous British brother who founded orphanages. One day he was in conversation and somebody asked him if he would tell the secret of the power in his life. This is what the biographer, W. E. Sangster, says:

> Hard pressed on one occasion to tell his secret, George Mueller said, "There was a day when I died, utterly died." And as he spoke, he bent lower and lower until he almost touched the floor. Continuing to speak he added, "I died to George Mueller, to his opinions, preferences, tastes, will. Died to the world, its approval or censure. Died to the approval or blame, even of my brethren. And since then I have studied only to show myself approved unto God."

There is a statement of a humble heart.

If you and I who are called by God's name humble ourselves, pray and seek his face, and turn from our wicked ways, then the question is: Where do we go from here? The battle will continue. The devil will actively seek to turn us back to our wicked ways. We must keep that rudder turned, the bearing right on, and the ship going in the direction that the Lord Jesus, guiding us through his Holy Spirit, indicates. And then, God says, "I'll hear from heaven, I'll forgive your sin, I'll heal your land."

The third passage of Scripture, another great massive truth, is in Matthew 15:7-9. The Lord Jesus says,

> You hypocrites! Well did Isaiah prophesy of you, when he said: "This people honors me with their lips, but their heart is far from me; in vain do they worship me, teaching as doctrines the precepts of men."

I see in this passage another warning: Beware of the trap of hypocrisy. Now, to be sure, the church has made many mistakes; the missionaries who have gone before us have made many mistakes; and many a mission board has made mistakes. But, with this Scripture, may I suggest that we look at ourselves?

How about us? Is what we declare with our lips incongruent with what we believe with our hearts? This kind of person doesn't hang together. With the lips one thing is said; with the heart another thing is believed. He honors God with his lips, he says he is a Christian, he takes God's name, but his heart is far from God. Doesn't that remind you of one of the Ten Commandments that says, "Don't take the name of the Lord in vain"? We dare not take God's name upon us if really deep down we are not committed to him. If we do, Jesus says of us, "In vain do they worship me."

We are into the realm of doctrine here; we are talking about the basic presuppositions, precepts, premises, on which we build our lives, the beliefs to which we are committed. Are these basic heart-beliefs merely the precepts of men? Where do we go from here? I hope that tomorrow and in the days ahead, we will be building upon sound doctrines.

Now let us consider the fourth portion of truth: Ephesians 4:11-16. Here the Lord focuses attention upon the gifts that he is giving his people. He explains why he has given the gifts and what our aspirations should be for them.

> And his gifts were that some should be apostles, some prophets, some evangelists, some pastors and teachers, for the equipment of the saints, for the work of ministry, for building up the body of Christ, until we all attain to the unity of the faith and of the knowledge of the Son of God, to mature manhood, to the measure of the stature of the fulness of Christ; so that we may no longer be children, tossed to and fro and carried about with every wind of doctrine, by the cunning

of men, by their craftiness in deceitful wiles. Rather, speaking the truth in love, we are to grow up in every way into him who is the head, into Christ, from whom the whole body, joined and knit together by every joint with which it is supplied, when each part is working properly, makes bodily growth and upbuilds itself in love.

From this paragraph, may I suggest two things to observe as we go from here into the future. First of all, this maturity we are to attain is a process of growth. Growth is slow; it takes time. And so our expectation should be realistic—tomorrow and next week and next month we can grow a little toward that fulness in him.

Also, growth is different for different people. This should encourage those of us who are sensitive by nature and introvert by style. We look around and see extroverts with effusive personalities. They can lead out in prayer; they can take a passage of Scripture and lead a Bible study easily. But it is hard for us to speak out in group prayer, and in a Bible study we tend to remain quiet. The Lord has made us all different. Our value to him is not determined by the stature which we have achieved so far. Introverts who are growing to mature introvert status in the Lord Jesus Christ are just as valuable as mature extroverts in Christ. The important thing is to be continually growing toward maturity.

My wife is an introvert type. And I have seen her crushed and bruised and beaten—not by other people, but by her own self as she tries to compare what she is in her timid, tender, quiet way with someone else who is strong and bold and can leap out ahead.

I think also of my father in this connection. He did not do anything great in life, I suppose, compared to other people. But he grew in Christ. I think of a little poem that I last heard about 30 years ago, and it was strange to me tonight as I was approaching this message, that poem came back to mind:

He built no great cathedral, that centuries applaud.
But in his daily living, his life cathedraled God.

May this be true of us as we grow up in every way into him.

The second observation relates to the reason we must grow in faith and knowledge: "that we may no longer be children tossed to and fro and carried about with every wind of doctrine." Too many of us are afraid of the whole area of doctrine. In order to grow we need to study deeply, probe Scripture, and under the touch of the Holy Spirit extract from this Word the doctrines upon which to build our lives. For in Scripture we will find the precepts, the premises, the presuppositions, and the basis of our faith.

If somebody should ask you to explain your basis of faith, could you write it out so that he could understand it? He might not necessarily believe your premises and presuppositions, but would he be able to follow what you were talking about? May I suggest that this would be a fascinating and valuable assignment for you to give yourself for the next month or year–construct your basis of faith with statements beginning, "I believe. . . ." I trust that these statements, these doctrines, on which your life is being built, will be rooted in Scripture.

Let's move on to a fifth chunk of truth in 2 Corinthians 3:18.

> And we all, with unveiled face, beholding the glory of the Lord, are being changed into his likeness from one degree of glory to another; for this comes from the Lord who is the Spirit.

In the Ephesians passage we noted the need to grow up to be like the Lord Jesus Christ. And if we are really growing up to maturity in the Lord, we are not going to forget him, as we are warned against doing in the Deuteronomy passage.

But now here in Corinthians is another dimension to this growing process, to this going on from here. Without this dimension we would be incapable of growing up into Christ. To be able to mature to the fulness of the stature of the Lord, we need the external action by an agent other than ourselves. And this verse in Corinthians identifies him: the Holy Spirit of God himself. It is he who changes us. We are on the receiving end. We are being changed into the Lord's likeness, gradually from one degree of glory to another. Our nature left to itself tends to grow in the opposite direction, away from the Lord's likeness, back to its own wicked ways. But the Holy Spirit puts new life in us, cleanses us, fills us, anoints us so that we can grow to be like Christ.

I hope that at this moment a prayer is in your heart: "Oh, Holy Spirit of God, make me more like the Lord Jesus Christ. I've got a long way to go. I know that you do it gradually, but here I am, ready for you to do it in me–one degree at a time. I want you to work in me so that as time goes by, as I go from here into the immediate future, you will make me different from myself, my old nature, and more like Christ, my new nature."

May I interject at this point that there is a difference between character and activity, between being and doing, between attributes and deeds. And it would seem to me that character, being, attributes, come first. And as we ask God to change our character and make us more like the Lord in our inner being, the deeds which will then issue from that character will be pleasing to him, that is, we will be changed from one degree of glory to another.

Let us now go back into the Old Testament, to a paragraph in the book of Psalms–Psalm 119:9-16.

> How can a young man keep his way pure? By guarding it according to thy word. With my whole heart I seek thee; let me not wander from thy commandments! I have laid up thy word in my heart, that I might not sin against thee. Blessed be thou, O Lord; teach me thy statutes! With my lips I declare all the ordinances of thy mouth. In the way of thy testimonies I delight as much as in all riches. I will meditate on thy precepts, and fix my eyes on thy ways. I will delight in thy statutes; I will not forget thy word.

Notice the recurrence of these nouns in the paragraph–*word, commandments, statutes, ordinances, testimonies, precepts* and *ways.*

Where do we go from here? I hope we will go from here to drive our roots, our minds, the sources of our thought, deep into the written Word of God–his commandments, ordinances, testimonies, precepts.

I am all for a regular daily Bible time. If I don't meet the Lord in the morning in his written Word, I find it hard to walk closely with the Living Word. I really believe that one of the most important publications of Inter-Varsity Press is the booklet, *Quiet Time.* May I fervently urge you to get a copy, study it and begin to build a "quiet time" into your daily schedule.

Some of you have realized great blessing in memorizing Scripture. Now I know that Scripture memorization is not a magic guarantee to growth in Christ. The devil used memorized Scripture to tempt Jesus in the wilderness, and it is possible to memorize huge Scripture passages and still be a Pharisee. But I am firmly convinced that we who love the Lord, want to remember him, and are yielded to the Holy Spirit to work in us will be better instruments in his hand if we have some Scripture memorized.

But perhaps we should backtrack here to a more basic problem, one that has become rather widespread in the United States. Are these Scriptures–these documents–trustworthy or reliable? It seems to me that we are in for trouble if we say that we are going to get our roots down deep and broadly into Scripture, but then as those roots are developed, we wonder whether what they are encountering is truth or error.

The question of the reliability of the Bible is difficult, but important. There are a lot of problems in the Bible we do not understand, many questions about it we cannot answer, many "apparent" discrepancies we cannot explain. (I emphasize the word *apparent* because the human mind is not great enough to plumb and explain all the "problems" in God's Word.) But I find that I must choose which side of the fence of this controversy I am going to come down on–the side which says, "Well, there's error in the Bible, and from here on I'll have to decide which part is error and which isn't," or the side which says, "Although there are many problems in the Scripture I don't understand, I refuse to judge God's Word by saying there's error in it."

This is a very complex question, and I hope that when you encounter it, you will prayerfully think it through. May I recommend James Packer's book, *Fundamentalism and the Word of God,* to help you resolve this question finally for yourself.

Let me make one more comment in connection with this passage in Psalm 119 which speaks about the mastery of God's Word–meditating on it, enjoying it, delighting in it. It is painfully evident that in the United States and Canada we do not have enough men who can expound God's Word to hungry young hearts who want to learn its truths. I wonder how many of you have received from the Holy Spirit the gift of expositing Scripture? One of my prayers is that Inter-Varsity and Christian pastors will be instruments to help young people become dedicated to long, hard study of the Bible, the classics and other bodies of literature so they can exposit God's Word–his precepts, his testimonies–to the next generation.

The seventh portion of truth which I would like to look at with you is in Mark 12:28-31:

> And one of the scribes came up and heard them [Pharisees, Herodians, Sadducees] disputing with one another, and seeing that he [Jesus] answered them well, asked him, "Which commandment is the first of all?" Jesus answered, "The first is, 'Hear, O Israel: The Lord our God, the Lord is one; and you shall love the Lord your God with all your heart, and with all your soul, and with all your mind, and with all your strength.' The second is this, 'You shall love your neighbor as yourself.' There is no other commandment greater than these."

The man's question was, "Lord, what's the most important thing in life?" And Jesus answered, "The first thing to understand about that is that you don't begin with yourself." And the most important thing as you go from here is to start thinking not about what you will do, but about God. We begin with God. And if we begin with him, we are more likely to end up on the right pathway and with the proper character than if we begin with ourselves.

Now what are we to do about God? Love him. We begin with that vertical love, the greatest love of all, to love the Lord our God with all our heart, soul, mind and strength–with our whole being, our whole person. From this upward love come two other loves–a horizontal love to others and an internal love to myself.

We are to love our neighbors–both Christian and non-Christian. It's the *how* that is tough. We have been told many times by many speakers in many meetings that we ought to love. And as we sit in our pews and in our chairs, we nod our heads up and down, "Yes, I think I ought to love my neighbor." But, for the most part, it is only when we go out the doors that we can love our neighbor. He is out there, not in here. Where do we go from here? We go out there to find and love our neighbor.

But what can we do when we get out there to really love him? If you define love as active concern for the best good of a person, then if I love my neighbor, I am actively concerned for his best good. And when I love myself, I'm actively concerned for my best good. And in this sense, therefore, it is certainly right to have love for one's self.

We should also realize that this is not situation ethics. We let God help us decide and guide us into what is good; we don't decide.

But how can we, as we go from here, take the initial steps in loving our neighbor? Here are two tangible suggestions. First, when you are back home, ask the Lord to guide you to one person who is suffering. He may be suffering emotionally, physically or economically. And then go and do something to help him because you love him and because Jesus told you to do it. This, to me, is the message of the Good Samaritan. The Samaritan was classified *good* by Jesus because he went out of his way to be actively concerned for the best good of a man who was suffering.

Of course, suffering people are all around and probably you have already thought of several, but I can think of one kind of suffering person that every one of us could help if we would. Our metropolitan areas are crowded with families in which the husband and father has deserted the wife and children. The mother alone is left to raise the children. Her boys have no father image. They may not even have an older brother, or if they do, the older brother may be a bad influence.

There is a desperate need in this kind of family for some kind of good male image. Perhaps you can love that family by going out of your way to help that kind of boy in your community. Many young girls growing up in such families need an older sister to identify with—to help them form a family image. One of you girls could help them bear the burden. Can't we ask the Lord Jesus, then, to help us choose at least one person that we could go out of our way to help?

The second suggestion is this: Ask the Lord to show you one problem, one social ill, one injustice that needs to be corrected. And then work on it. We all know numerous causes, but choose one to get involved in. I can think of the problem of absentee ownership. Perhaps you might be able to work in the area of zoning authority in the city—inspecting houses to see if they meet the building codes. There is almost a 100% correlation between the conditions of rented housing and absentee ownership. There is a cause in which each of us could get active if we would.

The eighth passage of Scripture that I want to look at briefly is 1 Corinthians 13.

> If I speak in the tongues of men and of angels, but have not love, I am a noisy gong or a clanging cymbal. And if I have prophetic powers, and understand all mysteries and all

> knowledge, and if I have all faith, so as to remove mountains, but have not love, I am nothing. If I give away all I have, and if I deliver my body to be burned, but have not love, I gain nothing.
>
> Love is patient and kind; love is not jealous or boastful; it is not arrogant or rude. Love does not insist on its own way; it is not irritable or resentful; it does not rejoice at wrong, but rejoices in the right. Love bears all things, believes all things, hopes all things, endures all things.

May I make three short observations: First, we must guard against loveless orthodoxy. When we come to know doctrine and with our intellects have all the answers and can tell other people what Scripture really means, when we have all the right knowledge and all the right faith—even then, if we do not have love, in God's eyes we have nothing. Second, we must understand that without genuine love, social activism—giving to the poor, self-sacrifice, even death—gains us nothing. Third, the correction is the real love talked about in the second paragraph.

As you reread the second paragraph, think about your parents, especially if your parents are not members of the body of Christ and you are. What is your attitude toward them? Patient, kind, not jealous or boastful, not arrogant or rude, not insisting on your own way, not irritable or resentful, not rejoicing in wrong, bearing all things? Let's ask God to help us love our non-Christian parents.

Let's move on to a ninth passage, Romans 8:5-8. As we go through this paragraph, notice that one idea occurs five times.

> For those who live according to the flesh set their minds on the things of the flesh, but those who live according to the Spirit set their minds on the things of the Spirit. To set the mind on the flesh is death, but to set the mind on the Spirit is life and peace. For the mind that is set on the flesh is hostile to God; it does not submit to God's law, indeed it cannot; and those who are in the flesh cannot please God.

In this passage of Scripture, God is speaking to us about the mind-set. This involves our intellect and our will; they mesh together, the gears connect. With my will I set the dial so that my mind will be thinking the things it should think, and dwelling upon the things it should dwell upon.

The tenth passage is in Colossians 4:2-4. Where do we go from here in evangelism?

> Continue steadfastly in prayer, being watchful in it with thanksgiving; and pray for us also, that God may open to us a door for the word, to declare the mystery of Christ, on account of which I am in prison, that I may make it clear, as I ought to speak.

In our evangelizing, I hope we can make the gospel clear so that people can understand.

The eleventh passage is in 2 Corinthians 4:1-2.

> Therefore, having this ministry by the mercy of God, we do not lose heart. We have renounced disgraceful, underhanded ways; we refuse to practice cunning or to tamper with God's word, but by the open statement of the truth we would commend ourselves to every man's conscience in the sight of God.

How often in evangelism are we tempted to practice cunning and by disgraceful, underhanded ways manipulate people to get decisions for Christ? We must refuse to tamper with God's Word. We want people to hear the bad news as they hear the good news because God's plan for life has a terrible dimension if they reject God, a wonderful dimension if they accept him. We must present an open statement of the truth.

The final passage is Revelation 7:9-12. This is a great passage to keep in mind as we go from here, as we participate in worldwide evangelism, as we look forward to the great day that is coming, as we anticipate it tomorrow, as we desire people from all over the world to be together with us.

> After this I looked, and behold, a great multitude which no man could number, from every nation, from all tribes and peoples and tongues, standing before the throne and before the Lamb, clothed in white robes, with palm branches in their hands, and crying out with a loud voice, "Salvation belongs to our God who sits upon the throne, and to the Lamb!" And all the angels stood round the throne and round the elders and the four living creatures, and they fell on their faces before the throne and worshiped God, saying, "Amen! Blessing and glory and wisdom and thanksgiving and honor and power and might

be to our God for ever and ever! Amen."

If the Lord Jesus Christ is residing within us, you and I are going to be there. People will be there from other nations, other tribes, other races, other languages, other classes. There will be no middle class, no upper class, no lower class. And together we will hear them sing, "Blessing and glory and wisdom and thanksgiving and honor and power and might be to our God for ever and ever! Amen."

PART IV

A SURVEY OF GOD'S WORK IN THE WORLD

STUDENT WORK AROUND THE WORLD

C. Stacey Woods
and
Samuel Escobar*

What is the IFES idea? It is students in faith accepting responsibility to evangelize their own universities. It is international student movements being formed in every nation, movements which are true to Christ and founded on his Word, but which witness in the context of the tradition and culture of their own nations. These movements are autonomous, not patterned after IVF in England, IVCF in the United States or IVF in Australia, but growing up out of their own church culture and tradition. The idea is that of a world fellowship of these student movements, helping one another by prayer, financial gifts and pioneer work in their neighboring countries. It is a fellowship of students, of faculty members, of partners, of missionaries, not

*C. Stacey Woods delivered this world report, asking Samuel Escobar to present the section on Latin America.

competing with one another, but working together for the furtherance of the gospel among the students of the world.

I would like to express thanks on behalf of the IFES to those missionary societies (there are quite a number) which are loaning missionaries to the IFES and to these younger national movements; these men are working side by side with the nationals in order that movements may be established. Today the IFES consists of 36 national student movements, and we are working in more than 80 different nations.

I. THE FAR EAST

First, I wish to speak of Korea, Japan, the Philippines, Taiwan, Hong Kong, Thailand, Vietnam, Indonesia, Singapore and Malaysia. Do you realize that in this area there are now 65 Asian staff members wholly supported from Asia, not receiving one cent of money from the West? Working alongside them as associate staff are some 31 missionaries from some 7 societies. To me this is a most remarkable example of cooperation and something for which we can only thank God: All of these 65 Asian staff workers are being supported from Asia itself.

When I think of these countries, I think of a scene a few weeks ago in Hong Kong, when representatives laid their hands on our first Indonesian staff worker, at the initiative of these Asian students. They commissioned this national for student work in his own country and they promised him their prayer and financial support. This is their missionary project for this year. To me this is something tremendous.

As we meet here tonight some 300 students over in the Philippines will be meeting in their third missionary conference. Already graduates from Inter-Varsity in the Philippines have established their own missionary movement, sending missionaries to Indonesia. This is something wonderful and very, very exciting. There are new Asian missionary societies which literally are growing up out of the Asian student movement in terms of graduates with vision, banding themselves together to evangelize their neighboring countries.

When I think of these countries, I think of The Way Press, with the literature already being produced there. In fact, they are mass-producing cassettes in English and Chinese for evangelism training and Bible study leader training. In many ways, they are far in advance of us here in the West.

When I think of training sessions, I think of the University Bible Fellowship of Korea. In their training conferences, 600 students were present. In Taiwan, some 800 students were present.

When I think of evangelism, I think of the recent mission in Kuala Lumpur. It was a unique university evangelistic mission. For several months Miss Ada Lum trained some 120 students in biblical evangelism. Mr. Chua Wee Hian was the evangelist. He spoke well; God blessed his ministry. But the heart of the meeting was not in the speaker. It was in the hands of these 120 students. And every day for two weeks after that mission ended, the university students were leading their friends to Christ.

So there is much we can thank God for in the Far East. Pray for them as they pray for you and me.

II. **EUROPE**

Europe is, I think, the most diverse, different, tragic, challenging and divided continent that we can find.

First of all, consider Scandinavia. There are strong student movements in the four Scandinavian countries. And yet they are not interdenominational but state-church movements, because each of these countries is 97% nominally Lutheran. I have just visited there. In Oslo you will find a Christian Union of at least 600 students from one university.

And I can scarcely think of a single university in Scandinavia where there is not a Christian group of at least 100.

I think we have much to learn from the Scandinavian Christians. If you went to one of their evangelistic meetings, there would be no appeal for people to make decisions; rather, after the meeting was over, you might find two or three hundred students on their knees, quietly seeking the Lord, because they believe rightly that it is not just a matter of *my* receiving Christ, *Christ* must receive me. We must seek the Lord who seeks us.

These people live a life where guilt and grace seem to be constantly in tension. They feel the need for daily repentance; they speak of living day by day under the forgiveness of God. And I found myself greatly enriched during my last visit through contact with them. Personally, I believe North American evangelical Christians with their tendency toward "easy assurance," "cheap grace," false doctrines of victory over sin and the ignoring of sin in a Christian's life have got much to learn from Scandinavia.

Second, consider Great Britain. I think the movement in Great Britain is probably the most wholesome and balanced and the strongest movement in proportion to the population that one finds anywhere. What is the continuing secret of the blessing in Great Britain in the universities? No new method, no new technique, no new attempt at using media, for that matter—but an emphasis each day upon the quiet time, every student meeting with God. There is likewise an emphasis on united prayer in the daily prayer meeting in the university, an emphasis on a weekly exposition of Scripture by a man of God who can expound the Word, an emphasis on student-led Bible study groups in the dormitories and the simple weekly proclamation of the simple gospel message which alone is the power of God unto salvation. I think the greatest danger that faces us is the loss of simplicity, the loss of simple confidence in prayer, in the study of the Word and in the proclamation of the gospel.

Third, I would take you to the Netherlands. There you could see the failure of doctrinal orthodoxy apart from the Holy Spirit. And yet God has raised up Ichthus, a new movement in the Netherlands, linked up with the IFES. God has greatly blessed it.

In Latin Europe there is an altogether different situation, with a heritage of French rationalism, and of course the Roman Catholic Church. Here we are in dire need of staff help. The work in France is pitifully weak. It is just beginning in Belgium. There are signs of real life in Portugal and Spain. In Italy it has been very discouraging. Do you know the greatest area of encouragement in Italy? The response of Roman Catholic students. And in many of the few groups that are there, the majority of the students today are Roman Catholics. And for this we can really thank God.

Finally, I would mention Eastern Europe. We hear so many conflicting reports about that part of the world. Where does truth lie? Please do not believe everything you read. Apart from Russia, there is no secret church, or hidden church or underground church in Eastern Europe. There is an extraordinary degree of liberty provided that people live within the limits of the law.

And yet, of course, in the universities we find the most difficult place of witness. This last summer we had a group of students from Eastern Europe. They said, "How can we carry on Bible studies?" And so the question was asked, "Could you get together for a musical evening?" "Certainly." "Could you get together to read poetry?" "Certainly." And then they grinned. "Yes, we can get together to study the Bible." And they were taught techniques in Bible study this summer. And it is exciting to hear what is going on.

I could tell of one country where one of our staff is going to be the chief speaker at an evangelistic ski camp in Eastern Europe. There will be more than 90 students present. People say it is not possible, but it is actually happening. What we are trying to do is to reach students within the limits of the law. We do not believe in breaking the law, but within its limits much can be done. A station wagon loaded with literature goes in regularly. Only once has it been stopped; the guards took samples of everything and said, "Go on." Of course, this is an answer to prayer. But nothing has been hidden. When God undertakes, this is possible.

People say, "How can we get Bibles into Hungary?" I say, "It's a very, very simple thing. First of all, you buy a Bible, next you wrap it up and put an address on it, and then you put a stamp on it and you post it. That's how you can send a Bible to Hungary." You see, it is possible. What we are trying to do is to explore ways and means of reaching the students.

We have a staff worker. I will not tell you his name. We call him Daniel, because he goes into the lion's den. In a few days he will leave for a three-month journey into those countries, contacting students, encouraging them. It is an expensive but a wonderfully rewarding business. So pray for Europe. Pray that we will be able to send staff workers to Latin Europe, and pray for our quiet work in Eastern Europe.

III. LATIN AMERICA

What is student work in Latin America like? In the first place, Latin America in general is a changing world—a world in which masses are hungry, both physically and spiritually, and in which the established Roman Catholic Church is going through a radical change in her approach to theology and to politics.

In the second place, the Latin American evangelical church has grown and is having adolescence pains. It is in some ways a complacent church which is reproducing some of the evils of the mother churches. At the moment, there is a terrible lack of Bible teaching, a lack of adequate social ethics, a lack of theologically informed leadership, but there is growth.

In the third place, a characteristic inside this church as well as outside is youth in revolt–youth willing to change the world.

Coming more specifically to the student work, I will say that there has been growth; it has been small, but it is there and we thank God for it. There is growth, for instance, in regard to self-support. Latin America has been considered in mission circles as a place where much money is invested and self-support is not adequate. Now those in student work are starting to expect from missions, not money, but teaching or fraternal help; the students themselves are trying to pay the expenses for their own activities. That is something I would like you to pray for: that this concept of self-support, of dignity, and of giving to the Lord what belongs to him will grow everywhere in Latin America. We have seen it recently and very evidently in Chile and Mexico by the way these student movements are paying for their programs.

Another aspect is the coming of the missionary vision. We had a missionary conference in Argentina some years ago. As a result, there is a growing feeling that Argentine university students should do something to send the gospel–not leave the evangelization of the country in the hands of foreign missionaries, but take their responsibilities with all the sacrifice involved.

There is also a concern for the vast university masses. The university in Buenos Aires has 80,000 students, the University of Mexico is even larger, the university in Cordoba has 25,000 students, and the population of university students in Brazil is over 150,000. This means that we are challenged by masses. So now, without simplifying the gospel and without having a lack of concern for the individual, the great challenge is how to reach the masses–how to announce to all this population the message of God, and how to call them in the name of God to discipleship.

Recently we have experimented with the distribution of tracts.

And in Brazil and in Argentina, the results have been really great, because almost half a million students will be reached through tracts and will be offered a Bible course. The number that have asked for that Bible course has been surprising. In Argentina, after two weeks there were 250 students who wanted to take the Bible course.

Another area is literature. Here we have both what we call "big literature," that is, books like *How to Give Away Your Faith* (that will soon be in Spanish) and also what we call "small literature." There are many students who will not read the Bible from a black-covered book, but will from a mimeographed sheet of paper. Now in some places we are experimenting on how to saturate the university every week with the type of literature that goes home and everyone reads it because it is the way things are being done in universities.

Another thing that we have tried may be unorthodox in other countries. But in Brazil, Argentina, Mexico and Peru, pre-evangelistic missions have been held. Here an attempt is made to relate the gospel to what is happening inside the university world. There are messages about Marxism and Christianity, about the meaning of freedom, about existentialism. These lectures are presented as academic, not religious, affairs, and they have to be given seriously from the scholarly and academic viewpoint. The interesting thing is that all over Latin America after a lecture of this type when the floor is opened to questions, students themselves start to ask, "If that is not Christianity, what is really Christianity? What was the message of Christ? Why did Christ come?" And this is precisely what we want.

Now it is sometimes dangerous to relate the gospel to things that are of the moment. That was the case with a student in the north of Brazil. He went to ask for permission from the police in order to have a series of meetings in which some of these subjects were going to be dealt with. The commander of the police there asked him, "Are you a Protestant?" He said, "Yes, sir, I am an evangelical student." "Then tell me how many books there are in the Bible." And he had to go through the list. "How many in the New Testament?" The police were examining him to be sure he was not just an agitator covered with a religious dress.

I think that we have to realize that new ways of reaching people with the gospel are needed for the South American student world, which in some aspects is quite different from the university world here.

But I see a great future for the student work in Latin America. Some people do not realize the potential there is even in small numbers of Christians if they are dedicated.

Not long ago I was reading a book about the second coming of Christ. The author says that one of the bad signs of the times, a sign that shows the apocalypse is coming, is the advance of colored people in the world. He goes on to say that since Christians are the majority in the white part of the world, the advance of the colored people means the advance of non-Christians. The fact is that Latin America—a place of colored people—has a great potential for evangelization in the future. But pray for us as we try to reach students, not only to be saved by Christ, but also to be disciples of Christ who obey his commands.

IV. **AFRICA**

Do you realize that throughout the whole of North Africa until you come to Egypt, there is no really indigenous Christian church, no Arab Christian church? All we have in North Africa is one reading room in Algeria where we have classes in English using the Bible as a textbook. We are hoping to open several more such reading rooms.

In Egypt it is a different matter, for there you have the Copts—the original Egyptians, those who lived there before the Arabs took away their country. And among them we have a very active student movement. I could take you to student meetings where there would be seventy or eighty students witnessing to Christ in Cairo, Alexandria, and so on, but they are second-class citizens dominated by the Arab world.

In Central Africa God has been at work in an amazing way. How I wish I could take you to a chapel in one of the universities there. I think one of the noblest sights I have seen is that of some 200 men—a noble race in their national dress, striding into the church amidst the great roar of their voices as they sing the great hymns of the church. We have Bible teachers in both Ghana and Nigeria that I would match against any in the Western world. I think we have little idea of the greatness of the work of God in Africa among students, little idea of the depth and strength of the leadership and of the potential for the future. We can praise God for what he has done.

Did you know that the World Council of Churches is determined to keep us out of English-speaking black Africa? But God has put a fifth column there. In every university there are Christian graduates. They did what they normally do. Sunday afternoon they invited students in, took tea and biscuits, and had a Bible reading. Soon there were Christians, those Christians asked for their own Christian organization, and so movements were born in those countries.

Now we are trying to pioneer work in French-speaking Africa—a very much more difficult task, and yet very exciting. We have three workers at present. One of them had been there only two or three weeks when he was asked if he would become the Protestant chaplain of the university. Amazing opportunities are being opened to us in the Congo and the Cameroun. We are hoping there will be many more volunteers to go into French-speaking Africa.

In Portuguese Africa we are beginning to make a beginning. In Southern Africa, in the University of Rhodesia, we are the only surviving integrated university society in that university. Pray for them in that university.

Student work is alive and well and growing throughout most of the world. Let us rejoice for this in the name of our Lord Jesus Christ!

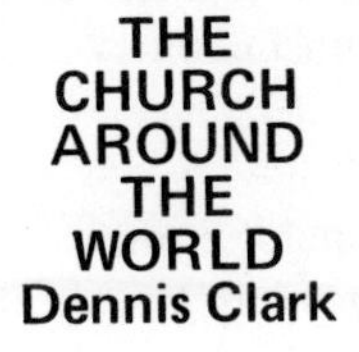

THE CHURCH AROUND THE WORLD

Dennis Clark

In four brief surveys I wish to cover some of the main regions of the world: Asia, the Muslim world, global implications of the media, the Marxist world, Africa and South America. But first I want to make clear my purpose in these surveys: It is to contrast the vigor of some churches in these other regions with the affluence and the sense of dissatisfaction found in Western Christendom. I shall keep in mind three main streams of personnel: (1) tentmakers—those who earn their living and in the context of their secular employment maintain a vital witness for Jesus Christ, (2) those who are called to the biblical ministry of evangelism, pastoral counseling and Bible teaching and (3) those involved in the communications media.

I would also like us to stay aware of the great changes that are taking place now in the '70s at the end of the colonial era. We are in a period of history when those serving in nations other than North

America must consider serving in the context of a multi-national partnership. We from the West must ring down the curtain on the power structures vested in Western missions, and we must enter into a period of servanthood when all decision-making is made by national leadership in the host country of our fellowship and service.

I. ASIA

I wish here to make three major points.

The vigor of the sending churches. At the Congress of Evangelism in Singapore, 1968, I believe one of the most stirring and momentous occasions was when Pak Octavianus of the Batu Bible School of Indonesia put forward his very simple thesis: that the gospel spread from Jerusalem to Europe, from Europe to North America, then from Europe and America to Africa, South America and Asia. "Now," he said, "my brothers, the time has come for some of us to take the responsibility of taking the gospel back to the pagan West." At that time there was a sense of burden that the younger churches in Asia would be sending churches. This is now the case.

In Korea very vital sending fellowships have been formed. In my hand is a prayer leaflet asking prayer for those from Korea now in Thailand, Iran and Hong Kong; and for one from the Ehwa Women's College now in West Pakistan.

In Japan I think of the downtown area, the Maranuchi district of Tokyo; on the ninth floor there is a vital church with the average membership under thirty years of age considering their new fields in Brazil, their new fields in Kenya, and already supporting those who have gone to India from a very small community in a great city and a nation of one hundred million. Here is a small Protestant community of just over a half a million, not only concerned with spreading the gospel to their own people but with taking this message to the other parts of Asia, South America and Africa.

From Indonesia out of a great revival movement there have come to West Pakistan those who minister the gospel with far greater power than any Western evangelist, for the latter have great problems in mastering the language and in understanding the cultural situation.

I am reminded of a word from Michael Griffiths of the Overseas Missionary Fellowship who complains of the problems in the third world when high-pressure Western evangelists who do not understand the environment of an entirely different culture try to jump on the bandwagon of the Indonesian revival and in their tactlessness unnecessarily stir up Islamic indignation and opposition. And his comment is that it is the national evangelist who today has the field at his feet.

In Burma, with no foreigners present at all, a multiplying church situation shows the power and the energy of men of God committed to spreading the gospel in their own nation. And from India, with its poverty, with its relatively small Christian community, there are those who have gone to Nepal and to other countries. I think of the Hare Krishna movement here in Canada and North America and the problem many students have in handling Eastern mysticism on their own campus. Perhaps this is the place where we will have two-way traffic; perhaps from India will come those who can more ably communicate the gospel in the context of this current obsession with Eastern mysticism.

The contrast between rural and urban Asia. There is a need for a balance between the two, and for personnel training programs that meet the needs of both. The highly-sophisticated Ph.D. returnee to the big cities of Asia has spiritual needs different from the illiterate peasant still struggling on $60 a year to rear a family and not yet benefited by the green revolution.

The situation in Asia that calls for leadership in theology. Western theology has been packaged in the Reformation and Renaissance structures of thought. The books written have all come from the West, and Western cultural accretions around the biblical core have been exported and taught. The period now before us calls for a return to the biblical core, an abandonment of this constant procession of experts from the West and the acceptance of the fresh leadership of biblically centered theologians in Asia who will take the biblical core and apply it to their local situations.

I think of a very significant theological consultation in June 1970 in Singapore. Fifty delegates from some twenty-five theological colleges, most of whom were men in Ph.D. standing—Koreans, Filipinos, Japanese, Indians, Indonesians, and Thais—met to consider the establishment of a doctoral and postgraduate center for advanced theological training, so that this training in the future would be centered on Asia. This perhaps is one of the brightest prospects before us in the decade which we are entering. The time has come for the development of Asian-oriented theological literature so that evangelism in Asia will be undergirded with a biblical faith. These are some of the men who can handle the problems of contamination from Western liberal theology, men who will firmly say that we want to introduce quarantine measures here. Show us your quarantine card. Are you clean or not? If not, go home. These are the men who are going to grapple with theology in the context of their own situation.

I would suggest that we are in a completely new period of history. Those who are being exposed to missions for the first time should realize that one has to balance, on the one hand, the commission of Jesus Christ to take the gospel to the whole world and, on the other hand, the fact that the divine instrument is the church in every country. The old idea of the white man's burden must be replaced by the biblical concept of evangelism from the churches to the world. We are in a period of two-way traffic, a period today when the dedication, prayer life and fasting of the churches in Asia will put to shame many in the Western world who live in more affluent and comfortable circumstances.

II. MUSLIM WORLD

Probably one of the biggest problems black Christians face today is the fact that many of their friends have become Muslims. Some of us have worked for thirty years among Muslims. Do you know what to say to them? Can you greet them and say, "*Salaam Ale Quum*" [Peace be to you] ?

You see, the problem of Islam is thirteen hundred years old and still with us. Today a great arc starts at Senegal, moves up to Morocco, Algeria, across North Africa, into the Middle East, up into Turkey, to Bulgaria, Yugoslavia, across to Iran, right into Russian Central Asia, down into Western Pakistan and jumps to the South Philippines, Indonesia and Malaysia. All across this arc there is a deep tension with the Western world, and it makes the proclamation of Jesus Christ as the eternal Son of God extremely difficult. There are three reasons for this.

The first reason is the Crusades. Whenever I use this word, I apologize in the name of Jesus Christ to any Muslim brother present for the great blot on Christian history that the Crusades brought. I can never utter that word without wanting with them to spit on the ground. It was the greatest mistake of Western Christendom.[1] And yet that word arouses enthusiasm in people's mind as they think of Richard Coeur de Lion. Perhaps some of you don't know that Bernard the Butcher, as he was called by some–better known to you as Bernard de Clairvaux, writer of the hymn, "Jesus the Very Thought of Thee"–stirred Christendom to go with the sword to conquer the Holy Land.

But in contrast to Bernard stood Francis of Assisi, giving up affluent life, going in the name of Jesus Christ, with his simple robe, in bare feet, into the very camp of Saladin. He went into the Saracen camp, caring for the sick and the wounded and humbly begging them to forgive and to know that Jesus Christ had compassion and love. And in contrast to Richard Coeur de Lion was Raymond Lull, in 1315, just two centuries later, stoned to death in North Africa for preaching the gospel.

Why mention the Crusades? Because we face today the same problem. The deep tension of the Israeli-Arab conflict has resulted in a mistaken idea in many Muslim minds that Christendom with its Phantom jets is behind the conflict.

May I clear myself here and say that I know of the ovens of Auschwitz, I knew of the problems in Germany, I have the deepest sympathy for my Jewish friends and brethren. I have been in Israel, I have many Israeli friends. But I wish to make the point tonight that any communication to the Muslim world requires disassociation from imperialistic policies and alignments in a worldly cold war. It requires that tender love and compassion that Francis of Assisi had in contrast to Bernard and Richard Coeur de Lion.

Therefore if you go today to the Muslim world–and this is one area where I believe foreign personnel can work–you will have to take the step of disassociation that some of us took in 1941 when, by wearing Indian dress in India, we disassociated ourselves from the British Empire and gained respect as persons from the people whom we served who hated the British.

You can survive if you have love and present yourself as man to man. The Islamic world today calls for a fresh concern for compassion in the heart of the Christian.

Consider briefly Cairo, Egypt, where in the heart of the city every noonday the Salvation for Souls Society has a great stream of people coming to pray. Look in Lebanon at the Al-Muntahaleikum, a group of seventy young Lebanese who with fervor are digging trenches right on the border where the guerilla warfare is. When they are asked why as Christians they help, they say, "We do this in the name of Jesus Christ." It is then so easy to say, "Do you know Jesus Christ is God? We do this in his name," and to present a Christian witness.

Look at Turkey (where the church was born), Ephesus, Nicaea (the Nicene Creed), Lystra and Derbe; look at Peter's epistles to Cappadocia, Pontus; look at the epistle to the Galatians. Throughout Turkey, the church was exterminated; not a single Christian church exists there today of Turkish origin. Churches are non-Turk–Greek, Assyrian, Gregorian or Armenian. Say to yourself, "Can't we reoccupy for Christ?" I listed fifty job openings in Turkey. Have you thought of going there? Look at Russian Central Asia, untouched, and yet in Samarkhand in Russian Central Asia I met an American visitor doing research on Uzbeck. *Saddat* is a magazine in Uzbeck circulating to three hundred thousand indicating the readership in this language. And yet there isn't a Bible in Uzbeck. Is this not enough to show that there is an open door for initiative?

In Iran they say to me, "Look! At the point of the sword the Arabs forced Islam on us. Previously we were Jews, Christians or Zoroastrians. We are now rethinking this thing." Some young men say, "Why not go back and be a Zoroastrian again? Why not be a Christian?" There is an openness in Iran that we have never known before.

III. MEDIA

Film today is the brush of the modern young Christian artist. It is the brush that will be used in the modern TV-cassette era that will enable you in 1973 or 1974 to plug a one- or two-hour film into your TV set. This calls for young film producers, directors, scenario writers, sound men, editors. Your generation will use film as my generation used literature. There will be twin packs of literature and film. Who of you will take this challenge? Who of you will break into the secular market? Look at TV programming–who of you will take up this whole area of communications?

I need not speak of music. You have had demonstrations that music in one of its cultural contexts is a medium of communicating the message of Jesus Christ. But let me ask you about creative writing. How many of you are creative writers? In Africa one key person in Dar es Salaam, Tanzania, is working with sixty key African writers, and their products are coming out in a saleable form because they are the product of Africa. Many want to declare a moratorium on the constant sending of Western literature for translation. They say, "Let us prepare our own literature in our own cultural media for our own people."

In Asia there are Christian writing schools. There is one in India, another in Hong Kong, another in the Philippines, and others in South America.

This introduction, then, in brief presents to you the challenge of the media for the work of Jesus Christ in the third world, here in the U. S. and in my country, Canada.

IV. MARXIST WORLD

Whenever I talk about this subject, there is always an immediate reaction. People think, "Is he from the John Birch Society? Or has he sold out to the Commies?" Let me make my position clear. As far as political systems go, I am not a capitalist (I ended last year with $100 in the bank). And I am not a Marxist. Why? Because in every Marxist country to which I have gone, I have argued as persuasively as I could: "If, comrades, you could have left religion out of it, if you had given freedom of religion, I could have accepted all the rest." But in no case have I found them ready to cease ruthlessly harassing men and women who actively believe in God and practice it. This is the issue.

Let us look at the counterpart of the Crusades to which I have referred above. In the days of Richard Coeur de Lion the lances were raised heavenward poised in battle. And opposing them were Saladin and the Saracens on their horses with their lances raised to heaven. Today the missiles are raised. And two great powers are locked in a kind of pseudo-religious crusade for liberty and freedom. Hence we have the cold war and hot wars. What is the Christian's position here? We want men like Francis of Assisi who, fulfilling the Sermon on the Mount, will love their enemies.

Let us look today into the Marxist world which I have seen first hand. I have talked with men and women by the hundreds throughout the Soviet Union and East Europe and I have listened to the situation in mainland China and Cuba. I am reminded of this verse: "The light still shines in the darkness, and the darkness has never put it out" (John 1:5, J. B. Phillips). After fifty years of hopeful expectation by Marxists, religious faith and the demand for freedom of choice have refused to decline and die. Even some atheists have become skeptical and have their doubts also. In Sophia, I asked, "What are those notices on the telegraph posts?" The Christians replied, smiling, "They are our Marxist comrades' insurance policies." I said, "Explain more." "Well, you see, to protect their relatives, they have a proper Marxist burial into the ground–finished. But then they go to the priest and they have a proper notice put up and the burial rites read in case there is something the other side of the grave." They have their doubts!

The biggest problem in the Marxist world today is what they are going to do with their youth. Despite all the tourist guides told me, I met hundreds of believing young people, prepared to forfeit their university careers for active Christian witness.

Here are two or three brief pictures of actual facts. I have a picture, of brother Kharma, whose tongue was cut out in 1964. I guess they never thought when they gave the body back to the relatives that they would photograph it. But why the torture? Because in prison he ceased not to mention Jesus Christ and pray in his name. I also have a letter from the Christians who is great boldness wrote last year to the churches, to all Christians in the world, from the Soviet Union, proclaiming their problems. And I have a list of 176 prisoners–this is one year old; the latest list I have, confidentially, is not yet translated into English. It adds 46 more. These people are in prison for their faith in Jesus Christ. I know of a letter (dated October 23, 1970) from the Soviet Union from a brave man professing his faith and writing to members of the government (Brezhnyov, Podgorny and Kosygin). There is indeed a battle today between those who believe in God and those who try to resist him.

You may know of the brave man, Alexander Solzhenitsyn, who wrote *One Day in the Life of Ivan Denisovich, The First Circle* and *Cancer Ward.* I have in my hand one of his prayers. Did you know he believed in God? "How easy it is," he says, "for me to live with You, Lord! How easy it is for me to believe in You! When my thoughts get stuck or my mind collapses, when the cleverest people see no further than this evening and do not know what must be done tomorrow, You send down to me clear confidence that You exist and that You will insure that not all the ways of goodness are blocked." And although they prevented him from receiving the Nobel prize, he continues his bold faith in God.

The researcher, Michael Bourdeaux[2], who was a student in Moscow has documented facts and shown that today the Reformed Baptist Movement, though illegal, is active throughout the whole Soviet Union. I have preached in several areas (one 200 miles from the Soviet-Chinese border). In one church they said to me, "Brother Clark, speak only half an hour because there are five other preachers tonight." I said, "Is this your custom?" "Yes," they said, "every man in our churches learns to preach because, you see, if there is only a pastor and they put him in prison, you're finished. But if every male is a preacher, they've got to put all the males in prison and that's too many, because they are rather useful, hardworking proletariat." In her latest book,[3] Svetlana Alliluyeva (now known as Mrs. Peters), Stalin's daughter, reveals something of her Christian faith and commitment to Jesus Christ: "Dostoevski suddenly captivated the younger generation, the nation so soaked in blood that as a counterbalance the Sermon on the Mount resounded with force." There is a situation just opposite to ours in North America: reaction from violence, turning to Christ, belief in the Sermon on the Mount.

Do you realize that in Russia there is no possibility of using the communications media–printing, radio, public meetings? There are very few Bibles or hymn books. And yet the Christian faith has spread very extensively. Would you ask yourself why? Would you therefore say our own political system is important to the propagation of the gospel? When that strip of agricultural experiment produces a better crop of wheat than the affluent, soft West, who are we to argue the superiority of our political systems?

Our churches don't know how to pray and fast; our churches vote $100,000 for buildings, carpeting, organs. But there you see God has his chosen people dedicated to Christ, serving him faithfully.

Let me give one or two pictures of the cost of such obedience. In one country in East Europe, I met a pastor. He said to me, "Brother, I've lost my permit for preaching." I said, "Why?" He said, "I had sixty converts last year. They told the hierarchy to take it away from me." But I went to his home on the outskirts of a large city. He showed me where he had dug in the ground and hid Bibles. He was in the Bible-running game. I went to another place. This pastor had just gotten his permit back last year. He said, "Do you know, I preached the resurrection of Christ at the grave, with a thousand Marxists present, and so many believed that they told the top boys to take my permit away. And that's what they've done."

I have been in congregations where in the middle of the service I have seen girls get up one after the other and read poems they have composed. The interpreters told me those poems were moving, full of love for Jesus Christ. They were willing to lose their jobs and to lose their opportunity for a university career. Vitality and sacrifice are characteristic today in East Europe, in the Soviet Union and mainland China.

Someone said to me, "When will God open the door?" I said, "To whom? Do you think it's shut?" In Tanzania I met key leaders. They said, "Some of our African sisters were recently in Peking at the cost of the Communist party on business from Tanzania. And, thank God, they had the chance to witness to their comrades." You think it's closed to you from Western Christendom? Why shouldn't it be opened to other national Christians?

How many of you here are studying Russian? Why not? I meet young people in Kiev, Tashkent, Moscow who are fluent in English, who have no hope of going overseas to spread their ideology. Why are you not studying Russian to take an exchange scholarship and communicate? Why do you not go as tourists? Today the door is wide open for those who want to go–if they are wise and if they know how to operate. Why don't you study Russian? Why don't you consider East Europe the place for witness?

And finally I will mention a devoted Chinese brother in Hong Kong. I saw him reading the Bible aloud in a studio and asked why.

The reply: "He is dictating the total Bible from Genesis to Revelation so that many believers in mainland China who had their Bibles burned in the cultural revolution can write by hand and reconstruct their Bible in their own land."

"The darkness has never put it out": The light shines very brightly.

V. AFRICA

By the year 2000, the total Christian population of Africa will be 351 million. (So says *U. S. News and World Report,* December 28, 1970, basing its figures on *Schism and Renewal in Africa,* a very important book by Dr. David B. Barrett.) At the moment, the population of Christians is about 100 million, of which over half are Protestants. This will give you some idea of the vitality of the churches in Africa.

My first contact with African Christians was in India where they came in the service of Jesus Christ in a group called the Ruanda Revival, of which Festo Kivengere is to some the best known person. Under the Spirit of God, great movements that brought humility, brokenness and confession of sin swept a number of churches in East Africa. This is one picture I see.

Another picture I see is the school system still wide open to definite Christian instruction–something you cannot imagine in the U. S. or even in Canada. But there teachers are invited and paid by local governments to teach the Christian faith. I remember one Canadian Christian I met in Kampala. He was adviser to the principal. He had come out under one of our Canadian CIDA programs. He is one of hundreds in this capacity.

Let me give you one other picture. In a university in a certain country where there are a number of Chinese from mainland China building a railway, a Christian is head of the Physics Department. He is a brilliant man, a determined Christian in his witness. He told me that it was rather embarrassing to the mainland Chinese consular official to have to call him on the phone and ask him to supervise the installation of a telescope that had been donated from mainland China. During the installation of this telescope in the observatory, an official was quite surprised to find a physicist who believed in a God. There is amazing witness to other nations (including the Soviet

Union) in the university systems of Africa, where mainland Chinese serving as professors are there with those from the U. S., Britain and Canada.

I think of another picture: a brilliant African with a Ph.D. in mathematics. We were in his home and he took me to the church where I preached. The Prime Minister of that nation regularly attends that church. Many leaders have come out of Christian background and education and are themselves believing Christians.

VI. SOUTH AMERICA

Here I'll give just two pictures. One is the dynamic of the great Pentecostal movement. Can you imagine a midweek prayer meeting with 3,000? Can you imagine a balcony with 500 young people in the choir and 100 guitars? And can you imagine what they have been doing an hour before the service in groups on corners of streets? They have been proclaiming the gospel of Jesus Christ with their guitars. And the people come in streams and the church fills up. They bring with them those who have listened to the message. That is a picture that can be repeated not only in Chile, but in many other countries of South America.

Second, let me mention the great Roman Catholic Church. There are three main streams, at least–there may be others. On the right are the conservatives, aligned to the power structures, the wealth and the status quo, unable to change, clinging to what they have. On the left are the revolutionaries, following Che Guevara with their machine guns, kidnapping foreign embassy officials for ransom, determined to lift the wealth from those who have it and give it to the poor. And in the middle, some compute the number to be 20 million at least, Roman Catholics, reading the Bible, of whom many are believers. Those of you who are Protestants, can you come to terms with the possibility that the Holy Spirit's strategy there is not the proselyting of Roman Catholics to become Protestants, but the bringing of Roman Catholics to a faith in the living Lord? And that they may remain in their churches? Could you serve under those circumstances? Could you conceive that this is God's plan? It may well be the same in the great block that I have not touched in my survey at all–the 200 million in the great orthodox churches of the Middle East, the Soviet Union, Ethiopia and the other countries such as Greece.

VII. CONCLUSION

We have seen the sovereign Lord Jesus working in great power throughout the whole earth. Our faith should be strengthened that in this decade of the '70s God is working in great power through his churches, his base of operation in all nations from which the Word of God will spread to all nations. We have seen the pattern changing to a two-way traffic.

So I make a plea first to my brothers and sisters here who come from the churches in Asia, the Middle East, Africa, South America, and the isles of the sea: Are you going back determined to maintain professional excellence and to witness for Jesus Christ by a pure life, to proclaim the message with your lips and to teach your fellow believers what you have learned here in the North American continent? And to my brothers and sisters here in Western Christendom—Europe, Canada and the U. S.: Are you going to determine to work with all your might here at home? You are the ones whom God may call either into the secular stream to be a witness to other nations, or into full-time Bible-teaching ministry for which there is more demand than supply, or into evangelism in a full-time capacity. Are you ready for situations that call for multi-cultural, multi-national teams who will demonstrate that Christianity is not a Western religion at all, but the heavenly order for all the nations? When men see an African, a Chinese, a Japanese, an Indian, an Egyptian, an Afghan, an American, a German and a Canadian together on the platform proclaiming the message, the stigma that Christianity is a Western religion will give place to a recognition that it is a word from God. Can we see this as our main objective in the next ten years?

I will finish with a testimony, a verse and a question. I have been in Christian work for thirty-six years. I started to preach when I was sixteen. I never had seminary training; I didn't finish high school; I learned the hard way. When I was 23, I went to India; I studied Islamics in a mosque on the floor. Are there not others who will follow what I have tried to do? In Colossians 1:28-29 (Phillips), Paul says, "We proclaim Christ. We warn everyone we meet, and we teach everyone we can, all that we know about him, so that, if possible, we may bring every man up to his full maturity in Christ Jesus. This is what I am working at all the time, with all the strength that God gives me." Will you?

Notes

[1] See Zoe Oldenbourg, *The Crusades* (New York: Ballantine Books, 1967).
[2] Michael Bourdeaux, *Religious Ferment in Russia* (New York: St. Martin's Press, 1968) and *Patriarchs–Prophets* (New York: Praeger, 1970).
[3] Svetlana Alliluyeva, *Only One Year* (New York: Harper and Row, 1969).